MEDIUM AEVUM MONOGRAPHS
NEW SERIES X

THE TRAGEDY OF KNIGHTHOOD

Origins of the Tannhäuser-legend

By

J. M. CLIFTON-EVEREST

Senior Lecturer in German
at the University of Sydney

Published by the Society for the
Study of Mediæval Languages and Literature
Oxford
1979

This volume is published with the aid of a grant from the Australian Academy of the Humanities

ISBN-13: 978-0-907570-04-2 (pb)

© 1978 J.M. Clifton-Everest

This reprint issued 2016

...ire ad conspectum cari genitoris et ora
contingat; doceas iter et sacra ostia pandas.

Verg. Aen. VI, 108-9

Nu wyl ick hen tho Rome gaen
God moete dysse reyse walden.
Thom Geystliken vader Pawes Vrban
de myn ssele mach behalden.

Low German Tannhäuser-ballad,
(broadsheet, c. 1530)

IN MEMORY OF MY FATHER

CONTENTS

Introduction — v

Chapter
I. The *Venusberg* — 1

II. *Le Paradis de la Reine Sibylle* — 21

III. *Guerino il Meschino:* the test of moral fortitude — 39

IV. Fairyland and the fairy-mistress story — 54

V. The demonic fairy-mistress — 74

VI. The German ballads — 92

VII. Tannhäuser and Venus — 111

Conclusion — 129

Appendix — 136

Bibliography — 172

Index — 177

INTRODUCTION

In the *Stadtarchiv* of the city of Essen is a small paper manuscript containing the somewhat corrupt text of a ballad in twenty-three stanzas of Low German. It affords the earliest extant German version of the story of Tannhäuser, the knight who entered the legendary *Venusberg*. Summarily it tells of how he came to repent of his sojourn there; how he obtained a grudging leave from Lady Venus; and how he travelled to Rome in order to confess himself to the Pope. But absolution was not at once granted to him, so that he returned, disconsolate, to the *Venusberg*. Later, God pronounced his pardon with a sign, but the knight, already once more inside the sinful mountain, "could not return".

Evidence for dating this manuscript is largely circumstantial, but there are no real grounds to doubt the common verdict that it belongs to the middle of the 15th century. It is at all events indubitably older than the Tannhäuser-ballads which came in considerable numbers off the German printing-presses of the early 16th century. All the surviving ballads are essentially variants of the same text, although the differences of detail are sometimes very important indeed — (representative texts are reproduced in Appendix IV). Though the song is less well-attested in the 15th century than in the 16th, it was not necessarily less popular then; a rapid expansion in the use of the printing-press adequately accounts for the relative profusion of texts after 1500. The earliest print to bear a date is from Nürnberg in 1515, but there are several more undated from about that time or soon afterwards. Of the ten or so broadsheets which survive from the first half of the 16th century (the same period sees three further manuscript texts), no two represent the same impression; even allowing for the comparatively small runs of the early presses, this suggests a low incidence of survival and points to the probable existence of further impressions of which all trace is lost. Both High and Low German prints survive, the former in greater numbers: all in all, the ballad must have enjoyed great popularity.

The literary shortcomings of these texts, even of the best of them, scarcely require critical exposure. Without in any way decrying the art of the balladist, one may fairly assert that his literary objectives are generally of a different and less sophisticated order than those which most widely excite the interest of scholars. Moreover, both the professional scholar with a particular interest in the genre and the connoisseur of folk-song are likely to rank many a text of the period above the Tannhäuser-ballad with respect to formal qualities. Whatever different and even superior versions may have existed at one time or another, the ballads were never products of the highest literary aspirations; they belonged among the crude entertainments of the *vulgus*, to employ the very term of the 15th century German writer who first wrote of this matter. The particular virtue of the legend lies less in the artistic merit of those versions which chance to survive, than in its intrinsic drama, which succeeds in transcending even the most inauspicious literary form. The conflict in its hero's soul, tragically torn between the contrary human promptings of flesh and spirit, engenders an awesome tension, all the more poignant in a medieval universe whose morality and eschatology know only uncompromising extremes the unrelieved dark of eternal damnation, and the indescribable radiance of ultimate salvation.

Significantly enough, it was this stark drama nourished by the opposed passions of body and soul which prompted the best-known and the most successful attempt to raise the legend up to the highest pinnacles of art: Richard Wagner's opera. Wagner's hero, wavering in his human weakness between the sinister carnal gravity of the subterranean *Venusberg* and his soul's soaring aspirations for celestial bliss, finally wins a victory for the spirit through the death of the body. It is an optimistic conclusion which reveals much of the particular preoccupation of Wagner and his public: nobody at that time can have been altogether blind to the supposedly German character of this story of a Faust whose two souls find expression in song. The sombre figure of the German knight, who dared, and eventually vanquished, the moral perils of the gloomy mountain, appealed forcefully to the romantic nationalism of 19th century Germany, steeped as it was in medievalism and concern with its own Germanic ancestry. Tannhäuser's salvation is a moral victory for the torn German soul. In this way, through the sheer persuasiveness of Wagner's art, the story of Tannhäuser maintained a hallowed place in the body of German legend.

Historical scholarship first showed real interest in the matter as a consequence of evaluating quite different evidence from Italy. Its first conclusions, reached outside Germany, were immediately at variance with the prevailing view there. An Italian romance, *Guerino il Meschino* by Andrea da Barberino, belonging to the first years of the 15th century, was found to display a remarkable affinity to the story of Tannhäuser in a fictional account of its hero's visit to a mountain in the Appennines; more important still, the Frenchman Antoine de la Sale in his *Paradis de la Reine Sibylle*, composed in 1440, describes a visit to the same mountain, where he heard a tale, duly retold, from the local inhabitants — it is to all intents and purposes a version of the Tannhäuser-legend. It was contended that the legend first came from Italy and was therefore not Germanic at all. Further historical investigation then revealed that in the 15th and 16th centuries the Germans widely associated the *Venusberg* with this same Italian mountain, and actually travelled there in large numbers to "visit" the realm of Venus.

Naturally enough, these conclusions did not find ready acceptance in Germany; indeed, they gave rise to a controversy which nearly a century of subsequent scholarship has failed to resolve satisfactorily. One cannot evade the impression that national pride played no small part in the matter. Two more or less opposed theories were formulated, and their respective causes were espoused at times with fervour. German scholars — *e.g.* Kluge, Siebert, Meyer, Naumann, Lang, *etc.* (their published contributions are detailed in the Bibliography and, where individually important, mentioned in the course of this study) — adopted the view that the legend was a purely German one which had been imported to Italy and located there by German travellers. Others, largely of non-German nationality —*e.g.* Paris, Dübi, Söderhjelm — asserted that the story began in the South, whence it migrated over the Alps to be connected eventually with the German knight. As late as 1948, F. Desonay claimed quite vehemently that the legend is in no way German in origin, and much more recently still, J. W. Thomas repeated the contrary view with equal assurance.

The failure of modern scholarship to settle this matter may not of course be blamed on the obtuseness of those investigating it, or simply on nationalistic prejudice, though an inherited obsession with the precise national origins of the legend has certainly hindered the investigation of other interesting aspects. The cause lies rather in the inadequacy of available information: useful evidence is parlously scant, and frequently equivocal. For this reason there is no real need to enumerate the arguments of the individual protagonists of each of the two opposing schools; they are repetitive in the extreme, for each has at his disposal only the barest handful of facts. Variation of argument within each school is possibly only in such matters as whether the *Venusberg* is regarded as a distinct legendary phenomenon of conceivably different national origin from the legend itself. Those who favoured a German origin for the legend pointed out that the knight Tannhäuser was a historical poet of the 13th century, a contemporary of Pope Urban IV, whom the High German ballads also name; the legend must consequently have grown up round his name and thus predates the Italian evidence. Those of the other persuasion noted that there was no mention of the legend in Germany prior to the appearance of the Italian sources, which accordingly took historical precedence. These arguments — and virtually nothing else of consequence was adduced — are very far from constituting proof or refutation (and it must be conceded in fairness that not all the earlier writers make such claims); they yield in fact nothing more than hypothesis.

Just such unproven and unprovable hypotheses have hitherto been the besetting problem of scholarship in this matter, due almost entirely to the paucity of information. Where the few facts afford little historical coherence, the explication of a hypothesis readily does so; though it also insidiously tends to obscure the limits of real knowledge. Too many scholars in the past have taken one of the tenuously based theories of the legend's national origins and attempted to compose a full chronicle of its development, using simple conjecture derived only from the theory where the facts failed. Needless to say, while such attempts prejudicially favour the chosen theory, they do nothing to strengthen its scientific foundation.

Much the same process may be observed where other aspects of the legend have been made the subject of examination. One of the most valuable insights into the legend's beginnings was the observation, also first made towards the end of the last century, that it belongs, in certain crucial respects, to the genre of the fairy-mistress story. But even this indisputable fact has led only to another hazardous hypothesis, first advanced by A. H. Krappe in the 1930's. The fairy-mistress story is extensively a Celtic phenomenon; an immediate Celtic source of the legend was accordingly postulated, duly sought, and eventually found (or at least its close relative was discovered). In this way a third point of origin entered the controversy, this time of ethnic rather than national type. Although this theory found another champion quite recently, its foundations are weaker even than those of the other two, and it is disproved in the course of this study.

The search for further evidence in the matter has generated still further hypotheses. P. S. Barto examined German sources concerning the *Venusberg* and reached the conclusion that it is derived from the Paradise of the Grail; he proceeded to argue that the Tannhäuser-legend's origins from the surviving evidence. In this study such an exercise Seductively spectacular as it is, his theory lacks any real substance, and has met with no agreement from others. More recently W. Pabst, concentrating likewise on the legendary hollow mountain, but investigating the Italian sources, discerned in the diabolical figure of Venus the re-named shade of a frustrated Dido. In this case the evidence is most dubious of all, and Pabst's theory has been strongly criticised and virtually disproved.

It is simply not possible to write a fully coherent history of the legend's origins from the surviving evidence. In this study such an exercise has been more or less eschewed in favour of the primary problem of ascertaining facts, however disjunct. The evidence is discussed in the natural divisions yielded by its sources; it is ordered in such a way as to facilitate overall argument, for which purpose necessary regard was obviously paid to chronology. But no general theory of the legend's early evolution is advanced, and no revelation, neatly linking all the evidence and answering all the questions, should be expected. Naturally enough, new theories and suggestions arise with regard to various points, and they are explored; but they do not constitute the basis for further argument beyond what is appropriate. Only in the *Conclusion* is some attempt made to integrate the results so as to produce a general picture, but the limitations of such an endeavour should be fully apparent to the reader who proceeds to that point with due regard to the nature of the arguments.

All too frequently, it is to be regretted, the quest for facts affords nothing more than probabilities of varying, and often very slender, reliability. Very much remains altogether obscure, and seems likely to remain so without the discovery of totally new sources of information. Indeed the shortage of valid information is a major reason for the brevity of this study; the numerous fleeting references to Tannhäuser and to the *Venusberg*, found in sources of the 16th century postdating the appearance of the printed broadsheets — insubstantial allusions which filled many earlier histories of the legend — have been carefully perused, but then mostly discarded; in almost every case they are valueless in ascertaining the circumstances of the story's beginnings. They would swell the text, and particularly the bibliographical apparatus of the footnotes, to no scientific avail. However, with regard to the earlier evidence, it is fair to say of most categories that a sufficiently close examination has never previously been undertaken. Certainly the *Paradis de la Reine Sibylle* of Antoine de la Sale has been neglected as to its detail, and the relationship between the legend and Sibylline episode of *Guerino il Meschino* has not been fully explored; the extent of the legend's correlation with the typical fairy-mistress story has been largely ignored in the pursuit of a Celtic "source"; variations of text among the German ballads have received insufficient attention. These matters I have attempted to illuminate.

A word concerning the translations I have made of passages quoted in the text: since the purpose of these quotations was to demonstrate precisely the contents and quality of the evidence they contain, I have on the whole endeavoured to follow them as closely as possible in translation, in order that no ambiguity or weakness in the original should be obscured. Virtually no heed was paid to English style, since deviations made in such an interest may prevent the reader unfamiliar with the foreign language from achieving maximum familiarity with the facts involved and their basis in evidence. The unevenness, and occasionally doubtful grammar, of the originals has been reproduced as accurately as possible. In several places the actual meaning of individual points, generally incidental ones, is uncertain: whenever possible the obscurity has been faithfully reproduced in English, but where this could not be done, one plausible rendering has been selected for the sake of completeness. Needless to say, no use is made of these last points in constructing argument.

Some justification is also desirable for the term "legend", employed throughout with reference to Tannhäuser's story. It is purely a convenience, adopted due to its wide use by others, and it has no definitive significance. Various definitions of a *genus* "legend" have been formulated and applied in literary studies, and the word has quite different meanings in different languages and with regard to different periods. None of these is intended here, for the immediate purpose is precisely to ascertain facts which would elucidate the nature of this very shadowy phenomenon; the use of a definitive term could easily prejudice that search from its outset.

The interval since the completion of this study has seen the appearance of another work in Germany treating the legend and its origins: Dietz-Rüdiger Moser, *Die Tannhäuser-Legende: eine Studie über Intentionalität und Rezeption katechetischer Volkserzählung zum Buß-Sakrament*, Berlin, 1977 (see Bibliography).

As his title indicates, Moser's approach to the subject is essentially different from that taken here; indeed, the two are to some extent complementary. For this reason no substantial alteration has been made to the present work in order to accommodate his conclusions. However attention has been drawn to them in the footnotes where deemed appropriate, and a few further observations seem justified here.

On two matters in particular Moser's contentions touch crucially on the ground covered here. Firstly, there is fundamental agreement in postulating an earlier, lost version of the legend which did not portray the Pope's response as a false and damnable repudiation of the sinner for all time. Secondly, Moser asserts that a "source" of the legend is to be found in the episode of the *Waldbüßer* (forest penitent) from a legend circulating widely in the late Middle Ages describing the life of St. John Chrysostom; the earliest extant manuscript of this story dates from the mid-15th century, but it is incomplete, lacking the all-important final part. Moser's confidence in this is not easily shared. The *Waldbüßer-Episode* includes none of the narrative features constituting the Tannhäuser-legend, with one exception: the Pope's apparent repulsion of a contrite sinner, to whom God subsequently shows His pardon by a wondrous sign (both sign and pardon are missing from the earliest manuscript). Moser seeks to buttress his claim with arguments derived from the theological intention which he believes underlies the composition of both legends: the Tannhäuser-legend, like the *Waldbüßer-Episode* and some more of the popular folk-tales of the period and afterwards, arose allegedly from efforts by educational groups within the Church (*e.g.* the Orders) to propagate in a form that was popularly assimilable the correct doctrine in matters of atonement and forgiveness. This view focuses Moser's attention almost exclusively on the Pope's utterance and on the miraculous sign which follows it; he assumes that the Pope's intention in an original version was to oblige the sinner to perform a sufficient atonement before receiving absolution. Such a conception of the legend's beginnings is by no means improbable in its outline, though it is one-sided and its arguments seem simplistic and even deficient. The story of the knight in the *Venusberg* must surely have first reached an advanced stage of development from other, very different sources, before it could readily acquire the conclusion found in the *Waldbüßer-Episode*. In fact the pope's role in that version of the latter which Moser reproduces is already uncomfortably ambivalent, in as far as he makes no gesture calling for a sign from heaven and no motivation is supplied for his uncompromising rejection of the sinner. In this respect the story seems further removed from the "original" version of the Tannhäuser-legend postulated in this study than are the stories described here in Chapter VI, where divine pardon manifest through the eventual fruitfulness of a dry branch is anticipated by the words and actions of the Pope.

All in all, it seems unlikely that the *Waldbüßer-Episode* can have exercised more than an incidental influence on the legend. Indeed it conceivably had less to do with the original version than with the critical tendency which culminated in the anti-papal travesty of the Reformation.

As is to be expected with an historical literary study calling on such far-flung and recondite sources, my indebtedness to others may scarcely be accounted in a few lines. Numerous colleagues have assisted me in linguistic matters where their competence surpassed my own. Especial debts are owed to Professor B. K. Martin for his aid in making a just assessment of *Tom the Rymer*, and to Professor A. J. Dunstan, whose patience proved no common thing when called on to unscramble the sorry omelette of Hemmerlin's Latin in the *Dialogus*. The chapter treating *Guerino il Meschino* is but a poor tribute to the warming efforts of the late Professor Frederick May: most of all for that part, but at many other points beside, he dipped constantly and without stinting into his capacious memory to guide my argument with wisdom. It is a cause of regret to me that he could not see the final product of those labours.

Without the very generous financial assistance of the *Deutscher Akademischer Austauschdienst*, which enabled me to visit Germany in the winter of 1973/4 and to gather there the material to make a beginning, it seems unlikely the work would have been attempted; my thanks are accordingly due. For innumerable subsequent needs I was dependent on the services of the Fisher Library, University of Sydney, whose selfless staff displayed a fine forbearance in handling my incessant and tiresome requests for overseas loans.

The entire manuscript was read painstakingly by Professor D. H. Green, and the countless emendations and improvements which resulted I must simply score up to the mounting tally of my obligation to his unexampled enthusiasm and kindness.

Finally, a debt so personal as to be undischargeable is owed to my wife Joyce, who has shared with me times beyond telling both the stimulation and the frustration of pursuing discussions without clear issue, and whose support and encouragement never flagged.

I.
THE *VENUSBERG*

No single element may be more readily isolated from the composition of themes and motifs which constitutes the Tannhäuser-legend than the phenomenon of the *Venusberg*. The sinful mountain-paradise penetrated by the knight will be progressively illuminated throughout the course of the present study by evidence of quite differing types, but there also exists a distinct body of information concerning it directly. Much of this results from its association with a specific and real geographic location, and is derived from sources of a factual, rather than literary character. Thus, whereas many of the other sources allow no more than uncertain inferences, the information to be gained here is relatively dependable.

The role played in the legend by the hollow mountain and its evil character is patently quite central. The tale told by the German ballads describes essentially one man's entanglement in a specific moral predicament owing its very existence to the phenomenon of the *Venusberg*. That predicament, though it is evidently harsh in the extreme, is virtually unexplained in the ballads, let alone elaborated. It appears to be implicit simply in the notion of the place: the mountain's moral attributes were apparently so well-known by the mid-15th century that the ballad had no need to explain them.

The name *Venusberg* first appears in about the second or third decade of the 15th century. The only real location to which the earliest allusions ascribe it is a mountain in the Umbrian Appenines near the town of Norcia. Nevertheless *Venusberg* is an entirely German appellation, for the Italians knew this place as the mountain of the Sibyl, and the range bears the name *Monti Sibillini* to this day. One early reference to the *Venusberg* appears, it is true, in a letter of Aeneas Silvius Piccolomini, the later Pope Pius II, but even here the German origin of the term is evident, for Aeneas writes in consequences of an enquiry from Germany; the name *Venusberg* was clearly unknown to him hitherto, though, from the activities associated with it, he soon deduces that the Norcian mountain is meant.[1] Aeneas' letter, of 15th

---

1) *Cf.* Appendix I.

January 1444, is the earliest reference to the *Venusberg* which can be precisely dated; but the name also appears in the *Precepta* of Johannes Nider (d. 1438)[2], and is treated to a quite full description in the *Dialogus de Nobilitate et Rusticitate* of the Zürich canon Felix Hemmerlin, who began his work some time after 1440 but did not complete it until about 1450.[3]

The profusion of direct allusion to the *Venusberg* at this time stands in sharp contrast to the complete absence of the name in the 13th and 14th centuries.[4] This fact alone casts some doubt on the claim that the Tannhäuser-legend began life as a ballad in the late 13th century, for it is at once hard to see why a legend so very popular about 1440 should entirely escape mention for the preceding century-and-an-half. It has been convincingly shown that the much cited passage in Gottfrid's *Tristan*, often seen as a reference to the *Venusberg*, does not necessarily involve a hollow-mountain at all.[5] The first literary text to situate Venus and her ladies inside a mountain appears only about the year 1380; but this work, *Der Tugenden Schatz* by Meister Altswert, presents her as a purely allegorical and literary figure displaying exemplary moral qualities, and the name *Venusberg* does not yet appear in any form.[6] The utterly sinful mountain, housing a temptress Venus and known as *Venusberg*, first appears only several decades later; when it suddenly does so, the comparative abundance of allusion suggests that some popularising change had immediately preceded this time.

---

2) *Precepta Divine Legis* (Cologne, Ulrich Zell, 1470?), precept. I, cap. 11, qu. 3; A. Amman, *Tannhäuser im Venusberg* (Zürich, 1964), p. 223, dates Nider's allusion before 1411, on the grounds of a manuscript of the *Precepta* in Munich. However, according to information received directly from the Bayrische Staatsbibliothek, the date 1411 was erroneously entered in the library's Catalogue of Manuscripts. The ms. concerned belongs to the first half of the 15th century, but neither it nor the composition of Nider's work can be dated more precisely.
3) *Cf.* Appendix II.
4) The same period sees the first extant text of the ballad, at least one other German poem based on the legend (*cf. infra*, p. 120), and the work of Antoine de la Sale which, though it does not include the name *Venusberg*, may be said to reflect the phenomenon quite precisely.
5) Gottfried von Strassburg, *Tristan und Isold* ed. F. Ranke (Berlin, 1961), vv. 4802 10; the passage has commonly been seen in this light since the suggestion of E. Schröder, *ZfdA*, 61 (1924), p. 178, but *cf.* O. Löhmann, "Die Entstehung der Tannhäusersage", *Fabula*, 3 (1959/60), p. 246.
6) *Der Tugenden Schatz*, ed. W. Holland and A. Keller, Bibliothek des literarischen Vereins in Stuttgart, 21 (Stuttgart, 1850), *cf. infra* p. 125; the verse "Dirre berg was fro Venus allein ..." (p. 83, v. 7) is an attributive description rather than a name.

The Italian tradition of the Sibylline mountain in the 15th century is less well attested than the German one and, with the important exception of the romance *Guerino il Meschino*, which is discussed in a later chapter, the texts evidencing it stress a somewhat different aspect of the mountain's character.[7] The different names indicate sufficiently the distinguishing preoccupations of what may be seen as two fairly separate traditions. The Italians are concerned with the prophetic and occult powers of spirits inhabiting the place, who may be conjured by necromancy; the classical figure of the Sibyl, who also has her abode there, represents or embodies this occult and prophetic reputation. Aeneas Piccolomini, for example, referred above all to necromantic events at the mountain. In a letter dated 1472, Luigi Pulci sarcastically outlined to Lorenzo di Medici a visit he made to the Norcian Sibyl in the company of Lorenzo's superstitious wife.[8] He describes a room in which the "Sibyl" sat and declaimed in the Greek language, much to the awe of credulous visitors; Pulci plainly considered the entire affair a confidence trick. But it is striking that his testimony, the only indication at this time of a *popular* tradition in Italy, makes no mention of the Sibyl's inhabiting the interior of the mountain. Much later, in the 16th century, Giangiorgio Trissino in Canto XXIV of his epic *L'Italia liberata di Goti* still saw Norcia as the true home of prophecy.[9]

For the Germans the *Venusberg* encloses a paradise of delights, principally, it appears, of a carnal nature, for the goddess of erotic love holds sway in the place. Felix Faber, a Dominican from Ulm who writes in 1483, tells of "quodam Tusciae monte, non longe a Roma, in quo dicunt dominam Venerem deliciis frui cum quibusdam viris et foeminis." He tells of Tannhäuser, who lives there "ut dicunt, usque ad diem judicii." While he certainly does not explicitly exclude others from knowledge of the legend, he significantly refers to a *German* ballad and to the *German* nationality of those who believe the story ("hac fama dementati sunt Alemanni").[10] Johannes Nider, an ecclesiast from Swabia, questions in his *Precepta Divine Legis* "an veritas subsit hiis que dicuntur de monte veneris ubi cum pulcherrimis feminis

---

7) M. Wis, "Ursprünge der deutschen Tannhäuserlegende", *Neuphilologische Mitteilungen*, 61 (1966) 8 58, discusses the attestations most fully.
8) L. Pulci, *Morgante e lettere*, ed. D. de Robertis (Florence, 1962), p. 980.
9) *L'Italia liberata di Goti,* (Venice, Tolomeo Janiculo di Bressa, 1548), fol. 99ff; also Ariosto, *Orlando Furioso*, ed. G. Lipparini (Milan, 1962), Canto XXXIII, str. 4, p. 583.
10) *Cf.* Appendix III.

dicuntur quidam frui luxuria et voluptate ad placitum".[11] The verbal similarities found here to Faber's description are in fact characteristic of most accounts of the mountain-paradise. Hemmerlin, too, speaks of the beautiful women and perfect pleasures found in the mountain, and refers especially to English and German men living there. His testimony is deserving of particular interest in that he seems aware of both Italian and German traditions, as well as of both names, and he presents his material (Appendix II) in such a way as to suggest that they are to some degree distinct. He speaks first of the "mons Sibille" near Norcia and alludes, by a cross-reference, to his later mention of the adjacent lake, a haunt of necromancers also described by Antoine de la Sale (*cf. infra*). He goes on to speak of the violent storms which are provoked by intrusion of humans into the area, a part of the local necromantic tradition which can be traced back into the 14th century, when it is mentioned by Pierre Bercheur (+ 1361).[12] Only then does he proceed to discuss the caves leading into the interior of the mountain, mentioning that it is also widely known as "mons Veneris" and that he himself had been there. He explains the name by citing the belief that Venus practises her erotic charms in the mountain, and adds his own view that malevolent spirits are at work there, assuming the guise of lovely women in order to corrupt men. He goes on to substantiate these claims with the testimony of a certain contrite Swiss, Simplicianus, who asserted that he had lived there for a year with two German friends amidst great pleasure, but now came to Hemmerlin in search of absolution. The detailed description of the paradise found inside the mountain is in fact explicitly based on the account of this Swiss man.

Of course the legend attaching to the Norcian mountain can scarcely have been a simple and uniform one, indeed it doubtless assumed various forms. The attempt to distinguish two traditions on broadly national lines should not be understood to imply mutual exclusiveness: in fact Andrea Barberino's *Guerino il Meschino* plainly draws on the legend of the mountain-paradise, while Aeneas' letter shows that the necromantic associations of the place were not unknown in Germany. By the 16th century, when German interest in the black arts was considerably greater, a distinction is not longer reasonably possible at

---

11) *Op. cit.*: "... whether there is any truth in those things that are said of the *Venusberg*, where certain men are said to enjoy licence and sensuality to their pleasure with the most beautiful women".
12) P. Bercheur, *Opera Omnia* (Mainz, 1609), Tom. I: *Reductorium Morale*, p. 611f.

all.[13] It is also most important to observe that the 15th century reports of both the "mons Sibille" and the *Venusberg* are not generally penned by those who lend extensive credence to them. Andrea Barberino is a romancer, while Pulci, though previously an adept of necromancy, now pours scorn on the entire matter. From Germany we have for the most part the reports of churchmen anxious to expose the falsehood of a popular legend (Faber is particularly vehement in his condemnation of such dangerous gullibility). The belief was evidently prevalent in a fairly uneducated class, who did not record their ideas or their experiences on visiting the mountain, and among whom the existence of a more or less distinct German tradition is all the more plausible. It is worth observing that Aeneas Piccolomini's German enquirer, the only one of his race to mention necromancy at the mountain at this date, was by way of exception no simpleton, but an influential and learned doctor interested specifically in the occult. Whatever reports of the mountain had reached him seem to have mentioned the name Venus, and may thus have mingled both traditions. But his ostensible concern was necromancy, not erotic delights.

Moreover, whereas the interest in the mountain-paradise among the Germans was certainly strong, the lack of Italian evidence does not permit the opposite conclusion there. Pulci testifies to some sort of popular Italian tradition concerning the mountain, and the absence of earlier Italian references to it may simply reflect a comparative lack of concern at such matters on the part of Italian churchmen and moralists.

The number of allusions to the *Venusberg* in the 15th century is furthermore no clear indication of the extent of the belief in Germany, for it was plainly widespread. Faber, writing towards the end of the century, unequivocally states that "multi simplices ad hos famatos peregrinentur montes"; Nider seems to regard the legend as familiar,

---

13) The numerous allusions of 16th century German humanists, who generally see the *Venusberg* as a school for the occult, are of no use to this study: *cf.* P. S. Barto, *Tannhäuser and the Mountain of Venus* (New York, 1916), cap. 2; F. Pfaff, *Die Tannhäusersage*, Verhandlungen der 49. Versammlung deutscher Philologen und Schulmänner in Basel, 1907 (Leipzig, 1908), p. 105; H. Dübi, "Drei spätmittelalterliche Legenden in ihrer Wanderung aus Italien durch die Schweiz nach Deutschland", *Zeitschrift für Volkskunde*, 17 (1907), p. 260; Amman, (*op. cit.*), p. 28ff; in 1669 Sigismund von Birken, in his *Brandenburgischer Ulysses (Anzeiger des German ischen Museums*, 88, 1860 p. 149) unequivocally states that at Norcia the natives themselves know the name *Venusberg* (*cf.* F. Kluge, "Der Venusberg", *Bunte Blätter* [Freiburg, 1908], p. 60).

and Hemmerlin declares the name common.¹⁴ An Italian source as late as 1550 still shows how Germans in particular seem drawn to the mountain.¹⁵

Hemmerlin's *Dialogus* offers a chance to probe a little further back into history. The author states that Simplicianus visited him while Pope John XXIII (a schismatic Pope) and his *curia* were at Bologna (c. 1412). But the suspiciously close resemblance of the man's story to the Tannhäuser-legend prompts some caution. Possibly the Swiss man genuinely existed, and was either a wilful liar or subject to delusions. However it is also possible that Hemmerlin himself fabricated the incident, including his part in it, for his own reasons — perhaps for the didactic benefit of the story, since this is his general aim in writing. Certainly Barto is right in pointing out that Hemmerlin's assertion, made after 1440, that the mountain was then called *Venusberg*, may not be taken as firm evidence that this was so in 1412.¹⁶ The expression "communiter dicitur" undeniably suggests that the name was in use some time previous to the composition of the *Dialogus*, and the citation of a specific earlier date, which has no further relevance to the story, makes it likely that Hemmerlin was actually in Bologna in 1412. Thus while it is quite reasonable to suppose that he heard the name at that time, it is not certain.

However there is much firmer evidence, from the same period as the papal visit to Bologna, of a legendary mountain-paradise in Italy, although its location is different, and its name is not *Venusberg*. It is to be found in the *De Schismate* (1410) of Dietrich von Nieheim, a Saxon prelate who lived for some time at the papal court in both Rome and Avignon. Dietrich states that, in the neighbourhood of Pozzuoli, "cernitur mons sancte Barbare in plano campo et rotundus, quem delusi multi Almanni in eorum vulgari appellant Der Gral asserentes, prout eciam in illis partibus plerique auctumant, quod in illo multi sunt homines vivi et victuri usque ad diem iudicii, qui nisi tripudiis et deliciis

---

14) W. Pabst, *Venus und die mißverstandene Dido: literarische Ursprünge des Sibyllen- und Venusberges*, Hamburger romanistische Studien, 40 (Hamburg, 1955), p. 94, suggests that Hemmerlin actually invented the term "mons veneris", but this has little justification in the face of the words "communiter dicitur".
15) Fra Leandro Alberti, *Descrittione di tutta l'Italia* (Venice, Lodovici de gli Auanzi, 1568), f. 278v.
16) Barto, (*op. cit.*), p. 40.

sunt dediti et ludibriis diabolicis perpetuo irretiti."[17] Discussion of the name "Grail" must be deferred for the present; more immediate interest attaches to the location and nature of the mountain.

It was the suggestion of W. Pabst that Dietrich knew of the Norcian mountain-paradise from the romance *Guerino il Meschino*, where it is known as the realm of the Sibyl, and that he arbitrarily sought to relocate it at the original home of the Cumean Sibyl.[18] However this view is quite untenable. Dietrich's work is quite objective in character; the passage concerned appears in the course of an extensive description of the hot springs and baths of the area and reveals intimate knowledge of its topography — e.g. precise distances are given. He gives no cause to doubt his truthfulness; indeed, by attributing the mountain-paradise to diabolical activity, he shows himself hostile to the legend and would scarcely have introduced it into his work were it not in truth a prominent feature of the region he describes. He is, moreover, well informed concerning the Cumean Sibyl, for he mentions her traditional proximity to Pozzuoli and even discusses her at length elsewhere,[19] yet he sees the Grail-mountain and the Sibylline *hospitium* as geographically quite distinct.

However, although Pabst is certainly incorrect in his explanation of its origins, he is surely right in seeing here essentially the same legendary phenomenon as is attested at Norcia slightly later. The verbal similarities in the descriptions admit no doubt as to this; the peculiarly German obsession with the place and the author's sceptical attitude are all too familiar. It is also remarkable that the German belief endows the mountain with a different name from the local Italian tradition.

Dietrich reveals in general a marked interest in the mountain-caves of the area, which is of course highly volcanic in nature, such that the hills around are honeycombed with labyrinthine passages. As a young man, he tells the reader, he entered one of these caves with twelve companions, crawling naked on hands and feet due to the warmth and

---

17) *De Schismate*, ed. G. Erler (Leipzig, 1890), p. 156: "... in flat country is to be seen the humped mountain of Saint Barbara which many deluded Germans (in as much as their numbers are increasing in those parts) call "Der Gral" in their tongue, asserting that many men live, and shall live, in it until the Day of Judgment and are given over entirely to dancing and delights and are ensnared for ever in devilish sensuality".
18) Pabst, (*op. cit.*), p. 97f.
19) *Op. cit.*, lib. I, cap. 32.

the noxious fumes that filled the top of the passage; after proceeding some distance they reached a spring of water so hot as to harden instantly an egg placed in it. In this particular mountain, which is stated to be only four miles from the *mons sancte Barbare*, any person entering while a South wind blows is inevitably suffocated; such was the fate that befell "tribus notabilibus militibus Almannis tempore regiminis dicti Ottonis [Otto IV, 1198-1212] domini ducis, qui venientes de sepulchro dominico montem ipsum utique intrare volebant ..."[20] These tales testify to a certain German passion for penetrating mysterious regions within the bowels of a mountain; the story of the three luckless German knights also suggests how the fate of such adventurers might fortify a popular belief in a paradisical realm from which men do not, or may not, return. Above all, these stories display the character of Dietrich's text, and show that there is no cause to doubt his testimony of a popular tradition concerning the Grail-mountain.

In fact, further evidence connecting this same locality with both the *Venusberg* and the Grail is to be found in the 16th century. Johann Fischart in his *Geschichtsklitterung*, speaking expressly of the district of Pozzuoli, reports how visitors "den Gral oder Venusberg besuchen, und die guten tropffen besehen, die das feuer in Vesuvio aufblasen."[21] The passage is facetious, and gives no further details, but it at least broadly corroborates the earlier statement of Dietrich and, interestingly enough, affords the only instance of any real location ascribed to the *Venusberg* other than that at Norcia, before a later era when it was transferred to a number of places in Germany.[22] It is not possible to establish if the name *Venusberg* was attached to any mountain in Campania as early as the 15th century. But the *De Schismate* at least proves unequivocally that a German tradition of a mountain-paradise, very similar in character to later descriptions of the *Venusberg*, was already well established near Pozzuoli in 1410.

---

20) *Ibid.*, p. 155: "... three notable German knights at the time of the reign of the said lord, Duke Otto; coming from the Holy Sepulchre, they insisted on entering the mountain ..."
21) *Geschichtsklitterung (Gargantua)*, Text der Ausgabe letzter Hand von 1590, ed. U. Nyssen (Darmstadt, 1963), p. 326: "... visit the Grail or Venusberg, and look at the good fools who fan the fire in Vesuvius"; *cf.* Barto, (*op. cit.*), p. 17.
22) *Cf.* K. Amersbach, "Zur Tannhäusersage", *Alemannia*, 23 (1895), p. 75ff.; Pfaff, (*op. cit.*), p. 104; E. Schmidt, "Tannhäuser", *Charakteristiken*, 2. Reihe, (Berlin, 1912), p. 27.

At just about the same time Andrea Barberino completed his romance *Guerino il Meschino*, the first surviving text to locate the subterranean paradise in the Norcian mountain. Pabst argued that the Umbrian location of the mountain was Andrea's own invention, though this is probably incorrect and the Norcian tradition, though it may not be very much older, in all likelihood pre-dates the romance.[23] In any event it is quite reasonable to suppose that a very similar belief obtained in Germany with respect to two different Italian locations simultaneously; only a small proportion of the believers can have visited either mountain, and ignorance of Italian geography was surely widespread, among travellers and non-travellers alike. It is in fact worth noting that, while in 1410 Dietrich speaks of the growing numbers of Germans in the vicinity of the Grail-mountain, only by Faber (1483) are the large numbers of Germans visiting Norcia first stressed.

Attempts to pursue the tradition of the mountain-paradise further back into history, retaining some significant link with the later *Venusberg*, produce increasingly uncertain results. The three German knights who, according to Dietrich von Nieheim, entered the volcanic mountain near Pozzuoli at the turn of the 12th century testify only to a certain German enthusiasm for speleology, and perhaps also for the marvellous; there is no indication of precisely what they hoped or expected to find inside the mountain. On the other hand, there is the valuable literary allusion to a hollow mountain in the following cryptic strophes from the so-called *Wartburgkrieg*:

> Felicia, Sybillen kint,
> und Iunas, die mit Artus in dem birge sint
> die habent vleisch sam wir ouch gebeine.
> Die vraget ich, wie der künic lebe,
> Artus, und wer der massenie spise gebe,
> wer ir da pflege mit dem getranke reine,
> Harnasch, kleider unde ros. sie lebent noch in vreche.
> die gotinne bringe her vür dich,
> daz sie dichs underscheiden sam sie taten mich,
> daz dir iht hoher meister kunst gebreche.

---

23) Pabst, p. 22f.; *cf.* Löhmann, (*op. cit.*), p. 225ff.

> Felicia ist noch ein maget.
> bi der selben wirde hat sie mir gesaget,
> daz sie einen abt in dem gebirge saehe.
> Des namen hat sie mir genant:
> taet ich iu sam, er waer iu allen wol bekant.
> der schreip mit siner hant vil gar die spaehe,
> Wie Artus im gebirge lebe und sine helde maere,
> der sie mir hundert hat genant,
> die er mit im vuorte von Britanjelant:
> sie sint dekeinem vilan sagebaere.[24]

These strophes date from about the middle of the 13th century. They do not, of course, depict a paradise identical in character to those of the 15th century texts, but two firm links with the later evidence may be discerned. In the first instance the *Wartburgkrieg* is concerned with the Grail: the text stands in a close (though still unclear relationship with the strophic romance *Lohengrin,* in which Arthur's haven in a hollow mountain expressly houses the Grail. The question concerning the mysterious source of supplies for Arthur's host is plainly to be answered by the Grail's traditional and miraculous power as provider. In *Lohengrin* the mountain is said to lie in the fantastic East:

> ... hoch ein gebirge lit
> in der innern India, daz ist niht wit.
> den gral mit all den helden ez besliuzet,
> Die Artus braht mit im dar.
> man vint da vil schoener vrouwen lieht gevar.[25]

---

24) T. Cramer, *Lohengrin: Edition und Untersuchungen* (Munich, 1971), p. 200f.: "Felicia, the daughter of the Sibyl, and Juno, who are in the mountain with Arthur, have flesh and bone like us. I asked them how the king, Arthur, lives and who nourishes his retinue, who furnishes them with pure drink, with armour, clothing and horses. They still perform deeds of valour. Summon the goddesses before you that they may reveal it to you as they did to me, so that the skills of the great masters are not seen to fail you".
"Felicia is yet a maid. By that same virtue she told me that she saw an abbot in the mountain. She told me his name and if I did the same to you, he would be known to you all. He wrote with his hand of the great splendour, how Arthur lives in the mountain and his renowned heroes whom he brought with him from Britain, and of whom she named for me one hundred; they may not be told to one of low birth."

25) *Ibid.,* p. 546; *cf.* also p. 34ff. for a discussion of the relationship between the two works: "... high stands a mountain in Inner India, which is not far. It encloses the Grail with all the heroes, whom Arthur brought thither with him. Many beautiful ladies of fair hue are found there."

This location is derived from the *Jüngerer Titurel* of Albrecht von Scharfenberg, in the course of which the Grail is transported to India; the idea underlying it is possibly the legendary role of the East as the site of the Garden of Eden, the Terrestrial Paradise to which Alexander the Great supposedly forced a passage, only to be refused admittance. Such a fanciful location is typical enough of the literary world of romance and does nothing to render either less or more likely a popular belief of the 13th century which located a mountain-paradise in Italy. The mountain of the *Wartburgkrieg* is assigned no location at all; attempts have been made to connect the name *Felicia* with Norcia, but they are less than convincing, and Pabst is probably right in claiming that the poem is much too early to have been inspired by the Norcian mountain.[26]

However the name "Sybille", recalling the Italian name for the Umbrian mountain, provides a second obvious point of contact with the later evidence. The fact that the occurrence of this name in the German text remains virtually unexplained serves only to highlight the connection. "Sybille" similarly provides a slender link between the German text and the Grail-mountain near Pozzuoli, on account of the latter's proximity to the Sibylline Grotto. The possible role of the Sibyl in the genesis of the legend is discussed in a later chapter.

The most prominent differences between the mountain of the *Wartburgkrieg* and that depicted in the 15th century sources are to be connected with the literary nature of the former. While the later reports describe a popular belief, the earlier mountain is a literary fiction which combines fairyland and courtly elements in a manner characteristic of 13th century romance. The Arthurian mountain appears to be simply the fairy realm to which the "Hope of Britain" retired after his life in this world, and where he perhaps awaits his return; according to the most common form of the Arthurian legend, he dwells with his fairy half-sister Morgan, whose magic powers cure him of the "mortal" wound received in his last fearful battle with Mordred. This fairyland quality provides a further link with the Tannhäuser-legend, for, in as far as the latter is descended from a fairy-mistress story, the *Venusberg* is derived from a fairyland. Moreover, just as the life of the legendary Arthur in the mountain is by fairy power sustained indefinitely, so too

---

26) *Cf.* A. Reumont, *Saggi di storia e letteratura* (Florence, 1880), p. 383; Dübi, (*op. cit.*), p. 263; Pabst, p. 99.

the inhabitants of the mountain-paradise, in the 15th century reports of Dietrich von Nieheim, Johannes Nider, and Felix Faber, are mysteriously capable of life until Judgment Day. All in all, there seem to be good grounds for connecting the mountain of the *Wartburgkrieg* and *Lohengrin* with the legendary mountain-paradise which became known as the *Venusberg*.

Frequent attempts have been made to associate the Arthurian mountain of these 13th century German texts with the legendary association of Arthur and Mount Etna.[27] It is generally agreed that the Arthurian matter was brought to the Sicilian *Regno* (which, it should be remembered, comprised all of Southern mainland Italy including Campania) by the Normans at the time of their conquest.[28] Gervase of Tilbury, who had actually been in the service of the Norman royal house in Sicily, first records in the early 13th century the tale of a groom searching for a runaway horse on Etna. The man is confronted by Arthur, reposing on a couch within a marvellous palace, and is told by him how, since his last battle with Mordred, the king has dwelt there with wounds that bleed anew each year. The situation of the palace is paradisical — "spatiosissimam planitiem jucundam omnibusque deliciis plenam" — and it is reached by an "arctissima semita sed plana".[29] Despite some strong argument, it is less than clear that the place is felt to be inside the mountain, indeed, if such a wonder were intended, Gervase might reasonably be expected to draw more unequivocal attention to the fact.[30]

Caesarius of Heisterbach, in his *Dialogus Miraculorum*, relates a similar tale to that of Gervase, whom he postdates by only a few years. In this version the pursuing servant does not see Arthur himself, but meets an old man who informs him that the horse is to be found with the legendary king "in monte Gyber" (a common medieval name for

---

27) A. Graf, "Artu nell' Etna", *Miti, legende e superstitioni del medio evo* (Turin, 1893), II, p. 303 25; for a full bibliography of this matter cf. R. S. Loomis, editor, *Arthurian literature in the Middle Ages* (Oxford, 1959), pp. 61 and 68, and E. G. Gardner, *The Arthurian legend in Italian literature* (London, 1930), p. 12ff.
28) *I.e.*, either by the Norman invaders themselves, or by Breton *raconteurs* in their wake; cf. R. S. Loomis, "Morgain la fee in oral tradition", *Romania*, 80 (1959), p. 340f.
29) *Otia Imperialia*, ed. G. W. von Leibnitz, Scriptores Rerum Brunsvicensium, vol. 2, (Hannover, 1707), Dec. II, cap. 12, p. 921: "... a most wide and pleasant plateau, full with every delight"; "... very narrow but level path".
30) *Cf.* R. S. Loomis, "King Arthur and the Antipodes", *Modern philology*, 38 (1940), p. 298.

Etna).[31] In this case it certainly seems more likely that Arthur is considered to reside actually inside the mountain, though it should be noted that the Latin preposition *in* must very frequently be construed as "on". In fact none of the other texts linking Arthur with Etna, all of which are of later date, indicates that he dwells inside the mountain. The hero of the romance *Floriant et Florete*, from the later 13th century, is a favourite of Morgan, who dwells at *Mongibel* (Etna); there she has an enchanted castle to which the wounded Arthur will one day be brought.[32] In a Tuscan work of about the same time, the *Detto del Gatto Lupesco*, Arthur is likewise sought *at*, rather than explicitly *in*, "Mongibello";[33] in the *Chevalier du Papegaut* Morgan is known simply as "la fée de Montgibel".[34] It is by no means impossible that Caesarius of Heisterbach, correctly or incorrectly, understood the name *Mons Gyber* to belong to the castle or palace, as well as to the mountain on which it stood. At all events it seems most venturesome to postulate, from one questionable preposition in Caesarius' text, the existence of a whole legend of Arthur's dwelling inside Etna.

Nevertheless the 13th century certainly did associate the interior of the volcano with supernatural occurrences. But these are of a hellish nature, and quite distinct from the paradise of pleasure found in the Grail-mountain and *Venusberg*. Since very early times volcanoes were believed to be the mouths of Hell, and this idea seems to have clung to Etna in particular.[35] "Infernus Theoderici" was the name by which St. Willibald knew the neighbouring volcano of Stromboli in the 8th century, and later Otto of Freising reported how Theoderic the Ostrogoth was seen riding into the crater of Etna.[36] Later still, Thomas of Eccleston told a similar tale of Frederick II[37] — both rulers died as

---

31) *Dialogus Miraculorum*, ed. J. Strange (Cologne, 1851), dist. xii, cap. 12.
32) *Floriant et Florete*, ed. H. F. Williams (Ann Arbor, 1947), vv. 8242-50.
33) *Cf.* Gardner, (*op. cit.*), p. 14.
34) *Chevalier du Papegaut*, ed. F. Heuckenkamp (Halle, 1896), p. 11.
35) The belief is recorded in the 12th century by Sigibert de Gembloux and Alberich de Trois Fontaines, *cf. Monumenta Germaniae Historica*, ed. H. Pertz (Hannover, 1844, rprt., 1963), vol. VI, p. 353 and vol. XXIII, p. 829; to Etienne de Bourbon, Etna is "locus Purgatorii", *cf. Anecdotes historiques, légendes, et apologues tirés du recueil inédit d'Etienne de Bourbon,* (Paris, Societé d'histoire de France, 1877), p.32.
36) *Cf.* Gregory the Great, *Dialogues*, IV, cap. 30, Migne, *Patrologiae Cursus Completus*, series Latina, vol. 77 (Paris, 1896), col. 368f; Otto von Freising, *Chronica sive Historia Duabus Civitatibus*, ed. A. Hofmeister (Darmstadt, 1961), p. 380.
37) *Tractatus de Adventu Fratrum Minorum in Angliam*, ed. A. G. Little (Manchester, 1951), p. 96.

heretics of course. Such tales may be connected with certain beliefs concerning the great German rulers of the past which developed in the course of the 13th century and are analogous with that the Britons entertained of Arthur: they will one day return to restore order and prosperity to their former realms.[38] Usually they are depicted in a long sleep inside a hollow mountain awaiting, with their warriors, the call to arms. Charlemagne and Frederick Barbarossa naturally figure prominently in such stories, but both Theoderic and Frederick II also attract something of the legend, the latter albeit without the element of the hollow mountain.[39] In fact the idea seems to have been readily transferable, for it was further connected with both Olger the Dane and King Wenzel, the latter of whom was long believed to sleep inside the Blanik mountain in Bohemia.

Relative chronology certainly suggests that the legend of the sleeping king was inspired by that of Arthur.[40] But the hollow mountain with which it is usually associated has more than one possible source; in addition to the hellish volcano, the fairy-mound of Celtic tradition may have had a role to play in particular. There is also evidence that Arthur himself was sometimes taken to be the denizen of a subterranean realm in the Norman-British tradition. The principal testimony of this at an early date (c. 1169) is the *Draco Normannicus* of Etienne de Rouen, in which Arthur rules "antipodean" peoples with weird and uncanny physiques.[41] It appears to reflect an Arthur of folklore, a pre-courtly figure of decidedly ghoulish nature.

Obviously the legend of the sleeping king may very well be connected with the Arthurian mountain of the *Wartburgkrieg*; although the German text does not refer to Arthur's eventual return, it is a very widely known part of the legend. But there is no evidence associating the *Venusberg* in particular more closely with the legendary abode of a dormant ruler. Presumably all the beliefs involving hollow mountains — to the examples already given may be added loosely some

---

38) *Cf.* F. Kampers, *Die deutsche Kaiseridee in Prophetie und Sage* (Aalen, 1969), p. 67ff.; Loomis, "King Arthur and the Antipodes," (*op. cit.*); A. H. Krappe, *Mitteilungen der schlesischen Gesellschaft für Volkskunde*, 35 (1935), p. 90.
39) *Cf.* J. Grimm,*Deutsche Mythologie*, 4th edit. (Gütersloh, 1875), cap. 32, p. 794ff.; E. S. Hartland, *The science of fairytales* (London, 1925), pp. 184 and 212ff.
40) Kampers, (*op. cit.*), p. 85.
41) *Cf. Chronicles of the reigns of Stephen, Henry II and Richard I*, ed, R. Howlett (1884 9), ii, pp. 696-707; for this and other evidence *cf.* also Loomis, *Arthurian literature*, (*op. cit.*), p. 69, and "King Arthur and the Antipodes," (*op. cit.*).

folktales collected at later date — mutually supported each other.[42] But neither the hellish volcano nor the cave of the sleeping king points forward to any crucial feature of the *Venusberg*; they involve neither the paradise of pleasure, nor the place of temptation, which combine to form the mountain of the Tannhäuser-legend.

The list of useful sources for the early history of the legendary mountain-paradise is thus soon completed. But some points do emerge which deserve further consideration. The Grail is the first of these, for it helps to show the continuity of tradition reaching from the Arthurian mountain of the 13th century texts to the 15th century evidence. Unfortunately, the facts amassed by P. Barto concerning this point have been unduly neglected, no doubt because the theory he derived from them proved unacceptable.[43] The evidence of a widespread association in the 15th century of the legendary mountain-paradise and the Grail cannot be overlooked; and the fact that it is given the name Grail exclusively in German texts is of particular interest. The *Venusberg* is explicitly connected with the Grail not only by Fischart in the 16th century, but also by a 15th century chronicle which relates the story of Helias (a later name for Lohengrin) but does not assign the mountain to a location: "... duesse Jungling Helias sy gekomen uthe dem Berghe, dar Venus in den Grale iß."[44] Perhaps the most important allusion of all is the brief entry in Diefenbach's *Glossarium* which defines a "gral": "eyn ghelogen dink dat eyn koning sy, dar de lude leven in vrolicheyt wente an den jungesten dach".[45] The source used was dated as early as 1425 and the wording, particularly in the last phrase, unmistakeably echoes the descriptions of both the *Venusberg* and the Grail-mountain, although any idea of a hollow-mountain is missing. The unnamed king may conceivably be Arthur, whose diminishing importance has obscured his identity.

The Grail was introduced into German literature by Wolfram von Eschenbach in his *Parzival*. For him it is a magical and religious object

---

42) *Cf.* Amersbach, (*op. cit.*), p. 75ff., and W. Golther, "Geschichte der Tannhäusersage und Dichting," *Bayreuther Taschenbuch*, 12 (1889), p. 14.
43) Barto, (*op. cit.*), p. 9ff.
44) Caspar Abel, *Teutsche und Sächsische Alterthümer* ... (Braunschweig, 1732), vol. 3, p. 56: "... this youth Helias came out of the mountain where Venus is in the Grail"; *cf.* Barto, p. 63.
45) L. Diefenbach, *Glossarium Latino-Germanicum Mediae et Infimae Aetatis* (Darmstadt, 1973), p. 268: "A fictitious thing, that there is a king, where people live in joy until the Last Day"; *cf. ibid.*, p. XV.

having, in addition to the power of providing nourishment, that of indefinitely sustaining life: whoever beheld it might not die within seven days.[46] In Wolfram's work both Anfortas and Titurel afford instances of men kept alive in this manner. In the related text of Albrecht von Scharfenberg the five-hundred-year-old Titurel is obliged to request the Grail-knights to withhold from him the sight of the Grail, in order that he may at last pass on to Heaven.[47] The same function of the Grail is adumbrated in the cited passage from *Wartburgkrieg*. A late 14th century Catalan-Provencal poem, *La faula*, which has been included by some scholars among the works associating Arthur with Etna, portrays the wounded king sustained and kept continually young by the recurring visits of the Grail; here Arthur has the legendary role of Maimed King, which had become that of Anfortas in *Parzival*.[48] In the late 13th century the German poet Heinrich von Meissen (Frauenlob) seems to conceive of the Grail as a place to which past heroes retire, although he evinces scepticism, or at least ambiguity, on the matter of whether they are actually alive:

> Wa kam mit Parcivale
> ris' Sigenot unt der wilde man?
> Sie kerten zuo dem Grale,
> der tot hat si erslichen.

> Swie hohe ir muot do swebte,
> unt waer noch Artus solcher tugent,
> als er do milte lebte
> mit siner tavelrunde
> man vünde noch wol Parcival
> und alle herren in dem Gral ...[49]

---

46) *Cf.* in particular the passage 469, 14 28   *Parzival*, ed. A. Leitzmann (Tübingen, 1955), vol. 2, p. 104.
47) Albrecht von Scharfenberg, *Der jüngere Titurel*, ed. K. A. Hahn (Quedlinburg & Leipzig, 1842), p. 607, str. 6177ff.
48) *Cf.* W. J. Entwhistle, *The Arthurian legend in the literatures of the Spanish peninsula* (London, 1925), p. 81 4.
49) Heinrich von Meissen, *Leiche,Sprüche, Streitgedichte und Lieder* (Quedlinburg and Leipzig, 1843), pp. 161 and 143: "Where came the giant Sigenot and the Wild Man, with Parzival? They went to the Grail, death has crept up on them"; "However high their spirits then soared, were Arthur still so virtuous as he then generously lived with his Round Table, one would still find Parzival and all the lords in the Grail ..."

It seems possible therefore that the original role of the Grail in the legendary mountain-paradise was precisely that suggested by the riddle in the *Wartburgkrieg*. The paradox of an immortal life in the flesh is so common a component of descriptions of the mountain-paradise that it appears to be fundamental. Life in the flesh (with pleasures that are all too fleshly) is an intrinsically mortal state, yet in the mountain it may endure till Doomsday: such an unorthodox state of being is attributable only to the wondrous power of the Grail. Presumably, from being the object which ensured perpetual life, it progressed to become the very name of the fairyland realm where eternal youth was possible for all who came there. Felix Hemmerlin, Johannes Nider, Dietrich von Nieheim, and Felix Faber all make it abundantly clear that the men living in the mountain (if not the women too) enjoy a natural life in the flesh, and all but one of them adds the phrase "till Judgment Day". The same state is expressed by Diefenbach's definition of a Grail. All the larger texts, which are fully discussed later, also make this point in one way or another: in *Guerino il Meschino* the Sibyl confidently affirms "non sono corpo fantastico, ma sono, e fui de carne e ossa come che tu sei",[50] apparently in order to point out to the hero that she is a creature of free will and cannot therefore be compelled by his invoking the name of God — the verbal similarity with the *Wartburgkrieg* "die habent vleisch sam wir ouch gebeine" is striking. Elsewhere the Sibyl tells Guerino that she has already lived 1200 years.[51] In Antoine's *Paradis de la Reine Sibylle* the knight, visiting a realm of flesh-and-blood people, learns that it will endure till the end of the world.[52] Even a later Czech text describing the journey to the Sibylline paradise hints at the same theme, recognisable despite the story's gross corruption. Here the travellers ask concerning the common report that the Sibyl presents a beautiful human aspect only from the front, while seen from the rear she is revealed as a hideous spectacle. In response she leads them to a tent where she strips naked, and they are able to convince themselves of her palpably human body from all sides.[53]

---

50) From the earliest known print (Padua, 1473), cap. 152; cf. infra, cap. 3: "My body is no apparition, but I am, and (always) was, of flesh and bone as you are".
51) *Ibid.*, cap. 145.
52) Antoine de la Sale, *Le paradis de la Reine Sibylle*, ed. F. Desonay (Paris, 1930), p. 26.
53) W. Söderhjelm, "Eine tschechische Version der Reise ins Sibyllenparadies", *Neuphilologische Mitteilungen*, 10 (1908), p. 77.

The Grail then, while it is in no way intrinsically connected with the Tannhäuser-legend itself, plainly had a major part to play in the German belief in a mountain-paradise. Yet the Grail exhibits of course no trace at all of the demonic nature which attaches to the *Venusberg* in the Tannhäuser-legend. The world of the Grail was originally courtly and innocent, in Germany even sanctified; at its worst, it is only the mystery of the Arthurian court of the romances, exemplified in the mountain of the *Wartburgkrieg*. These Arthurian beginnings suggest that the demonic nature of the mountain was not authentic, but a later accretion which evolved, it appears, from moral interpretation of the place.

The reasons for this degradation, like those for the development of a legendary mountain-paradise itself, are probably complex and certainly not fully ascertainable; the precise time at which it occurred remains quite obscure even with the assistance of the different evidence to be discussed later. But at least the 15th century German sources cast some light on the nature of the change. All the churchmen describe a popular belief, according to which the mountain-realm and its pleasures are quite real; the view that it is in fact a diabolical illusion, or a snare to trap men's souls, is by and large submitted as their own enlightened explanation. Only in the fictional, but obviously didactic, story of Hemmerlin's Simplicianus does the simple visitor himself clearly recognise the evil into which he has fallen. Obviously, when the legend of Tannhäuser was itself widely known, the popular belief must have incorporated the recognition that the mountain was diabolical. It appears possible that the writers depict a belief of extreme *naïveté* largely in order to derive from it didactic capital. Dietrich von Nieheim briefly states that the Grail-mountain is a trap of the devil, but expressly indicates that the Germans are deceived by it. The interests of Johannes Nider are more scientific, and he adopts his typically academic approach precisely to the matter of the supposed reality of the *Venusberg*; his conclusion is to explain it all, including the apparent corporeality of the beautiful women there, as diabolical illusion, and he gives a brief *exemplum* to demonstrate such a revelation:

> Respondet Wilhelmus [William of Auvergne] ... quod fictitium est totum, licet demonum opere tales homines illudantur modis tactis in primo dubio ut in veritate eis fieri videatur quod tamen in apparentia sit, unde refert quod quidam miles se sic putabat

frui quadam femina luxuriose qui evigilians se reperit in luto quodam realiter amplecti quoddam cadaver mortue bestie.[54]

In Hemmerlin's case, it is the power of demons to employ such tactics which, forming his immediate subject, prompts mention of the *Venùsberg* at all. Felix Faber fulminates at human gullibility but, writing in an age that had already grown more humanistic, he is disinclined even to honour the legend with the fatuous suggestion that devils are at work, preferring to blame the mendacity of travellers. His euhemeristic insistence that Venus is long dead further indicates how he feels himself confronted with a firm belief in her existence.

The 13th century literary fiction of a romantic and courtly mountain-paradise, innocently housing King Arthur and the Grail together with its essentially fairy female denizens, does not betray what moral censure, if any, it attracted from those who felt themselves called to judge in such matters. But the popular belief which ascribed reality to such a place and attracted ordinary men to seek out its perpetual pleasures for themselves is recorded only later and by those who condemned it; in their unfavourable judgment the essentially pagan and fairy realm is revealed as a diabolical machination designed to lure men to perdition. Even the claim of perpetuity for its pleasures undergoes modification, in order to indicate quite unambiguously that no such sinner could at the last escape the wrath of God. The fairyland realm of immortality had no conceivable place in Christian orthodoxy, unless it were on the side of the devils. In fact, medieval ecclesiastical writers were inclined to construe all fairies and their activities as essentially diabolical, until the time of such rationalists as Faber, who ventured to call them fictitious.[55] Notwithstanding the obscure notion of the sustaining Grail, the immortality of the flesh remained a doctrinal absurdity. Only the spirit possessed immortality, and the mortality of the flesh was unalterable; any promise, such as that made by the mountain-paradise, to combine the best of both natures must represent a pernicious snare employed by demons to rob men of both body and soul.

---

54) *Op. cit.*: "William answers ... that it is all false, although such men are deceived by the work of demons, their manner of perception being changed in the first moment of doubt, so that what is in fact appearance seems to be happening to them in truth; and he tells of a knight who in this way thought he was enjoying a certain woman with lasciviousness, who awoke to find himself in a mire, really embracing the corpse of a dead animal"; (the meaning of "modis tactis in primo dubio" is very obscure).
55) *Cf.* J. A. McCulloch, *Medieval faith and fable* (London, 1932), cap. 2.

With the degradation of the mountain's moral quality went hand in hand, it seems, a degeneration of the pleasures it supposedly provided. The courtly perfection and pleasures of the Arthurian mountain in the *Wartburgkrieg* are not greatly emphasised; they are largely incidental to the writer's immediate purpose, it appears, and probably self-evident to the 13th century adept of Arthurian literature — in any case they are axiomatic at the court of Arthur. When the legend emerges in the 15th century, in texts of a quite different sort, the mountain is a place of sensual and wicked indulgence. Perhaps the "tripudiis et deliciis" of Dietrich von Nieheim still betray a lingering awareness of the original innocence of a place that bears the name "Grail". But for Nider and Faber, as well as Hemmerlin, the mountain is a mire of demonic debauchery.

This transformation of a realm of perfect delectation into a perfidious and diabolical trap for the human soul is a process charged with disillusionment. It is the didactic potential of that disillusionment which seems to have inspired so many of the 15th century allusions to the legendary *Venusberg*. The German churchmen exploit the disillusionment, contrasting the simple innocence of the popular belief with a reality that is most sinister. Nider extends this exploitation further with his *exemplum*, instancing in a literary miniature the experience of such disillusionment. But it is the Tannhäuser-legend itself, in the same spirit as the others, which gives full literary form to the disenchanting history of the *Venusberg*: the honourable knight, who penetrates the mountain in search of Fro Minne and her ladies, finds himself, to his horror, in the clutches of the devil.[56] The succeeding events of the story result from his efforts to escape this plight.

---

56) Such considerations lend broad support to the view, advanced by D. Moser in his very recent work, *Die Tannhäuser Legende: eine Studie über Intentionalität und Rezeption katechetischer Volkserzählungen zum Buß Sakrament* (Berlin, 1977), p. 12ff., concerning the theological intention underlying the legend's composition; but the specific claim *(ibid.)* that the story was authored by bodies within the church seeking to reinforce orthodox tenets among a simple populace threatened by heterodoxy cannot be demonstrated from the evidence.

THE TRAGEDY OF KNIGHTHOOD 21

II
LE PARADIS DE LA REINE SIBYLLE

The earliest and the fullest surviving version of the Tannhäuser-legend is that given by Antoine de la Sale in his *Paradis de la Reine Sibylle*. Yet this well-written French text can scarcely be said to have enjoyed the attention it consequently merits: while the affinity between Antoine's story and the German ballads has been universally recognised, scholars have for the most part done little more than argue from the simple existence of the former, and from what Antoine says of his sources, either *pro* or *contra* the legend's Italian origins. The Frenchman's work has been frequently described, but never given the scrutiny it deserves.[1]

Reservations about terming it a version of the Tannhäuser-legend are less than warranted; with only one important exception, every essential narrative component present in the ballads is to be found there.[2] Where the French text shows immensely greater detail, subtlety and embellishment, the ballads — which disagree sufficiently among themselves to constitute different versions — do not contradict, but only pass on cursorily with the bald terseness and energetic parataxis characteristic of balladic narrative. While the sophisticated psychology and the detailed, colourful descriptions in Antoine's versions are virtually inimical to the balladic style, they are nevertheless quite compatible with the story given by the ballads. It is true that the *Paradis* makes no explicit mention of Tannhäuser himself, and that the Italian Sibyl appears in the place of the German Venus, but this is not necessarily a matter of more than names: the parts played by the Queen and the sinning knight, of whose particulars Antoine was able to ascertain no more than his German origins, are in every crucial point those of their counterparts in the ballads. More important is the difference in the manner by which the knight is brought to despair, and consequently to return to the mountain: Antoine makes no mention of

---

1) *Cf.* Dübi, (*op. cit.*), p. 252ff., Pfaff, (*op. cit.*), p. 106; E. Grisebach, *Tannhäuser in Rom*, 9th edit., (Stuttgart, 1904), p. 129; G. Paris, "La légende de Tannhäuser," *Légendes du Moyen Age* (Paris, 1903; rprt. Amsterdam, 1970), p. 113ff.; W. Söderhjelm, "Antoine de La Sale et la légende de Tannhäuser", *Memoires de la Société Neo-Philologique a Helsingfors*, 2 (1897), p. 111ff.; Kluge, *(op. cit.)* p. 37ff.
2) *Cf.* Kluge, p. 43.

the miraculous burgeoning of the Pope's dry staff. This matter is fully treated in a later chapter.

The *Paradis* is not in fact the first work to show the Norcian Sibyl in a Calypso-like role. In *Guerino il Meschino*, written several years previously, she is licentious and seductive both to a greater degree, and in a manner more personal, than is Antoine's Sibyl. But, being a proper version of the legend, the *Paradis* is best given priority in discussion; Guerino's story is not Tannhäuser's, although the Italian romance displays an obvious and material affinity with the legend. Indeed that affinity is best elucidated from a full knowledge of Antoine's story.

It has been suggested however that Antoine knew the romance and employed it a source for his work.[3] There are no proper grounds for this supposition, though it does effectively highlight what is perhaps the greatest problem in assessing the evidence supplied by the French text, and one that is central to any argument treating the legend's early history: it is difficult to determine satisfactorily the extent of Antoine's own originality in his story. He himself emphatically disclaims all originality. But the tale is told with much skill and artistry; it is fluent, balanced in its emphases, and rich in detail. Where so much imagination was employed in the telling, it is not safe to assume that every detail appears precisely in the form he received it, although the authenticity of most points he includes may be corroborated from other evidence, as will be seen subsequently. This small reservation apart however, attacks on the honesty of Antoine's declaration have little enough foundation. A brief consideration of the background and nature of the work will help to demonstrate this.

The *Paradis* was first composed with an introductory dedication to Agnes, Duchess of Bourbon, probably in 1437 or 1438.[4] It was subsequently incorporated into Antoine's extensive didactic work *La Salade*, written for the young John of Calabria to whom Antoine was mentor in about 1444.[5] The Angevin prince was of the Sicilian royal house, in whose service the respected knight had spent his earlier years.

---

3) Pabst, p. 32f.
4) *Cf.* C. Knudson, "Une aventure d'Antoine de la Sale aux Iles Lipari", *Romania*, 54 (1928), p. 99ff.
5) *La Salade* was first printed in Paris, 1527; critical edition: Antoine de la Sale, "La Salade", *Oeuvres completes*, ed. F. Desonay (Paris, 1935), Vol. 1.

In fact Antoine was already some fifty years old when he commenced his career as a writer. He had travelled extensively in Italy, and sets out in the *Paradis* to describe simply what he saw and learnt on the occasion of a visit to the Norcian mountain; he dates his own ascent to the cave on the 8th May, 1420. The considerable lapse of time between his visit and his record of it certainly admits the possibility that his memory failed at the occasional detail and called on the assistance of his imagination. But his account is so thorough that it may be presumed to rest on some record he made at the time. The tale of the German knight, which he declares he had from the local inhabitants, fascinates him but also calls forth a certain scepticism which is characteristic, but distinctly equivocal: his efforts to disprove scientifically, rather than ridicule, the alleged truth of the legend, as well as the cautious modesty with which his opinion is advanced, betray the uncertainty which remains in his mind. The objective and factual quality of all Antoine's writings, and his scrupulous scientific scepticism, have in point of fact been admired generally as unusual for his time.[6] His integrity seems virtually unimpeachable, and deception and fabrication are alien to his nature.

Internal evidence from the text, such as there is, also tends to support the view that Antoine does not seek to emend or alter the story, but only to report it faithfully. His own experience of the mountain included nothing supernatural or even abnormal; indeed, when his escorting company attribute an eerie cry, heard as they reach the grotto, to the inhabitants of the Sibylline paradise, he readily explains it as an acoustic distortion of the whinnying of the horses, tethered in a meadow some distance below.[7] Everything uncanny that he has to report of the mountain is expressly derived from sources whose suspect nature is made fully clear, *e.g.* from the lunatic hallucinations of a priest, and from the fabulosity of the "gens du païs" who "assez sont fortes a croire".[8] He refers briefly to information obtained elsewhere, but gives no details of it, except that it was less satisfactory than what

---

6) *Cf.* J. Nève, *Antoine de la Salle: sa vie et ouvrages* (Paris, 1903), p. 28; J. M. Ferrier, "Antoine de la Salle and the beginnings of Naturalism in French prose", *French studies*, 10 (1956) 3, 216 23; G. Paris, (*op. cit.*), p. 73f.; Pabst, p. 34.
7) *Paradis*, (*op. cit*), p.15.
8) *Ibid.*, pp. 17 and 21: "local inhabitants"; "... are hard enough to believe."

he gained at the mountain itself: "neantmoins que en autres pars les aye ouy raconter, mais non mie si tresproprement".[9]

Antoine begins his account with the story of the nearby "Lac du Pillate", resort of necromancers and the alleged last resting-place of the body of Pontius Pilate. The legend of Pilate's end need not concern us, but it is worth noting how Antoine seeks to discredit it scientifically by pointing out the crass historical inaccuracies it includes. His own journey to the Sibylline grotto and the details of the cave he entered are next described in the same scientific spirit: precise distances are supplied and Antoine even digresses to give some botanical details of certain Alpine flowers found on the way. With some emphasis he assures the reader that he did not venture beyond the outer cave — "si bien eusse voulu, sans grant dangier de ma personne je n'eusse peu".[10] In proceeding to relate what he was told by the local inhabitants, he makes the further cautionary observation that not all of them are credulous, some even ridiculing the tales.

His first source of this type is the verbal account of two young men of the vicinity who entered the cave with three others; Antoine makes no negative observation on the value of their testimony. Equipped with ropes, candles and supplies for five days, these young men penetrated the cave as far as a cleft, from which issued a wind so strong that they feared to be swept away and ventured no further. This escapade, which Antoine describes as a piece of youthful bravado, includes nothing that could not easily be explained by natural phenomena.

The only other specific witness of the cave's interior of whom Antoine speaks is a priest named Anthon Fumato, whom he describes thus: "... lequel par lunoisons n'estoit mie en son bon sens. Et en sa maladie aloit et venoit en plusieurs lieux, et disoit de merveilleuses choses qui sont acoustumees a dire a gens malades de telz maladies ..."[11] Few people lend credence to this priest's words, though Antoine

---

9) *Ibid.*: "... nevertheless I have heard them told in other parts, although not as correctly"; in *La Salade* (*op. cit.*, p. 63) Antoine specifies that he had heard of these matters in his youth.
10) *Paradis*, p. 15: "... even had I wished to, I would not have been able to do so without great danger to my person."
11) *Ibid.*, p. 17:"... who was not in his good senses, due to the influences of the moon. And in his sickness he came and went in various places, and said wondrous things, such as people sick with such disorders are accustomed to say."

points out that both his consistency over a number of tellings, and the corroboration of his experience by that of the German knight in the 'Tannhäuser-story' reported by others, stand in his favour. In fact the essence of the priest's story is that he accompanied two Germans into the cave, past a series of supernatural obstacles, and as far as the "portes de metal, qui jour et nuyt sans cesser batent, clouant et ouvrant",[12] where the two foreigners entered, though he remained outside. Since this hallucination of the priest was, in all likelihood, based on the story of the German knight, the corroboration of detail is of course not surprising; yet it is symptomatic of Antoine's objectivity towards all the facts, that he makes this point.

The mysterious obstacles described by Don Fumato each take the form of a test of courage. First came the windy cleft which deterred Antoine's previous witnesses. However, according to the priest, if one but ventures three or four paces into the dangerous storm the severity of the wind is quickly diminished. Following it comes a bridge of unknown material, which is only one foot in width and of great length, traversing a chasm at whose bottom a mighty river rushes with terrifying noise. But when one advances with both feet on to the bridge, it at once becomes broader and continuous to grow in width as one proceeds across it. At the same time the roar of the water becomes less intense. Then the adventurers reach two artificial dragons, one each side of the passage, of horrifying verisimilitude with eyes which illuminate the cave with their gleam. They too, of course, prove harmless and the visitors pass on to the metal doors, which "batent par telle maniere qu'il est proprement advis a celui qui y doit entrer que entrer ne pourroit sans estre entre deux acueilli et tout effroissié".[13] Here the two Germans led by Fumato halt in trepidation, but they eventually decide to proceed, requesting the priest, who declines to go further, to await them there for twenty-four hours. In the event, they pass the beating doors as easily as the other obstacles. Don Fumato falls asleep while waiting, and dreams that they emerge and request him to wait longer. On awakening he is uncertain of what has really happened and, after waiting a short while, departs from the mountain never to hear of the two Germans again.

---

12) *Ibid.*: "... metal doors which beat ceaselessly night and day, shutting and opening.'
13) *Ibid.*, p. 20: "... beat in such a way that he who should enter there is duly shown that he cannot enter without being caught between them and quite crushed."

The story of the German knight and his squire, which Antoine next relates, affords all the information he ever procured regarding the paradise itself. It is true that he later mentions two other men reputed to have entered it, but these reports are not backed by any information describing it.

Summarily he tells how the German knight and his squire successfully pass all the obstacles described by Fumato, and enter unscathed through the beating doors. They find themselves confronted by a further door, of great beauty, and glistening as though made of crystal, and, although from outside the beating doors they had heard a murmuring sound as if of people, they marvel to find absolute silence here. After waiting a while in indecision, they hear a voice near the door; the knight calls out, and is asked what he seeks and where he comes from. Grandiloquently he replies "qu'il estoit un chevalier des parties des Allemaignes, et que la estoit il venu pour veoir les choses merveilleuses de ce monde, comme son estat le requeroit, pour acquerir honneur et mondaine gloire".[14] Earlier, Antoine described him as "chevalier des parties d'Alemaigne, qui sont gens grandement voiageurs et querans les adventurez du monde"; he had heard tell of this place and the "merveilles qui s'ensuivent; si conclut d'y aler, et ainsi le fist".[15]

The knight is thus not only quite oblivious to any possibility that he may be entering a sinful realm; he even regards his action as meritorious in the light of his chivalric calling. Precisely because he is a knight, it is incumbent on him to seek out such wonders; rather than transgressing any moral code, he is, in his own eyes, acting with positive virtue according to his station.

This feeling for aristocratic propriety is matched by the courtly tone of his reception into the paradise. The voice beyond the door requests them with exemplary politeness to wait while the news is conveyed to the queen; a host of further people then arrive "en treshonnourablez estatz", who repeat the question and, on receiving the same answer,

---

14) *Ibid.*, p. 24: "... that he was a knight from German parts and that he had come there to behold the wonders of this world, as his status required, in order to gain honour and worldly glory."
15) *Ibid.*, p. 21: "... knight from German parts, who are great travellers, seeking the adventures of the world"; "... wonders that arise from it; he decided to go there, and accordingly did so."

admit them. Before passing a third door they are taken to a side-chamber and completely re-clothed in rich new array; then they are led, to the sound of musical instruments, through fine chambers and gardens, past companies "de dames et de damoiselles, de chevaliers et d'escuiers" who have assembled to welcome them, into the presence of the queen herself, who receives them enthroned. All this description Antoine adorns with the superlatives proper to idealized courtly splendour; it is indeed a mountain-court of which King Arthur would have been proud. There is, as yet, no hint whatsoever that it houses anything untoward. The Sibylline Queen herself carries the air of a supreme secular ruler — "ainsi que s'elle feust dame de tout le monde" — and greets the German knight "telles que a chevalier s'appartenoit, comme celui qui bien savoit honnourer dames et seigneurs de pris",[16] showing pleasure at his arrival, and once more questioning him as to his name and origins. He is offered the opportunity to choose for himself a lady from among those without escort, but he politely declines at first, "disant que la n'estoit il mie venuz pour autre chose que pour cela qu'il avoit dit", perhaps because he feels such conduct is not in keeping with the honourable chivalric aims of his visit.[17] However this scruple, if indeed it is such, is short-lived, for both he and the squire soon select ladies to their pleasure.

If the knight sins at all in simply entering the mountain, it is because he accepts without question the propriety of a chivalric moral code which requires him to aspire to worldly honour and glory, by seeking out wonders. He is thoughtlessly blind to the moral implications of such a quest. And thoughtlessly blind he remains, persistently and dangerously long after his entry into the mountain. A warning seems to be intended, though it is disregarded, when the knight asks what will become of the Sibyl and her realm at the end of the world and receives the chilling reply: "Nous devendrons ce que est ordonné, et n'en vueillez plus savoir".[18] But the theme of unheeded warnings is subsequently highlighted in a far more drastic, and yet intricate, way: each Saturday all the ladies inside the mountain are transformed for a period of twenty-four hours into snakes and serpents, creatures of unmistakeably diabolical quality. That this is a warning of their true

---

16) *Ibid.*, p. 25: "... as if she were lady of all the world"; "... such as becomes a knight, like one who well knows how to esteem praiseworthy ladies and lords."
17) *Ibid.*, p. 26: "... saying that he had not come for any other purpose than that which he had stated."
18) *Ibid.*: "It will befall us as is ordained, and you should seek to know no more."

nature is unambiguously evidenced by the knight's eventually seeing in it the proof that they are the enemies of God. According to the custom of the place the knight is permitted to leave the mountain on any one of only three days: on the ninth day following that of his arrival, or on the thirtieth, or on the three-hundred-and-thirtieth; if he fails to avail himself of this last opportunity he is obliged to remain for ever. These figures demonstrate even more clearly the admonitory function of the ladies' transformations: the minimum days of sojourn are not three, as the simple numerical pattern might have prompted, but the multiple, which just exceeds one week and must therefore include a day of transformation. In this way, if the warning were heeded, the knight would be free to depart soon after his recognition of the evil; and vice-versa, if he wished to leave at the earliest opportunity, the true nature of the realm would be first revealed to him.

In the event, the German knight initially declares he will leave after the first term but, in his utter enjoyment, time flies for him and, heedlessly engrossed in pleasure, he fails to see the admonition; he defers departure to the second, and again finally to the third chance. Antoine quite explicitly attributes these delays to the knight's utter preoccupation with the pleasures of the paradise. When his change of heart finally eventuates, three hundred days have elapsed since his arrival, during which he must have witnessed forty-two transformations precisely. Such dilatoriness in recognising the devilish nature of the realm, despite so many opportunities, indicates a degree of moral apathy which is psychologically plausible only in terms of Antoine's emphasis on the knight's oblivious absorption in sinful pleasure.

But, although the weekly transformation of the ladies is quite expressly the feature which confirms for the knight the satanic quality of his company, his moral wakening is described as a more intricate process, preceding any mention of the transformations. Interestingly God Himself plays a part:

> Un jour, pensant a certaine chose de ses affaires, dont le cuer lui commança a douloir. Et de ce pensement l'ama Dieux tant, qu'il le mist au pensement de congnoissance, par lequel il se fut advisé d'avoir tant grandement mespris vers son Createur de plusieurs choses mondaines qu'il avoit faictes encontre son vouloir et ses commandemens, et souverainement du tresorrible pechié ou il

vivoit, par lequel il l'avoit de tous poins mis en oubli par l'espace
de iijc jours, pour soy acompaigner avec son ennemy; ...[19]

Only after this passage does Antoine proceed to mention the regular metamorphoses and the hero's recognition of their significance. A psychological process of some intricacy, in which God plays a vital part, is thus described. First, memory of the outside world induces sorrow in the midst of pleasure; at this moment of consideration, God in His love directs the sinner's thoughts along the proper course. Only with thoughts of God, who was hitherto forgotten, can the knight overcome his obtuse moral blindness and correctly recognise his plight.

His disenchantment at this point has a wide embrace. A naively sincere pursuit of "honneur et mondaine gloire", seemingly so proper for one of chivalric status, has led directly to the jeopardy of his soul. The perfect and pleasurable world, which he entered, believing it a laudable goal of courtly and knightly endeavour, and in which he so long dwelt enjoying its unalloyed delights in absolute innocence, is revealed as a threatening and sinister snare. Such disillusionment is, in the first instance, only a more literary expression of the view expressed by the religious writers of the 15th century regarding the legend of the mountain-paradise.[20] But it also has obvious figurative implications here; it touches more than simply the conventional ideals and aims of chivalry. In a long literary tradition preceding this time, chivalry had been conceived as the supreme instance of a life dedicated to the values of this world, frequently in explicit contrast to the religious life; it was the ideal form of secular human existence. Antoine stresses repeatedly the worldliness of what the knight seeks and finds in the mountain: he holds it his duty to seek out the "choses merveilleuses de ce monde";

---

19) *Ibid.*, p. 27: "One day, thinking of a certain matter of his affairs, his heart began to pain him. And, because of this thought, God so loved him that He made him to think of his conscience[?], by which he was shown that he had greatly defied his Creator in committing various worldly deeds against His will and commandments, and most of all in the appalling sin in which he lived, by which he had entirely forgotten Him for the space of three hundred days, in order to keep company with His enemy ..."
20) J. Siebert, in his edition and study of Tannhäuser's works *Der Dichter Tannhäuser Leben Gedichte Sage* (Halle, 1934), p. 238f., recognises the criticism of chivalry implicit in the legend and adduces it as evidence of the latter's early origin, by connecting it with the spirit of asceticism which set in after the worldly chivalric age of the emperor Frederick II. However the argument has little weight: this asceticism became a prominent part of the complex moral mood of the late Middle Ages, and was by no means restricted to the end of the 13th century.

he aspires to "mondaine gloire"; and he thereby unknowingly commits "plusieurs choses mondaines" contrary to the will of God. The mountain-realm itself offers worldly pleasures in limitless abundance: "les deliz mondains y sont tielz que cuer pourroit penser ne langue dire".[21] By such expressions, the paradise is made the more easily to seem a metaphor for this world, where man is allotted a space of time which he may squander in reckless enjoyment of the paradisical pleasures it offers. But unless he pays timely consideration to higher matters, and turns his back on the sinfulness of the place, he will lose all chance of entering the true paradise of eternal life in heaven. In a clear indication of the transitoriness of this world's pleasures, the Sibylline queen prudently evades an honest answer to the question of her realm's ultimate fate; she does not wish the visitor to consider his final destiny, lest he wisely choose to leave her while he may. It is the duty of a man in this world to take thought for those things that transcend its temporary physical pleasures, to evaluate its attractions accordingly and, seeing in them a mortal danger for the soul, to repudiate them.

In the second half of Antoine's story this universality of its moral content is sustained, indeed the hero's chivalric status is now all but incidental. The psychological emphasis shifts from his moral blindness to his constancy in remorse and repentance. Now that he comprehends his grave situation, time lies heavily on his hands and he can scarce endure to wait the remaining thirty days before his permitted departure. The pleasures of the mountain have all become repugnant to him. His squire, whose portrayal as an independent character commences only at this point, has experienced no change of attitude towards the paradise, but is persuaded reluctantly, but loyally, to accompany him from the place.

In contrast to the German ballads, there is no bitter altercation between the queen and the knight at the time of departure; the latter, it is true, is urgently implored to remain, but he naturally refuses. The exchange is apparently conducted with all chivalrous decorum, for "pour partir plus courtoisement, dist de retourner briefment".[22] At the moment of leave-taking the squire, who can barely tear himself away, repeats this promise without any such dissembling; both the promise

---

21) *Paradis*, p. 28: "... the worldly delights there are such that heart cannot conceive them, nor tongue tell ..."
22) *Ibid.*, p. 30: "... in order to leave more courteously, he said he would return shortly."

itself and the contrasting sincerity of the two travellers are proved tragically ironic by later events.

Once outside the mountain, the knight evinces a sense of urgency which is the proper antithesis of his dilatoriness during the first three hundred days in the paradise: just as he gave no thought then to the passage of allowed time, and to the needs of his soul when that time elapsed, so now he "estoit dolent de tout son cuer de l'offense qu'il avoit par tant de temps faicte a Nostre Seigneur, ne pensa jamais venir a temps en sa vraie repentance et de venir a confession".[23] Making straight for Rome he throws himself at the feet of a confessor in St. Peter's. The latter, on hearing his story, explains that he is not empowered to pronounce the absolution of such an offence, and directs the sinner to the Pope in person. Significantly, he nevertheless exhorts him to true repentance and trust in God's mercy.

At this point Antoine digresses to treat the question of the identity of the Pope concerned, and in doing so commits a factual error of some interest. He offers the names of three Popes, together with a date for each, asserting that his sources varied as to which one was actually involved. The first of them is Pope Innocent in 1352 (Innocent VI); the second is Urban in 1362 (Urban V); the third he names as "Urbain de Limozin" in 1377. In that year the regnant Pope was in fact Gregory XI, who indeed came from Limoges, but never took the name Urban.[24] Antoine plainly understands his "Urbain de Limozin" to be Gregory, despite the incorrect name, for he goes on to outline correctly the events at the papal election following his death, which led to the Great Schism. He further adds that this pope ordered the destruction of both the causeway, by which the necromancers reached the island in the Lac du Pillate, and the path to the Sibylline Grotto; he also excommunicated all who visited the mountain and retained to himself the sole right to absolve them. This error of naming, which Antoine repeated elsewhere in *La Salade*, invites no ready explanation. Probably Antoine, who is usually most accurate in historical matters, had in mind Gregory's successor, Urban VI, who was an Italian and not a Limousin.

---

23) *Ibid.*, p. 31: "... he was suffering with all his heart for the offence he had committed for so long against Our Saviour, and believed he would never get there in his true repentance and reach confession in time."

24) Antoine makes the same error in another part of *La Salade*; cf. *Paradis*, Desonay's Introduction, p. lxxiff.

The knight's interview with the Pope, which marks the point of divergence of Antoine's version and the German ballads, further reveals how the depth and pertinacity of the sinner's repentance is now the crucial matter. The Pope has heard tell of this knight who presses for an immediate opportunity to be confessed. On confronting him, he repeats the question first put by the inhabitants of the mountain, as to the knight's name, his quest and origins; the reply is significantly different this time: "... dont je suis ne qui je suis saurez vous par temps assez. Mais je viens a vous, vicaire de Dieu, pour vous requerir pardon et mercy des offenses que j'ay tant faictes a mon Sauveur".[25] Gone is the pride and sense of individual dignity that becomes a knight; the state of his soul is now an issue more urgent than the vanity of worldly status. The Pope, while grieving intensely at the knight's grave sin, is delighted to find him so repentant; however he resolves to deny him absolution for the present, and drives him from the audience "comme homme perdu".[26] This is not, Antoine promptly reassures the reader, because he cannot or does not wish to grant absolution for the offence, but rather in order to make an example of him; he seeks to demonstrate the enormity of this sin for the benefit of others, so that they may be discouraged from visiting the mountain in confident hope of subsequent absolution. It is the Pope's intention at all times that the knight should finally receive absolution. But the delay occasioned by his measure functions as a test of the sinner's steadfastness in repentance. The danger of the knight's despairing is made all too clear: indescribably grief-stricken, he is consoled by the ministrations of a certain cardinal who "le mist hors de desespoir".[27] Various representations are made on his behalf to the Pope, who clings to his policy, maintaining an appearance of adamant and lasting refusal. But still the contrite sinner persists in believing his offence pardonable; unremittingly he endeavours to gain the successful intercession of cardinals and prelates with the Holy Father.

In order to destroy this confidence and faith, the devil is compelled to resort to precisely the same tactic as was so successful in first winning the knight's dedication to the diabolical pleasures of the mountain: he employs deception, so that the genuinely remorseful sinner is tricked

---

25) *Paradis*, p. 34: "... whence I come, and who I am, you will learn in due course. But I come to you, Vicar of God, to beg pardon and grace for the many sins I have committed against my Saviour."
26) *Ibid.*, p. 35: "... as a man lost ... ."
27) *Ibid.*: "... kept him from despair."

into despairing of a forgiveness which was never to have been denied him. The squire, who has never ceased to yearn for the mountain-paradise, is inspired by the devil to bring false news of a papal plot to arrest and kill them both. The knight, deprived by this ruse of all hope of forgiveness, commits the consummating sin of despair: with all hope lost for the everlasting life of the soul, he hastens to save the remaining life of the body and flees away from the fictitious executioners of the Pope to the mountain. In this way he may delay at least until Judgment Day the horrible fate that awaits his soul.

Antoine makes it quite clear that the knight's return is caused by despair; the Pope, too, recognises this fact: "car, se parti estoit, c'estoit par desesperation".[28] Apportioning blame for this despair is a matter of some importance, in view of the variation at the conclusion of the legend between Antoine's version and that of the German ballads. Full consideration of this matter must be deferred to a later chapter where the ballads are discussed, but it should be noted at once that Antoine does not entirely exonerate the Pope, who "se sentoit moult coulpables".[29] On the other hand, the resounding damnation accorded to the Pope in the High German ballad for his part in the affair is foreign to the French text in every way. When, in the High German version, Urban IV indirectly tells Tannhäuser that he can never find forgiveness, there is no saving hint of a white lie; it remains a bald theological error (for no act of sin is absolutely unpardonable), which is all the more gross for its source in Christ's Vicar on earth. When Antoine's Pope rejects the knight's request, treating him "comme homme perdu", he dissembles with a laudable motive. His joy at the man's repentance is sincere, and he eventually sends for him in order to actually pronounce him absolved, unaware that he has departed. The Pope might be criticised for a failure to fulfil a pastoral duty by comforting and encouraging the sinner in his repentance; but the task of consolation is performed by the cardinal.

However, even if the actions of individual characters do not permit any simple allocation of guilt, the legend itself and the universal moral lesson it implies leave no doubt as to whose moral shortcomings are of central interest. Judged from a modern point of view, the Pope perhaps shows himself a poor judge of the weakness of human nature; but,

---

28) *Ibid.*, p. 37: "... for, if he had departed, it was from despair."
29) *Ibid.*: "... felt himself most guilty."

taking into account the figurative quality of the knight's role in this version, precisely that human weakness is exposed by the Pope's action as a moral flaw of tragic potential. Antoine does not further consider the Pope's culpability, and makes no attempt to analyse it or to suggest a preferable course of action for him; attention falls on the knight's despair, which is made an integral part of the moral-theological theme of the story. The papal delay in granting absolution, far from being damnable, is a most efficient and proper test of the strength of his repentance — an efficient test, in that it reveals ultimate inadequacy. Antoine even gives some hint that the knight's anxiety during this period serves as some kind of atonement, when he states "mais neantmoins encores eust il assez souffert ..."[30]

Despair of forgiveness is, theologically speaking, a general human problem, and thus fully commensurate with those illustrated by the sojourn in the mountain-paradise. The man who dwells for a term inside the mountain, sinfully indulging *ad libitum* in its pleasures, becomes, by virtue of its figurative representation of the sinful world, himself a representative of man's worldly sinfulness. When he seeks papal remission of his guilt it is human sinfulness itself who kneels at confession, and the pardonableness of human sin is at stake. Such an extended view of the knight's role is supported by his disclosing to the Pope not merely his stay in the mountain, but "la somme de ces pechiez dont il estoit souvenant, depuis l'eure de sa nativité ...".[31] Orthodox doctrine affirms that all sin may be remitted, provided that the sinner is truly repentant and performs adequate atonement. But the matter of despair touches less on the mechanics by which the church administered the sacrament of absolution, than on the underlying theology of pardon. In the last resort only God can forgive; to despair of forgiveness is to despair of God's mercy. However His forgiveness is not merited, but is freely given as a voluntary act of grace; sincere repentance is only an essential precondition of receiving pardon, and it cannot buy absolution. Repentance and atonement are thus insufficient, and it is further essential that man has an enduring faith in God's gratuitous willingness to forgive. If he despairs of that, all reason

---

30) *Ibid.*, p. 36: "Nevertheless he would have suffered enough ..."
31) *Ibid.*, p. 34: "... the sum of the sins which he recalled, since the hour of his birth"; J. C. Payen, "Le problème du pardon dans Le Paradis de la Reine Sibylle d'Antoine de la Sale", *Fin du Moyen Age et Renaissance*: Mélanges de Philologies Française offerts à R. Guiette (Anvers, 1961), argues from this feature in favour of the great antiquity of the tale, but disregards its evident metaphorical function.

for repentance is lost. The knight's return to the mountain accordingly represents a despairing renunciation of the life of the soul, and an endeavour to seek consolation in the wretched pleasures of the body that remain to him: "... puis que n'ay peu avoir la vie de l'ame, que ne vueil perdre celle du corps".[32] For all that the Pope's action contributed to it, the knight's despair is portrayed as a consequence of his own weakness in faith. Even before the squire's base trick is described, Antoine hints that his master's patience is nearly exhausted; he is constantly reminded by his servant of the pleasures of the mountain, so that "au chevalier enuera le grant deslay de son pardon".[33]

The conclusion of Antoine's tale differs little from the other versions. Messengers sent by the Pope fail to reach the knight before he has re-entered the mountain, and the transmission of his detailed story to posterity is conveniently explained by letters describing his experience, which he leaves with shepherds on the hillside. No mention is made of the Pope's fate, though the reader is informed that he ordered the destruction of the path to the grotto as a result of the affair.

Two other incidents are mentioned by Antoine concerning visitors to the interior of the mountain, but neither provides further information of the German knight. However one of them, which treats the great-uncle of a certain Messire Gaulchier de Ruppes, is of some interest for all its brevity: it has the same structure (characteristic of a fairy-mistress story) as the Tannhäuser-legend. The man apparently came back to the outer world after a long stay in the paradise, but later returned there as a consequence of some devastating disappointment, whose cause is not specified. It is quite possible, even likely, that this tale was inspired by the Tannhäuser-legend, although it may reflect a previous or independent fairy-mistress tradition connected with the Norcian mountain.[34]

Antoine also relates how he searched among the inscriptions on the wall of the grotto, in an effort to identify that of the unfortunate German knight. The name which he tentatively selected is scarcely of

---

32) *Paradis*, p. 38: "... since I could not possess the life of the soul, I do not wish to lose that of the body."
33) *Ibid.*, p. 36: "... the knight was vexed at the great delay to his pardon."
34) *Ibid.*, p. 50f.; the story is perhaps a conflation of such material with an earlier narrative concerning Gaulchier, *cf.* Desonay's Introduction, p. LXXIVf., and E. Langlois, *Nouvelles françaises inédites du XVe siècle*, Bibliothèque du XVe siècle, vol. VI (Paris, 1908), p. 34-38.

scientific value;[35] but, that he did so betrays some inclination on his part to regard the story as true. The same attitude is indicated by his efforts to inspect the letters left by the knight; he is informed that they were forwarded to the Pope, who destroyed them. On the other hand, Antoine concludes the *Paradis* with an emphatic statement of the legend's falsehood, using arguments from Scripture and from learned writings concerning the Sibyl. Perhaps his varying attitude to the story's truth is to be explained by a greater credulity in the young man who actually visited the mountain than in the older one who recorded the visit years later. His obviously acute awareness of the tale's moral import also suggests that, at the time writing, he saw it as a fable.

But this ambivalence at least lends further support to what he tells of his sources. Clearly he is repeating at second hand a story for whose truth he accepts no responsibility. More than once he faithfully includes in his account details whose significance plainly escaped him: a golden ring given to the knight by his own lady on his departure from the mountain, which he later surrendered to the Pope, is one example of this;[36] another is the linguistic gift acquired by those who dwell in the paradise — after nine days the visitor understands all tongues, and after three hundred and thirty days can actually speak them (this is very possibly a part of the necromantic tradition). However, although there is no reason to doubt Antoine's claims that his immediate sources were the oral statements of "gens du païs", the story's sophistication strongly suggests earlier literary origins. Far from being a simple popular tale of mysterious and magical beings inside the mountain, it is a religious moral story employing depth of understanding and literary subtlety in its portrayal of the psychology of pleasure, guilt, repentance and despair. The metaphorical use made of the mountain-paradise, the ironic contrast of the knight's innocent but worldly objective with the true nature of his achievement, as well as the precision with which the theme of disregarded warnings is managed, all betray the work of a highly artistic literary hand. A fine symmetry is established between the sinner's initial dilatoriness and his later urgency, and another between

---

35) *Paradis*, p. 40: "Herhans Wanban borg intravit"; variant in the ms. of *Salade*: "Herhans Wanbanbourg Borg", and in the incunables (1521 and 1527): Her Hans Wanbranbourg intravit"; (= ? *Her Hans van B(r)anburg*, presumably a Low German name).
36) A number of earlier scholars (*e.g.* Kluge, *op. cit.*, p. 44; Schmidt, *op. cit.*, p. 28) supposed the "vergette" to be a rod or wand, and connected it with the Pope's staff in the ballads; but for Antoine it is most certainly a ring, *cf.* Dübi, *op. cit.*, p. 259.

his delay in leaving the mountain and the fatal delay in granting absolution. Of course, it is not possible to prove conclusively that some features of this sort which are less essential to the story— *e.g.*, the complementary questions posed by the Pope and the Sibylline Queen as to the knight's identity — are not the contribution of Antoine's own imagination. But since an anterior version of considerable sophistication is to be postulated, it is both simplest and most plausible to attribute them in the first instance to that version.

It is also clear from Antoine's story that the earlier literary version which he indirectly, and doubtlessly imperfectly, transmits, can scarcely have been a political one. There is no suggestion of a conflict of Guelf and Ghibelline, or of a knight of the Hohenstaufen allegiance suffering vindictive treatment at the hands of an anti-Hohenstaufen Pope — a theory that has been commonly advanced to account for the naming of Urban IV and the *Minnesänger* Tannhäuser in the High German ballad.[37] If Antoine's source had given greater prominence to criticism of the Pope's action than does his own version, he would scarcely, in his efforts to exculpate the pontiff, have drawn attention, as he does, to the possibility of actually blaming him.[38] On this point, as elsewhere, there is no reason to accuse Antoine of distorting his source in any way. It is not simply the Frenchman's telling which makes the tale a primarily religious one, depicting the human moral predicament in general terms; such must also have been the character of the anterior literary source, for the fundamental elements of the story point clearly in that direction. This view is also supported by the testimony of Felix Hemmerlin, recorded about the time of the *Paradis* and, like Antoine's text, allegedly conveying facts gathered two or three decades previously. Simplicianus' tale involves not only a total lack of anti-papal sentiment, but the sinner's remorse actually wins the reward of absolution; the state of Simplicianus' soul occupies the centre of the stage throughout, and no other person's guilt intrudes.

But the most important question regarding the *Paradis* remains that of its sources, both indirect and direct. How much of the original version has become distorted in the dubious transmission of the "gens du pais"? May one lay at their door the curious fact that the lady of the

---

37) *E.g.* R. M. Meyer, "Tannhäuser und die Tannhäusersage", *Zeitschrift des Vereins für Volkskunde*, NS 21 (1911), p. 14.
38) *Cf.* Kluge, p. 46.

mountain is a Sibylline Queen, whom Antoine, despite his puzzlement, at once identifies with a prophetic Sibyl but who nevertheless shows some of the allegorical properties of the German "Fro Venus"?[39] Are they also to be blamed for obscuring the name of the German knight? These matters do not admit of sure answers, and they may only be tackled in the light of all the evidence at the conclusion.

---

39) *Paradis*, p. 51.

III

GUERINO IL MESCHINO: THE TEST OF MORAL FORTITUDE

Guerino il Meschino is a rambling but highly imaginative romance composed by Andrea da Barberino, probably in the first decade of the 15th century.[1] It is the earliest known text to locate a mountain-paradise at Norcia, though whether this location of the Sibylline realm was entirely Andrea's invention, as has been suggested, seems most doubtful.[2] The question is not without interest, in view of the usual subsequent identification of the Norcian mountain with the *Venusberg*, but it is not central to a search for the origins of the Tannhäuser-legend; the tragic story of the German knight is in no way intrinsically tied to the Norcian location, or indeed to any real location at all.

The most cursory comparison of the story furnished by the *Paradis de la Reine Sibylle* with the Sibylline episode in *Guerino* at once reveals fundamental external differences. The former is a fully self-contained tale, faithfully retold from obscure sources by a writer whose only apparent independent contribution is a candid, but naively equivocal scepticism regarding its veracity. The latter, on the other hand, constitutes only a fairly well integrated component in an extended narrative by an author of some originality, who freely employs his lively imagination to mould and adapt quite diverse material to a broad theme. The simple but crucial fact that Guerino, his hero, commits no sin at all while actually inside the mountain, serves to indicate how far removed is his story from that of Tannhäuser. On entering it he has no illusions as to its true nature and consequently experiences no disenchantment; since he resists all the temptations with success, he knows no pangs of remorse, and no test is set for his steadfastness in repentance. Indeed any need he has of forgiveness arises solely from his entry of the place — morally a mere technicality in view of his reasons for doing so.

Andrea's manner of composition is eclectic in the extreme, but one other literary source in particular gave inspiration to the Sibyl-episode of *Guerino*: — the catabasis of Aeneas and the Sibyl in Book VI of the

---

1) For the date of the work *cf.* G. Osella, "Il Guerrin Meschino", *Pallante*, fasc., IX and X (Turin, 1932).
2) *Cf.* Pabst, p. 22ff., and the criticisms of his view made by Löhmann, (*op. cit.*), p. 225f., and Wis (*op. cit.*), p. 17ff.

Aeneid. It may be argued that Vergil's work plays the role rather of an allusion than of a source, but it is nevertheless vital to the passage and may not be discounted.[3] Andrea explicitly draws attention to the parallel more than once; it is part of his aim to demonstrate how his Christian hero, Guerino, can not only match the awesome adventure of the eponymous pagan founder of Latin civilisation, but even surpass it, for he later achieves greater success in the Christian Hell with the superior moral strength of his Christianity. It should be noted at the same time however that Aeneas' adventure had no discernible direct influence on Antoine's tale of the German knight.[4]

The course of Andrea's work as far as the Sibylline episode may be very briefly summarised.[5] Guerino is of noble birth, but, having been abducted as a small child, he grows up obscurely in Byzantium, in ignorance of his lineage. In his youth, however, he so excels in chivalric valour and service that he becomes a favourite of the Emperor. Eventually he wins the hand of the Emperor's daughter by his victory in a tournament, but the reward is lawfully denied him, because he cannot prove his nobility. He consequently embarks on a long series of adventures in quest of his father, a search that leads him through the length and breadth of the world. It is plainly the objective in this quest which inspired the literary analogy with Aeneas: just as the classical hero sought the knowledge and aid of the oracular Sibyl to penetrate the Nether-world and seek out the shade of his father Anchises, so Guerino, with essentially the same problem, also looks to her prescience for help. The motive for Guerino's entry into the mountain is entirely explained by this parallel with Aeneas, and it has nothing at all in common with the adventurous hedonism of the German knight.

However, unlike that of Aeneas, Guerino's world is essentially Christian, and his pagan Sibyl suffers a negative moral evaluation in consequence. Her oracular powers are revealed as nothing other than an occult knowledge accessible only through sorcery, that is, through forbidden intercourse with evil forces. On arrival in Italy, Guerino at once learns that the Sibyl now lives in the Norcian mountain, the traditional haunt of those malevolent spirits whom the black arts render amenable to the human will. On his journey to the place he is repeatedly

---

3) *Cf*. Pabst, p. 53ff.; Löhmann, p. 236.
4) Nevertheless this gives no grounds whatsoever for Pabst's strange assertion (p. 53) that Antoine was ignorant of Vergil.
5) A full summary is given by Osella (*op. cit.*).

warned of its wicked and sinful nature, which he accordingly acknowledges. His failure to gain his objective inside the mountain (it is, at the same time, a moral success) results from his realisation that the knowledge possessed by these diabolical powers can be procured from them only at the soul's peril. The Sibyl makes perfectly clear her knowledge of his father's identity, but adamantly refuses to divulge it until he yields to her sexual importuning. This he just as adamantly refuses to do; a true Christian knight, he refuses to barter his soul for the worldly glory of acknowledged nobility and an imperial marriage. He will not, for success alone, succumb to the sordid temptations of a half-hellish realm where wretched souls eke out their time in shallow pleasures until their inevitable damnation at the Last Day. Appropriately enough, when Guerino's search eventually meets with success, a similarly subterranean location is involved, but the source of his information is wholesomely Christian, in distinct contrast with the pagan powers of the Sibyl: he finally learns of his father by visiting St. Patrick's Purgatory in Ireland.

In thus employing the legendary mountain-paradise as an exacting test of his hero's virtue, Andrea evidently had no cause to use many of the psychological motifs that are so essential to Antoine's tale, whether or not he knew of them. Nevertheless the two stories have so many similarities, that there can be no doubt that they drew on common material, and closer examination of the Sibylline episode in *Guerino* is necessary in order to ascertain the implications of these similarities. Unfortunately the text of the work, which proved immensely popular until quite recent times, has endured almost ceaseless modification and alteration since its composition; a critical edition is a pressing desideratum. The manuscripts are numerous and in many cases nearly inaccessible, so that the text here used and referred to is, *faute de mieux*, that of the first printed edition (1473).[6]

A number of the mountain's physical features described by Antoine are recognisable in *Guerino il Meschino*. The topography is described by Andrea with a fantastic exaggeration which renders comparison with the Frenchman's scientific report difficult; however, both emphasise the perilous windy ridge with deep chasms on either side, and some real

---

6) The copy obtained was that of the Bayerische Staatsbibliothek, Munich, which lacks a title page; the imprint on the final leaf runs: "... in Padua a di XXI. de Aurille M.CCCC.LXXiii. Bartholomeus de Waldezochio civis Patuus Martinus de septem arboribus Prutenus F.F.''

knowledge of the climb seems to underlie Andrea's account, even if it was not at first hand.[7] His claim that all the winds dwell on the mountain (*Cap.* 138) seems to be another version of the report concerning storms and tempests found not only in the *Paradis*, but also in Hemmerlin and Bercheur.[8] Similarly, the ferocious gale that earlier visitors experienced issuing from the mouth of the cave (*Cap.* 139) plainly corresponds to the windy cleft mentioned by Antoine. On his passage through the mountain Guerino, like Antoine's nameless knight, encounters a raging torrent of water, though no reference is made here to a bridge, or indeed to how he crossed it at all (*Cap.* 143). He is also confronted by two frighteningly life-like artificial "demonio", which evidently correspond to Antoine's dragons. Finally he reaches a metal door which, unlike the "portes de metal" in the *Paradis*, does not beat unceasingly but is opened at his knocking to admit him to the Sibyl's realm. Andrea's story also includes numerous elements mentioned neither by Antoine nor in any other description of the mountain-paradise; individually they are of no interest here, though their presence serves to indicate that the sources employed by the Italian writer are by no means restricted to Vergil and the legend of the mountain.

By the time Guerino actually reaches the metal door he is already very well informed with regard to the nature of the region he approaches. The importance of this warning prior to entry, alien as it is to the spirit of Antoine's story, is so great for Andrea's version that he makes it, in effect, a permanent installation of the place: each of the two "demonio" flanking the doorway bears an inscription (perhaps inspired by the inscribed portal in *Inferno* Canto III): "cui intra in questa porta e passa lanno che non ense non morira in fino al di del iudicio & alora morira in anema e in corpo sara danato".[9] This threat is a familiar feature of the mountain-paradise, though it may be noted that the term of one year corresponds more precisely to Hemmerlin and to the German ballads than to Antoine's tale. But for Guerino the warnings began even earlier: the innkeeper at Norcia anxiously tells him that nobody ever returns from the place; a certain "official del castello" (perhaps identifiable with the "chastel nommé

---

7) *Cf.* Wis, (*op. cit.*), p. 30.
8) Bercheur, (*op. et loc. cit.*).
9) *Guerino*, cap 143: "... whoever enters at this door and spends a year without leaving shall not die until Judgment Day, and then he shall die in soul and body, and be damned."

Montemoynaco" of Antoine,[10] or the "castello Montefortin" of Hemmerlin) informs him that all who go there are excommunicated (*Cap.* 141). From the point of view of Guerino's own story, this last statement seems to prepare the way for his sketchily described visit to Rome on leaving the mountain. Yet, at the same time, it plainly corresponds to Antoine's report of a Pope who excommunicates all who visit the place, retaining sole right of absolution. Most important of all are the admonitions and advice of the hermits through whose dwelling the visitor must pass on his way to the cave. They greet Guerino and the innkeeper, who accompanies him only to this point, with the question "quale de uui che vole andare a perdere lanima el corpo?"[11] Then, after informing him that he will be obliged to remain there for a full year, but should on no account delay longer, they arm him spiritually for his ordeal, by advising what prayers and invocations are necessary to escape the false enticements, and by warning him above all to "guardarte dala luxuria pero che elle no sono tanto uitiate che se tu non te sapera graudare [=guardare] tu porti pericolo de non tornare zamai ..."[12]

Guerino, then, shares nothing of the well-meaning, but naive innocence of the German knight at the time of his entry, and his adventure develops accordingly. Whereas Antoine, in describing the knight's reception, endeavoured to let the reader participate in his delusion, by lingering on the splendour and pleasures of the place and by giving no explicit indication of its sinfulness until the moment of the hero's disenchantment, Andrea makes no attempt to conceal the dangers which threaten Guerino. One of the maidens who admit him addresses him "con uno falso riso", and even as he first beholds the Sibyl in her beauty, he thinks to utter the efficacious words: "Ihesu cristo nazarero libera me da questi incantamenti".[13]

Andrea's realm is markedly less courtly than Antoine's. Courtly etiquette is of course largely the behavioural norm in a romance of this period, and it is true that Guerino kneels before the Sibyl, who takes him by the hand as though a lady of station. But any emphasis on

---

10) *Cf. Paradis*, p. 9.
11) *Guerino*, cap. 141: "... which of you seeks to go and lose both body and soul?"
12) *Ibid.*, cap. 142: "Beware of lust, by which they are not so weakened that if you do not take care you are in danger of never returning."
13) *Ibid.*, cap. 144: "... with a false smile"; "Jesus Christ of Nazareth, free me from these spells."

courtly decorum, such as to suggest the place has idealistic attributes of courtly type, is absent; fine music, and opulent clothing, which Antoine accentuates, are not mentioned by Andrea. The disenchantment with a worldly ideal which resulted from the German knight's adventure, is inapposite here; Guerino faces simply a trial of his virtue or, more specifically, a test of chastity. In place of Antoine's hosts of gracious ladies and knights he therefore meets at first only beautiful maidens, whose sexual attractions are given much emphasis. Other pleasures are not altogether omitted from the place: the luxuriant garden of unseasonable fruits, a part of the tradition found in both Hemmerlin's account and, with less prominence, in Antoine's, is met with; Guerino is also shown an abundance of gold and precious stones, and prompted to give his estimation of such wealth in a scene distinctly reminiscent of one in the *Paradis*. But these features are more or less irrelevant to Guerino's ordeal or, at the best, they serve only to arouse his appetite generally and weaken his resistance to sexual seduction. In the *Paradis* the matter of the knight's sexual accommodation was circumscribed with every courtly discretion; his "compagnon" was properly chosen from among those who were unattached, and was otherwise not distinguished in any way. The sexual nature of Guerino's ordeal calls for a very different state of affairs: the Sibyl herself, potential source of the knowledge he above all seeks, assumes the role of seductress and lies beside him exposing her beauty in an effort to vanquish his virtue. At one point he actually feigns love for her, in order to trick her into divulging the secret of his parentage. She encourages him, hinting at her knowledge with a full account of his life-story hitherto, but withholds the crucial information, vainly awaiting his sexual corruption. Plainly his success here is possible only through sin.

With difficulty, Guerino defends himself from their lust until the first of the weekly transformations, on the Sabbath. This event had in fact already been foreshadowed by the hermits outside the mountain who told him: "se pure te defendi .vii. ziorni tu vederai que cossa ele sono".[14] But since Guerino was by that stage already well aware of their true nature, these words of the hermits must betray what was the function of the metamorphosis in Andrea's source: to betray the inhabitants' evil nature. Guerino's staunch and virtuous resistance is perhaps fortified by witnessing the metamorphosis, but otherwise its

---

14) *Ibid.*, cap. 142: "If you can defend yourself for seven days, you will see of what substance they are."

admonitory role is quite superfluous here. Andrea, as will be seen, personally puts the motif to a very different use. Moreover, he commits an inconsistency which reveals unmistakeably how he has failed to marry his source with his own different intention: the hermits use the feminine pronoun (it will be recalled that only the ladies are transformed in Antoine's story), but Andrea describes the male denizens of the mountain also undergoing metamorphosis. Indeed, although there was no specific previous allusion to any male residents other than Guerino himself, it is a man who first tells the hero of the imminent transformations and then actually becomes horribly changed in his sight.

The metamorphosis is conceived simply as punishment for sin, so that all sinners inside the mountain are equally affected; Andrea then uses the idea for a somewhat crude tract on the Seven Deadly Sins, and apparently borrows inspiration from the punishment of the thieves in the Eighth Circle of Dante's *Inferno*. In addition to the man whose transformation he actually witnesses, Guerino sees six distinct kinds of reptilian monster, each of which represents by some symbolic action or feature one of the Sins; indeed the description supplied in each case invariably incorporates the name of that Sin. The first man plainly instances *Pride*, for "li parea Superbia bestia & la diuina posanza lo feze humili ..."[15] Later the Sibyl, with an earnest didacticism far more typical of Andrea's time than of her character otherwise, systematically explains each of these monstrous forms to the hero. She tells how all of them are there on account of a sin which God punishes with an appropriate metamorphosis.

Another theme is touched on in the course of the Sibyl's explanations which is of considerable importance to the Tannhäuser-story: it seems that the denizens of Andrea's mountain, like Tannhäuser and Antoine's knight, have resorted there in despair. In fact this theme is introduced much earlier in the episode and recurs with some persistence throughout. The "official del castello" whom Guerino met on the way to the mountain reproaches him with despair, since he sought to go "dove non uano altro che ribaldi, o gente disperata", and the hero defends himself with the innocence of his purpose: "lanima mia non e desperata"   "sapiate che io non uo alla

---

15) *Ibid.*, cap. 147: "It seemed to him a proud creature, and the divine power made it humble."

Sibilla per nessuna falanza anci uo per ritrouare el mio padre".[16] Shortly afterwards the hermits compel him to a similar explanation: "o sancto padre iu non ua per uanita, ni per superbia, ne per desperatione, ma solo per ritrouare de que generatione io sono nato".[17] Now, in explaining the seven types of sinner in her realm, the Sibyl repeatedly mentions how they came in despair at their sinfulness; only in the case of the *Angry* is the reference to despair lacking, and it is hard to see any specific intention in this omission.

Of the proud man she has some personal details to tell, and it seems likely that Andrea had some known character, real or fictional, in mind; but she adds that he came finally to the mountain "como homo desperato". Similarly of the *Avaricious*: "fono tanto auari che se desperono e ueneno qui per lavaritia"; of the *Slothful*: "ueneno qui per desperatione de accidia"; of the *Lustful*: "essendo molto biasmati & minazati se desperono deliberono uenire in questo loco solo per questo vitio de al luxuria"; and so on.[18] The notion of despair due to sinfulness is in no way germane to Guerino's plight, and must have had some place in Andrea's source to have found inclusion here at all.

When, by assiduously following the advice of the hermits, Guerino has successfully resisted the blandishments of the Sibyl for nearly a year, but has consequently learnt nothing of his father, he confronts her for the last time in a scene of some interest. In a moving appeal, he alludes to her oracular powers in days of classical antiquity, thus giving the opportunity for overt comparison of himself with Aeneas. In reply, she reproaches him with being a "uilano caualiero", declaring "el duco Eneas troyano fu de piui zentil natione die te & lo condusi per tuto lo inferno e mostroli lo suo padre Anchise".[19] There is evident irony in this notion of *gentilezza* put in the mouth of the evil pagan seeress, and Guerino steadfastly bears the slight on his knighthood. He attempts a

---

16) *Ibid.*, cap. 141: "... where only scoundrels and desperate men go"; "... my soul has not despaired"; "Know that I do not go to the Sibyl on account of any crime, but solely to find my father."
17) *Ibid.*: "O holy father, I do not go out of vanity, nor pride, nor despair, but only to find of what parentage I was born."
18) *Ibid.*, cap. 151: "They were so avaricious that they despaired and came here on account of Avarice"; "They came here from despair at Sloth"; "They were much cursed and threatened, and they despaired and resolved to come to this place purely from the sin of Lust."
19) *Ibid.*, cap. 152: "... base knight ... Duke Aeneas of Troy was of more gentle birth than you, and I led him right through Hell, and showed him his father Anchises."

further bribe, in words that call to mind the demand made by Venus in the German Tannhäuser-ballads: "comemzo a promettere che la li lo insegnasse che lui li daria al mondo bona fama & diria la sua nobelta e teria celata la sua trasmutatione".[20] But the attempt is rebuffed — the inhabitants of the mountain are indifferent to their reputation in the world. Finally Guerino's anger bursts forth in the words "o iniquissima o renegata fada maledeta da lo eterno dio",[21] as he vainly attempts to coerce her by invoking the power of God, in the passage described in a previous chapter. Then, amid maledictions on both sides, he leaves the place.

His journey to Rome, undertaken as soon as he leaves the mountain, is described summarily. It is justified only in terms of the previous warning that all who visit the place are excommunicated, for he has manifestly not otherwise sinned. Nevertheless, Guerino throws himself at the feet of the Pope in extreme remorse, claiming "non e mazior peccatore de mi"[22] and reminding him of the high power to forgive, bestowed by Christ on St. Peter. It seems exceedingly probable that Andrea's source-material involved a character who, like Antoine's knight, actually sinned inside the mountain. But in Guerino's case the Pope, in view of what he is told of the hero's quest, and of the hermits' testimony to his unblemished virtue, pronounces him absolved. At the same time it is worth noting that Guerino is also obliged to wait three days before he obtains a papal audience; in the ballads this is precisely the span of time that tragically proves too long.

Although Andrea evidently freely adapted his material to fit his own story, he apparently used a source similar in very many respects to the tale of the German knight in the *Paradis*. Pabst contended that, since (in his view) Andrea actually invented the Norcian Sibyl, the Italian work must have been a source of the *Paradis*, as the latter includes the "Reine Sibylle".[23] But this is most improbable; one should speak rather of common source-material, though this does not in either case necessarily represent the immediate source. Andrea plainly had before him a source in which the hero sinned and required pardon; the

---

20) *Ibid.*: "He began to promise that, if she told him, he would give her a good reputation in the world, and tell of her nobility, and keep secret her transformations."
21) *Ibid.*: "O iniquitous and despised fairy, cursed by the Eternal God ..."
22) *Ibid.*, cap. 157: "There is no greater sinner than I."
23) Pabst, p. 39ff.

transformations of the ladies also evidently served primarily to betray their diabolism (as will be seen later, this is the original function of the motif), so that the hero must have entered the mountain in innocent ignorance of its sinfulness. Together with all the corroborative detail, this constitutes some case for the claim that Andrea's source was a version of the Tannhäuser-legend. On the other hand, there is no positive evidence that is described the knight's return to the mountain, or included the figure of Venus and much of the subtle detail found in Antoine's story. The presumed source appears to have had generally the same characteristics as the tale of Simplicianus, told by Hemmerlin, although the latter also lacks the metamorphosis-motif and includes both the figure of Venus and some hint of the mountain's metaphorical role. If Andrea omits these last points, it is perhaps only because they were not consonant with his particular aims.

All that may be said with scientific certainty is that Andrea knew the story of a hollow mountain containing a worldly paradise where men live on in the flesh, enjoying sensual pleasures until Judgment Day; beautiful women dwell there under their leader, and entice men to this sinful indulgence; they also experience a weekly transformation which warns visitors of the sinful nature of the place; the visitor must depart after one year, or is condemned to remain till the end of time; men commonly repair there in despair of their sins;[24] an automatic sentence of excommunication falls on every visitor, unless he procures absolution at Rome. With only few exclusions and additions, the same list would also summarise the affinity of Hemmerlin's story with the legend.

More must be said of Pabst's theory concerning Andrea's sources. He suggests that the Italian romancer derived the figure of the Sibyl from a certain "regine d'ancelles" in the 14th century French work, *Huon d'Auvergne*; the "regine" was in turn, he believes, based on the figure of Dido in the *Aenead*.[25] Thus Pabst contrives to trace the lineage of the Venus in the Tannhäuser-legend back to a frustrated Dido.

---

24) The agreement of Andrea and Antoine, both of them early sources, in indicating despair as the reason for an unending stay in the mountain is not at once easily reconciled with Moser's belief (*op. cit.*, p. 30ff.) that Tannhäuser's return thither was originally a matter of the sinner's reverting to the place of sin to await there his pardon; his view derives largely from analogous tales of repentant sinners.
25) Pabst, p. 66; "Huons von Auvergne Keuschheitsprobe", ed. E. Stengel, *Mélanges de philologie rom. et d'histoire littéraire offerts à M. Wilmotte*, vol. 1 (Paris, 1910), p. 685 713; *cf.* also the highly critical view of Löhmann, (*op. cit.*), p. 233ff.

Andrea, he supposes, misunderstood the true character behind the "regine" and substituted the Sibyl for Dido. Antoine de la Sale must have used as sources both *Guerino* and *Huon d'Auvergne*, since his lady is both "Sibylle" and "Reine"; Pabst altogether ignores Antoine's own declaration concerning the provenance of his tale.

There need be no doubt that *Huon d'Auvergne* was influential in Andrea's conception of the Sibylline realm, for he had previously translated the French text into Italian, and a certain affinity with his own Sibylline episode is clear.[26] Like Guerino, Huon penetrates a hellish region with the best of intentions, and there finds his virtue subjected to an exigent test; like Guerino, he is forewarned of the true nature of the place and resists the temptations. But *Huon d'Auvergne* contains none of the features which *Guerino il Meschino* shares with the Tannhäuser-legend: the region visited by Huon is not subterranean; there is no weekly transformation, though, at the conclusion, the unsuccessful tempters are suddenly revealed in their true shape as devils, and the entire illusion, which has no substantial reality, vanishes in flames. There is no reason to suppose that the "regine d'ancelles" had any particular influence on the figure of Andrea's Sibyl, indeed even her connection with Dido is slender in the extreme: only the briefest allusion, a mere literary comparison, is made to the tragic Carthagian queen.[27] It is therefore much more probable that Andrea's Sibyl was largely derived from the lady of the mountain in that other source, which he shared with Antoine de la Sale. As will be seen in the following chapters, that source may be described as a demonic fairy-mistress story, and there are reasonable grounds for arguing that it was connected with the Sibyl well before Andrea's time.

Another popular medieval legend used by Andrea in *Guerino il Meschino* is the legend of St. Patrick's Purgatory. Although Guerino actually journeys to the Purgatory later in the work, and consequently learns of his father's identity, the same legend possibly also influenced the Sibylline episode directly. It was known as well to Antoine, who mentioned it in another part of his *Salade*.[28] But it merits some consideration here, because it also provided at least one feature of the mountain described in the *Paradis*. It should be noted at once that there

---

26) *Ugone d'Alvernia*, ed. Z. della Lega (Bologna, 1882).
27) *Cf.* Stengel's edition, v. 6799.
28) *Cf. La Salade (op. cit.)*, p. 133.

are no grounds for supposing this to be an independent contribution of Antoine's imagination, rather than an authentic part of the story he heard.

The legend of St. Patrick's Purgatory is comparatively old, and its popularity on the continent sprang initially from a 12th century Latin text describing a visit to the Purgatory by the knight Owen.[29] This early work is apparently the ancestor of all medieval stories depicting a journey to Purgatory and Paradise actually undertaken by a living man. In the following centuries, particularly in the 14th, many more texts describing visits to St. Patrick's Purgatory were composed.

The Purgatory is a subterranean region, accessible from a pit on an island in Lough Derg, Ireland. In legend, it was revealed by God to St. Patrick as an aid in converting the intractable Irish from their wicked ways; a man who enters it, and survives the ordeals of the place to leave unscathed after twenty-four hours, performs full expiation of all his previous sins and need not suffer for them in Purgatory, after death. The experiences of Owen belong to an old and long tradition of medieval visionary literature treating Hell, Purgatory and Heaven. But whereas all previous texts in the tradition are of the type of Cicero's *Somnium Scipionis*, describing revelations made only to the soul while the body remains behind, usually in sleep, *Owen Miles* describes for the first time a visit to infernal parts by a man in the flesh. The text itself stresses this feature, which derives no doubt from native Celtic tales of mortals visiting the Other World: "in hac narratione a corporali et mortali homine spiritualia dicuntur videri, quasi in corporali forma specie".[30] Owen is even made to suffer physical torment.

The nature of the visitor's experience has a lot in common with those of Guerino and Huon. Owen is alternately tempted and tortured by the demons, who promise to commute his punishment in Hell if he agrees to renounce God and put himself unreservedly in their power. Plainly it is his steadfastness which undergoes a test, and in the event proves itself: "quicunque vere penitens et fide armatus fossam illam

---

29) Edit. E. Mall, "Zur Geschichte der Legende vom Purgatorium des heiligen Patricius", *Romanische Forschungen*, 6 (1891) 141ff.; the very extensive literature on the legend is listed by H. R. Patch, *The Other World according to descriptions in medieval literature* (Cambridge, Mass., 1950: rprt. New York, 1970), p. 114ff.
30) Mall, (*op. cit.*), p. 146: "... in this account spiritual things are declared to be seen by a substantial and mortal man, as though with the appearance of substantial nature."

bona intentione introierit, spacia unius diei et noctis ab omnibus in ea purgaretur peccatis, que in tota vita sua commiserat".[31]

At the farther limit of Purgatory Owen eventually reaches a perilous bridge traversing a foul river, beneath which lies Hell itself; the bridge leads to the Earthly Paradise. There can be no doubt that this bridge either directly or indirectly inspired the one crossed by the German knight in *Paradis*. Antoine's bridge has been connected with numerous mysterious bridges from Celtic tradition, particularly those of the Arthurian stories (best known is the Sword-bridge in Chrétien's *Lancelot*), yet none of these has the characteristics of the bridge in the Norcian mountain.[32] But the one spanning Hell in *Owen Miles* behaves almost exactly like Antoine's. Its appearance is daunting: "erat autem subtilis et angustus, ut, si eciam super terram protensus uno tantum pede ab ea esset exaltatus, nullomodo tamen, ut videbatur, quis super eum iter capere potuisset"; but Owen takes heart: "et cum ambularet in eo, in tantum ceperunt solidari gressus eius, ut facile se non diffideret transiturum, sed et cum paululum pertransisset, cepit adeo pons dilatari, ut eciam ea via pateret latissima".[33] Antoine says of his bridge: "que il n'ait mie un pie de large", but "aussi tost qu'on a les deux piez sur ce pont, il est assez large et, tant vait on plus avant, tant est plus large et moins creux ...".[34]

The bridge traversing Hell is in fact a traditional feature of considerable antiquity in eschatological and visionary writings, and it entered Celtic lore from such sources.[35] Muslim eschatology knows of a bridge by which virtuous souls pass over Hell to reach the Garden of

---

31) *Ibid.*, p. 148: "whoever enters that cave, penitent, and armed with the faith and with good intention, shall be purged in the space of one day and night of all the sins he ever committed in his whole life."
32) *Cf.* Löhmann, p. 229.
33) Mall, p. 175f.: "It was slender and narrow, so that even if it had been stretched only one foot above the ground, it seemed in no way possible for one to go over it ... and when he walked on it, since he was not easily discouraged from crossing, so his steps began to grow firm, and when he had gone a little way along it, the bridge began to expand and his path lay most broad."
34) *Paradis*, p. 19: "... that it was not a foot in breadth ... as soon as one has both feet on this bridge, it is quite broad, and the further one advances, the larger it is, and the less frail."
35) *Cf.*, L. Hibbard, "The sword Bridge of Chrétien de Troyes and its Celtic original," *Romanic Review*, 4 (1913), esp. p. 175; H. R. Patch, "Some elements in medieval descriptions of the Otherworld," *Publications of the Modern Language Association*, 33 (1918), esp. p. 635.

Paradise. The same bridge appears in the *Dialogues* of Gregory the Great, by whose transmission it became a commonplace in Christian literature.[36] Its function and appearance are essentially the same in all texts prior to *Owen Miles*: it is dangerously narrow, so that sinful souls tumble down to the river of Hell beneath and only virtuous souls cross in safety. But it is therefore only metaphorical, graphically serving to separate mechanically two groups already distinguished by the morality of their previous actions. Sometimes it is stated to appear narrow to the Damned, but broad and secure to the Blessed; however there is no question of it presenting an actual moral test. In *Owen Miles*, on the other hand, where a living man is involved, the bridge acts as a test of the human moral will. It appears narrow, in order to daunt his trust in God's aid, but when he nevertheless confidently sets out, it broadens in proof that his confidence is justified. In exactly the same way Antoine's bridge operates to test the knight's courage. Its Celtic propensity for shape-shifting was probably inspired by such animated Irish bridges as that crossed by the hero Cu Chulainn;[37] but its precise performance in *Owen Miles* is definitely a test designed for a living man with free moral will.

The broadening bridge is not met with in any other Christian location than St. Patrick's Purgatory and the Norcian mountain, and it is therefore reasonable to conclude that the latter is derived from the former. However the bridge crossed by Antoine's knight is far from intrinsic to the Tannhäuser-story and belongs only to the incidental features of the mountain-paradise. Indeed neither *Owen Miles* nor any of the later texts describing visits to the Purgatory contains further close correspondences to the *Paradis*. One of these later visits is of some passing interest, for all the temptations take the form of sexual provocations by comely maidens, while the visitor also finds himself threatened by demons in the form of dragons seeking to devour him.[38] This version, which belongs to the 14th century, bears a certain general resemblance to *Huon d'Auvergne* and *Guerino*, but there are no persuasive grounds for associating it closely with the Tannhäuser-legend; it conspicuously lacks the feature of the broadening bridge.

---

36) *Dialogues*, IV, cap. 36, (*op. cit.*), vol. 77, col. 384.
37) *Cf*. E. Hull, *The Cuchullin Saga in Irish literature* (London, 1898), p. 75.
38) *Cf*. M. Voigt, "Beiträge zur Geschichte der Visionenliteratur im Mittelalter," *Palaestra*, 146 (1924), p. 121ff.

All of these tales, *Guerino*, *Huon* and the various visits to St. Patrick's Purgatory, are related to the Tannhäuser-legend in the basic matter of the human visit to a diabolical region (which, in all cases but Huon's, is situated underground). But in the more crucial point of moral content they must be said to belong to a different *genre* of story: they describe a test of moral *fortitude*; the hero is fully cognizant of the moral nature of the place and stalwartly resists the temptations to which he is exposed. The moral disillusionment so crucial to the corresponding part of the Tannhäuser-legend is a different matter; it results from a test of moral *discerning*, which the knight at first fails. He is deluded by the apparent innocence of the place in a test that demands moral understanding rather than strength in virtue; he consequently sins, and must emerge to bear the resulting guilt. It was from such a story that Andrea Barberino extracted material for the location, and for much of the incidental detail, in his own narrative; however, as to moral content, the Sibylline episode in *Guerino* belongs decidedly to the quite separate type of St. Patrick's Purgatory.

IV
FAIRYLAND AND THE FAIRY-MISTRESS STORY

No less a scholar than the eminent Frenchman, Gaston Paris, first pointed out that the Tannhäuser-legend is structurally, and to no small extent thematically too, a fairy-mistress story.[1] Such stories tell of the meeting of a fairy and a mortal, and of their mutual love and happiness together; after a period of time the relationship is interrupted, generally by the will or agency of the mortal. But it is usually resumed eventually, often only after much suffering on the part of the man, and the couple subsequently live on in eternal joy in fairyland. Fairy-mistress stories are found in a wide variety of cultures throughout the world, but they form one of the mainstays of the Celtic narrative tradition in particular. The dissemination of this Celtic material on the continent in the 12th century, especially from the mainland Celtic stronghold of Brittany, was of immeasurable consequence for Western literature in general, for it supplied the raw material of much secular literature for many centuries; the part played in this by the fairy-mistress theme was by no means small. In addition to the numerous surviving texts which retain the outward character of the fairy-mistress story (many of which will be mentioned or discussed subsequently), its very profound influence is to be detected in the courtly romances of the High Middle Ages. It has been shown for example that the theme of a mortal's enticement and union with a fairy underlies the stories of such couples as Lanzelet and Pluris (in Ulrich von Zatzikhoven's *Lanzelet*), Gawein and Florie, Wigalois and Larie (both in Wirnt von Gravenberg's *Wigalois*), and Gawan and Orgeluse (in Wolfram's *Parzival*).[2] Most striking of all is the use made of the theme in the Yvain-romance (Chrétien de Troyes and Hartmann von Aue), where, as well as many of the associated motifs, the entire structure of the fairy-mistress story is preserved: — Yvain's hasty love for Laudine; his prompt winning of her hand; her later displeasure at his conduct and consequent repudiation of him; and his final re-entry into her favour after a period of anguished separation.

---

1) Paris, "La légende de Tannhäuser," *op. cit.*
2) *Cf.* G. Ehrismann, "Märchen im höfischen Epos," *Beiträge zur Geschichte der deutschen Sprache und Literatur,* 30 (1905) esp. p. 21ff; on this general matter *cf.* also J. R. Reinhard, *The survival of geis in medieval romance* (Halle, 1933) and L. Mackensen, *Handwörterbuch des deutschen Märchens* (Berlin, 1934), vol. II, p. 76.

A marked similarity has been noted between Yvain's story and the French *Lai de Désiré*, whose affinity with the Tannhäuser-legend is discussed fully in the following chapter.[3] The contrast between the legend and these romances, regarding the moral tendency derived from the fairy-mistress material, is also a question to be touched on later.

The original observation of Gaston Paris may scarcely be disputed, but in the heat of controversy over the legend's national origins it came to suffer neglect. Eventually an American Celticist, A. H. Krappe, examined a number of fairy-mistress tales drawing comparisons with the Tannhäuser-legend, but, true to the scholarly fashions of his time, his interest lay principally in identifying an actual source.[4] He pointed to the Middle Scots romance of *Tom the Rymer* which, though it could not itself be justifiably called the source of the legend, was in his view at least closely related to a lost British text which found its way to Germany and there spawned the Tannhäuser-legend. The theory has since been neglected again, although it aroused some further interest a few years ago when an attempt was made to explain the transmission of the putative insular source to Germany.[5] Krappe's belief in an authentic and unadulterated Celtic source for the legend has surely little foundation, for the story contains no markedly Celtic element which was not in fact circulating in medieval Europe in some form for a long time previous to the legend's appearance. Indeed, as will later be seen, even *Tom the Rymer* is very probably less pure in its Celticism than Krappe held. An ultimately Celtic origin for very many features of the Tannhäuser-legend need not be seriously doubted, but the immediate sources of the story are best sought in the narrative traditions spread over continental Europe in the Middle Ages.

Before proceeding to examine the fairy-mistress elements of the legend in comparison with analogous tales from the same period, it is helpful first to consider once more the specific phenomenon of the *Venusberg*. It was observed earlier that the mountain-paradise was connected in the 13th century with an Arthurian Other-world realm, whose fairy nature was implied by the Arthurian legend itself, even if it

---

3) *Cf.* R. S. Loomis, *Arthurian tradition and Chrétien de Troyes* (New York, 1949), p. 271 and p. 304f.
4) A. H. Krappe, "Die Sage vom Tannhäuser," *Mitteilungen der schlesischen Gesellschaft für Volkskunde*, 36 (1937) 106-132; also "La légende de Tannhäuser," *Mercure de France*, 284 (1936) 257-275.
5) Löhmann, (*op. cit.*) p. 239ff.

is not closely described in the scanty texts. In the 15th century descriptions of the mountain, although every trace of Arthur has gone and the Grail is no more than a name fast being replaced, it nevertheless retains sufficient fairyland attributes to betray unmistakeably its earlier nature.

Generally speaking the Celtic fairyland is never described other than in vague terms, and many of its features differ little from Other-world locations in quite different civilisations and cultures. The common picture is of a realm which is idealised in terms of normal human experience: while pleasures abound, pain and sorrow are entirely absent. It has been shown how descriptions of the Other World, whether they be Oriental, Islamic, Classical, Celtic or simply of the Western medieval tradition, all make extensive use of the same repetitive negative formula in characterising this ideal state:[6] "no snow falls, no strong winds blow and there is never any rain ..." says Homer of Elysium; in *Owen Miles* the Earthly Paradise is reported to have no night, no winter, no heat and no cold;[7] Tennyson employs the same formula in his *Mort d'Arthur* to evoke the fairyland serenity of Avalon. More immediately interesting is its application by Antoine de la Sale to the Sibylline paradise: "Froit n'y fait nul, ne aussi point de chault".[8]

The eagerness with which mortals are admitted, and even enticed, to fairyland and there detained for long periods, sometimes even in perpetuity, is a common feature of Celtic fairy mythology. This characteristic assumes a natural importance in the *Venusberg*, a place of pure temptation: Hemmerlin speaks unequivocally of the active part played by the resident spirits in coaxing men into the mountain; in the *Paradis* the very reputation of the place apparently acts as a devilish lure to draw the knight into the mountain where he, like Guerino and the Czech visitors to the Paradise, is then warmly welcomed.

The ideal pleasures with which fairies may so easily charm their guests have become in the *Venusberg* a further means to seduce them to sin. Both Hemmerlin and Antoine take some pains to stress the ideal quality of life inside the mountain; in the *Paradis* and in *Guerino* the good food and the wealth of the place are conspicuous assets, although the latter work, as well as Hemmerlin's story, permits the sexual

---

6) Patch, *The Other World* ... (*op. cit.*), p. 12ff.
7) Mall, (*op. cit.*), p. 181ff.
8) *Paradis*, p. 28.

pleasures largely to overshadow all others.⁹ This last point is of course no more than a characteristic preoccupation of Christian moral writers, but it is at the same time a very obvious form of ideal gratification, and may be found in non-Christian descriptions of the Other World: the Irish *imrama* (tales of sea-journeys to Other-world lands) commonly include an Island of Women among the places visited,¹⁰ and Muslim eschatology holds that each soul is allotted a sexual partner in Paradise.

The luxuriant summer-garden often found inside the mountain is similarly no exclusive feature, though the emphasis placed on its unseasonableness appears to be a more specifically Celtic trait. Gervase of Tilbury, an avid collector of British folk-tales, tells the story of a Derbyshire swineherd who, having lost a valuable pregnant sow, searched in a cavern and found a wide subterranean land where it was summer, although he had entered the cave in winter.¹¹ In *Guerino* the summer fruitfulness inside the mountain, while it is March outside, serves as another indication to the hero that the delights are all false.¹² Hemmerlin emphasises the same marvel, but in his case the selection of twelve varied climates seems even more of a paradisical ideal: every possible human appetite may find its fulfilment inside the mountain.

Antoine also makes mention of the opulent clothing freely to be had in the paradise, although the necessity of the knight's completely changing his apparel before finally entering the realm remains a somewhat curious circumstance. The feature is absent from *Guerino*, but reappears in the Czech account of the Sibylline Paradise, a text which otherwise has more in common with *Guerino* than the *Paradis*. Here the virtuous visitors stoutly resist the attempt to divest them of their own clothing. It appears likely that the acceptance of the rich raiment proper to the paradise represents some surrender to the temptations of the place.¹³

The most important gift which the fairies may bestow on a favoured mortal is that of sharing their immortality. The very prominent part played by immortality in the legend of the mountain-paradise has

---

9) *Cf. Guerino*, cap. 144.
10) E.g. *The voyage of Bran* ... ed. and transl. K. Meyer (London, 1895), vol. 1, p. 30; The voyage of Maelduin, *Immrama*, ed. A. von Hamel (Dublin, 1941), p. 20ff.
11) *Otia Imperialium (op. cit.)*, Dec. III, cap. 45, p. 975.
12) *Guerino*, cap. 144.
13) *Cf.* Söderhjelm, "Eine tschechische Version ..." *(op. cit.)*, p. 76.

already been discussed; it may be noted in addition how Antoine once more falls back on the ancient descriptive formula to indicate the eternal youth enjoyed by the ladies inhabiting his paradise: "Car elles jamais n'en vieillissent, ne scevent que douleur est".[14] But the immortality of fairyland has a further aspect, most commonly found in Celtic tales: time is distorted for the human visitor. The mortal guest in fairyland experiences a subjective compression of time, such that a sojourn believed to last only a few days is discovered, on return, to have endured as many years, or a visit of two years proves to be as many centuries.[15] When, in the latter case, the visitor reaches his home, he commonly undergoes a sudden commensurate ageing on touching native soil or human food. He may shrivel up, or simply fall to dust. Frequently the solicitudinous fairy gives specific injunctions to meet this contingency, but for one reason or another they are not observed, with tragic results.[16]

In the romances of the High Middle Ages (particularly those of Chrétien) the timeless character of the narrative is at least in part a reflection of the magical order from which much of the material came, a world where the dimension of time showed a mysterious flexibility unknown in the human world.[17]

The quite specific feature of subjective time-distortion is met with in both the *Paradis* and in Hemmerlin's account of the *Venusberg*. In both cases it has been adapted to the moral tendency of the legend. Hemmerlin's "simplicianus" summarily tells how the visitors are shocked by the warning that their permitted year has elapsed, for they believe they have savoured the delights for no more than a month; absorbed in pleasure, they sinfully failed to pay regard to the crucial matter of their chance to escape. In the *Paradis* the motif is used in the same way, but with immensely greater subtlety; in fact its application constitutes the best possible example of that sophistication and acute sense of symmetry characterising the *Paradis*. Unlike the Celtic fairyland, the Sibylline mountain demonstrates time-distortion not as a magical trick of the environment, but as a realistic function of the

---

14) *Paradis*, p. 28: "For they never grow old, nor do they know what pain is."
15) *Cf.* the numerous instances cited in E. S. Hartland, *The science of fairy tales* (London, 1925), caps. 8 and 9.
16) *Cf.* Reinhard, (*op. cit.*), p. 277ff.
17) *Cf.* P. Ménhard, "Le temps et la durée dans les romans de Chrétien de Troyes", *Le Moyen âge*, 73 (1967) 375-401, esp. p. 380f.

visitor's mind. While the knight is heedlessly abandoned to pleasure, subjective time flies for him, he is unaware of its true value for his soul and squanders it in empty delights; in this state, one day seems to him but an hour. In indication of the psychological, rather than magical, quality of the phenomenon, Antoine carefully reassures the reader that the knight "savoit bien le compte" of the three-hundred days thus spent.[18] But when his disillusion with the paradise is complete the reverse process applies, such as to effect a neat balance: he is now all too aware of the passage of time, for he urgently desires to procure absolution while he still may; time is precious and, of the remaining thirty days, every hour seems like ten days.[19] This reversed time-distortion, which is found in no other version of the legend, serves to highlight drastically the knight's change of heart and the turning-point of his career. The original fairyland motif has been in this way integrated with the moral and psychological theme of the legend. However the symmetry of these two modes of time-distortion is more subtle still, and appears to betray once again an ultimate literary source, which was the work of a creative and highly artistic mind. Not only is the knight's remorse shown as the appropriate reversal of his earlier thoughtless abandonment, but his initial pleasure is balanced with an equal later anguish of remorseful waiting, in such a manner as to provide mathematically precise moral justice. In the case of the first time-distortion the days subjectively become hours; in the second, every hour becomes fully ten days, but the actual days are only a tenth of the previous number. If an accurate computation is made, it can be seen that this does not give a true equation. Nevertheless the mathematical factors themselves are made to balance precisely, so as to suggest an arithmetically correct symmetry (*i.e.*, in each case an interchange of days and hours, with an additional factor of ten in the second instance, since the first period is ten times as long — three-hundred days, compared to thirty days). Just as the period of sinfulness is ten times longer than the period of remorse, so the time-distortion in the latter case is not only reversed, but ten times greater than the former. The evidence of Hemmerlin's story shows that time-distortion was an authentic feature of the legend, and not Antoine's addition. But whether Antoine is himself responsible for the mathematical intricacy with which it is applied in the *Paradis* cannot be certainly known; one may only reiterate: there are no real grounds for doubting his word when he claims to transmit the story faithfully from other sources.

---

18) *Paradis*, p. 27.
19) *Ibid.* p. 29.

The structure of the fairy-mistress story, a feature which goes some way towards defining the *genre* itself, is the most conspicuous element it gave to the Tannhäuser-legend. In describing this structure one may speak of three typical *stages*, separated by two *turning-points*. At the first of the turning-points the fairy and her mortal lover are parted, to be re-united at the second. (It should be noted, however, that many tales break off with a more or less tragic conclusion at the second stage). The initial meeting of the couple, which introduces the first stage, is normally achieved by what is known as the *fairy induction*: common devices for this are the magic boat which carries the mortal to fairyland, and the white stag or other enchanted beast, which he pursues to a lonely spot in the forest.[20] The fairy herself is always responsible for arranging this induction and thereby actually initiating the liaison, for she has previously noted and selected her mate on account of his exceptional qualities. This is true even of tales of the Swan-maiden type — where the hero finds the Swan-maiden bathing, is captivated by her beauty, and places her within his power by appropriating her clothing — for the fairy generally reveals subsequently that she had in fact planned the encounter.[21] In keeping with the Christian spirit of the Tannhäuser-legend, the knight entering the *Venusberg* is invariably portrayed doing so of his free moral will; the fairy induction has become simply the temptation posed by the mountain's existence.

Among those medieval fairy-mistress stories which show significant affinity to the Tannhäuser-legend it is possible to discern two distinct categories. (The distinction is made solely for the present purpose, and though it may in fact have some wider validity, that is not claimed here.) The difference between these two types resides primarily in the separation of the lovers, which marks the first turning-point of the story; but from this difference others follow, and extend the distinction. In one case the separation involves an emotional estrangement: in some way the fairy is offended by the mortal's actions. In the other the separation is purely geographical.

---

20) *Cf.* L. A. Paton, *Studies in the Fairy Mythology of Arthurian Romance* (New York, 1903, rprt. 1970), p. 15ff., and the extensive literature cited *ibid.*, p. 16, note 1.
21) *Cf.* Hartland, (*op. cit.*), caps. 10 and 11; S. Sturm, *The lay of Guingamor: a study*, University of North Carolina, Studies in the Romance Languages and Literatures, 76 (Chapel Hill, 1968), p. 15ff.

Category A

The best example of this type in the pure Celtic tradition is the Irish story of the *Debility of the Ultonian warriors*.[22] The most familiar continental examples are from among the French (Breton) lays, *e.g. Lanval, Graelent, Guingamor* and *Désiré* (the last of which must be more fully discussed later).[23] The Italian poem *Pulzella Gaia*, though it shows considerable structural refinement, also belongs fundamentally to this category.[24]

The first stage of the story takes place in the real world. In the French lays an induction of the Swan-maiden type is common, by which the mortal may be inveigled to a fairyland location, but, once a mutually convenient arrangement has been reached, he returns to his usual mode of life in the world, equipped by the fairy with the means to summon her at will. The first turning-point is actuated by the mortal contrary to his own intention, and involves his breaking a tabu which the fairy imposed on him at the outset of their liaison, *e.g.* he may not betray their love to another mortal *(Graelent, Lanval, Debility of the Ultonian warriors, Pulzella Gaia)*. It should be observed that the breach of this tabu or injunction thus plays a vital structural role, by actually causing the first turning-point.

The motif of a fairy ring is also commonly found in conjunction with the tabu. Magic rings are of course usual enough in fairytales and medieval romances, and they frequently possess just whatever supernatural powers the author requires of them. But in *Pulzella Gaia* and *Désiré* the specific function of the ring, which is made amply clear, appears to be quite fundamental: it is a fairy talisman, an element of *faerie* which the mortal must always bear with him and which affords a constant magic contact with the fairy-world. In *Pulzella Gaia* the ring grants Gawain's every wish and gives him continuous contact with his fairy-mistress; in *Désiré* the hero is warned that if he loses the ring he will have lost his beloved. The fatal transgression of the fairy's tabu,

---

22) Hull, *The Cuchullin saga* ... (*op. cit.*) p. 96ff; *cf.* E. Windisch, *Berichte über die Verhandlungen der Königlichen Gesellschaft der Wissenschaften, Phil.-hist. Classe* (1884), p. 336ff.
23) Marie de France, *Le lai de Lanval*, ed. J. Rychner (Geneva, 1958); *The lays of Désiré, Graelent, and Melion*, ed. E. M. Grimes (New York, 1928); *cf.* also T. P. Cross, "The Celtic elements in the lays of Lanval and Graelent", *Modern philology* 12 (1915) 585 644.
24) *Fiori di leggende: cantari antichi*, ed. E. Levi, serie prima (Bari, 1914), p. 31ff.

which generally ensues under the provocation of a jealous queen, directly concerns the ring: in *Pulzella Gaia* the fairy gift simply loses all its power, while in *Désiré*, where the motif of the jealous queen is not found, the hero suddenly discovers that the ring is missing from his finger and that he cannot summon the fairy. In most stories the hero finds himself in a mortal plight as a result of idly boasting his love, and the fairy is obliged to reappear briefly in order to effect his rescue, but she then departs, seemingly for ever. However, the fidelity of fairy love being more or less axiomatic, she finally relents and returns to transport him to fairyland and perpetual happiness.

Category B

A Celtic example of the category is the Irish *Voyage of Bran*.[25] But the type is common among romances of the 13th century and afterwards, and is often used with a freedom which tends to obscure the original structure. Amplification of some details, loss of others, and even the rearrangement of the component parts are all met with. *Floriant et Florete*,[26] *Partonopeus*,[27] and the sojourn of Ogier the Dane in Avalon may be cited as further examples.[28]

Whereas in category *A* the vicissitudes of fairy love and the relationship of fairy and mortal are generally of self-sufficient interest, in category *B* the fairy liaison is frequently no more than one notable episode in a mortal life which is otherwise of considerable repute. The mortal is frequently the hero of a narrative cycle (Ogier is an obvious example) and the story seems designed to enhance his prestige with a supernatural connection.

The first stage is enacted in fairyland, and the induction commonly effected with a magic boat; this occurs in both *Partonopeus* and the abduction of Arthur by Morgan, a story which belongs loosely to this

---

25) Edit. K. Meyer, *op. cit.*
26) Edit. H. F. Williams, *op. cit.*
27) *Partonopeu de Blois*, ed. J. Gildea (Villanova, 1967); *cf.* the German version of Konrad von Würzburg, *Partonopier und Meliur*, ed. K. Bartsch (rprt. Berlin, 1970).
28) An original work relating Ogier's exploits in Avalon is lost; but an unknown poet of the 14th century composed a work in alexandrines, based on the 12th century text *La chevalerie Ogier*, in which he inserted a long account of the hero's romantic affair. Regrettably this work has not been edited in modern times and for its contents one is obliged to resort to descriptions and summaries, *cf.* H. L. D. Ward, *Catalogue of romances ... in the British Museum* (London, 1883) vol. I, p. 607ff., and Paton, (*op. cit.*), p. 74ff.

category. Ogier is brought to Avalon by a shipwreck which Morgan has arranged on the rocks nearby. But other devices are also used: for example, Floriant is removed to fairyland as a new-born child. The first turning-point results from the mortal's desire or duty to re-visit the world; for the hero of romance it is usually a pressing need for his chivalric prowess which beckons, but for Bran it is simply a nostalgia for home. There is no breakdown in the relationship of fairy and mortal, indeed in most cases the latter confidently expects to return. As with category *A*, a tabu is associated with his activities in the human world, although the changed geographical pattern requires that this applies only in the second stage of the story. The second turning-point, which follows this, is not necessarily caused by a breach of the tabu, though tabu and turning-point are nevertheless usually closely related. The crucial point governing the second turning-point is generally the time-distortion of fairyland. The mortal learns that while in fairyland he has far outlived a natural human life, despite his own impression to the contrary, and he is entirely dependent on the fairy gift of immortality for his continued existence. A return to the real world endangers his precarious life, as, for instance, contact with the ground may cause an immediate reversion to purely human nature and the instantaneous death described earlier. The fairy places a tabu on his leaving the boat (*Voyage of Bran*) or forbids him to dismount from his horse.[29] In *Bran* one of the hero's followers, more homesick than the rest, imprudently leaps overboard and turns at once into dust; the remainder, heedful of this warning, sail back to the Other World. Thus, in category *B*, the second turning-point is dictated by circumstance, for the visit to this world is made under conditions that are reasonably supportable only for a short while. The tabu serves to make the visit possible. However, in the romances this conclusion is often altered beyond all recognisable similarity. Ogier, for example, receives from Morgan a ring bestowing on him eternal youth, and he lives with her for two centuries, which seem no more than twenty years to him. When he returns to France in order to wage war, he keeps the ring but is also given a firebrand and told he will die when it is burnt away. Eventually he wearies of this world and casts the firebrand into a flaming fire; as it is consumed, his body undergoes a rapid decline, but suddenly Morgan appears to rescue him and bear him off to *faerie*. It is not altogether clear whether an intended tabu attaches to the firebrand, or whether it is

---

29) *E.g.* in the story of King Herla, told by Walter Map, *De Nugis Curialium*, ed. M. R. James, Anecdota Oxoniensia: medieval and modern series, part 14 (Oxford, 1914), Division I, cap. xi; *cf.* the tale of Oisin in Reinhard, (*op. cit.*), p. 276.

simply a device to enable Ogier to leave this life at the moment of his choice.

If the Tannhäuser-legend is now examined in the light of these two categories of fairy-mistress story, it can at once be seen to belong, according to most criteria, to category *A*. The relationship between the fairy (Venus) and the mortal undergoes change, causing their estrangement at the second stage of the story. Even the tabu typical of category *A* is discernible, though much altered: when, in the next chapter, the *Lai de Désiré* is considered in some detail, it will be seen that there are some good grounds for regarding the lady's request that the knight sing her praises in the world (also found in an even further altered form in *Guerino*) as a derivative of the tabu on his divulging their love. The tabu is broken by the knight's confession, which involves an implicit condemnation of the lady. The motif is absent from the *Paradis*, although the magic ring is found in its stead. Antoine himself seems somewhat perplexed by this ring, and says of it that it was given to the knight by his "compaigne par le commandement de la royne, et lui dist la vertu que ceste verge avoit; mais oncques ne fut celui qui le peust savoir";[30] it is possible that some further explanation had been lost in the transmission of the story to the Frenchman. But the antecedents of the motif make its significance fairly clear. It is the only item which the knight is permitted to take with him from the mountain: — "Et n'emporta oncques chose de leans que une vergette d'or si tressubtil que a peine estoit oeil qui le peust apparcevoir"[31] — he is even obliged to depart in his original clothing, while the torch he receives to illuminate the subterranean path from the mountain becomes a useless object, incapable of re-ignition, on reaching the daylight. The ring is thus presumably a derivative of the original talisman, being the only tangible contact he has with the sinful realm. In surrendering it to the Pope he symbolically renounces all association with the mountain. Thus the confession, a direct violation of the lady's wish that he should laud her, and the surrendering of the ring both perform essentially the same function: they express the knight's repudiation of all commitment to the baleful place.

---

30) *Paradis*, p. 30: "... by his lady at the order of the queen, and she told him of the power which this ring had; but there was no-one who could know of it".
31) *Ibid.*, "... and he took away nothing from inside except a golden ring, so fine that the eye could scarce behold it."

However, despite its general affinity to type *A*, the legend in fact displays the geographical arrangement of category *B*: the first stage is enacted in the fairyland location of the mountain-paradise, and the knight, like Bran and Ogier the Dane, seeks voluntarily to return to the real world. This combination of elements from both categories is made possible because, unlike the category *A* story, in which the fairy seeks in anger to dissociate herself from her lover, it is the knight himself who here finds his affections alienated from the fairy by his realisation of her true nature, and he seeks to escape her realm. As a result, the tabu-motif becomes transferred to the second stage of the story, since this is now the part which takes place in the real world. Antoine's knight also makes an insincere, but dramatically ironical, promise to return, a motif which interestingly enough reappears in the earliest extant version of the German ballad without any explicit hint of insincerity; it seems possible that this results from the typical expectation of a hero in a category *B* story.

The tabu-motif or ring-motif, still discernible in the legend, has nevertheless lost its original function as evidenced in other category *A* stories. Delayed until the second stage, it can no longer actually effect the emotional estrangement of the couple; at the best it serves, as was seen, to emphasise the degree of that estrangement in the interview with the Pope. What then can be said to actuate the turning-points of the Tannhäuser-legend? The answer is to be found in the story's Christian tendentiousness; the crucial pivots are psychologically internalised to become the vital steps of the human mind or soul on the path to either salvation or perdition. The places filled in other fairy-mistress stories by magic, by heroism, by the fairy's desire for secrecy, by her immutable love and by the mortal's pride in her, are taken in the legend by the knight's awareness of his sinfulness and guilt and by his eventual despair in God's forgiveness and willingness to redeem him. But each of the two turning-points is connected with a specific narrative motif — the reptilian metamorphosis, and the confession of sin — both of which form part of what may be termed the demonisation of the fairy-mistress story. These motifs are dealt with in the following chapter; here we may turn to a different question, which is nevertheless related to the fairy elements in the legend: that of the part played by the Sibyl.

The connection of the classical Cumean Sibyl with the fairyland mountain-paradise may be explained in two general ways. It may, on the one hand, have been a more or less original part of the legend, or it may, on the other, have arisen subsequently, perhaps as the contribution of an individual writer or poet — Pabst suggests that this was Andrea Barberino himself. In the latter case one must assume that the original mistress of the mountain bore either no name at all, or a different one. *Venus* is of course the only other name allotted to her in the entire early history of the legend. The presence of Venus in the mountain is discussed more fully later, but it is at least immediately apparent that Venus, whether she be classical goddess or the medieval allegorical representation of carnal love, has little enough of the fairy about her. It is hard to see her as anything other than an intruder in the fairy-mistress story. Initially the same appears to be true of the classical Sibyl of course, but in her case one very clear link with the fairy world is afforded by the figure of the Fay Sebile, of whom Lucy Paton says: "There is little question that she is descended from the Sibyl".[32] It is this argument whose details must be pursued here.

Andrea Barberino identified the lady of the mountain with the classical Sibyl from the outset. Antoine, in his discussion of the Sibylline question at the conclusion of the *Paradis*, does likewise. Pabst based his claim that the Norcian Sibyl was Andrea's innovation substantially on the belief that the demonic Sibyl in *Guerino* represents a radical departure from an ingrained medieval tradition, which viewed her as an entirely christianised and virtuous character, responsible for no less than a prophesy of Christ's coming.[33] Certainly, the learned literature of the period sees her, just as it saw Vergil, in a favourable light, but Pabst is altogether too restrictive in considering only this learned tradition. His discussion of the Fay Sebile is too brief and, although he concedes her possible influence on *Guerino*, he declines to consider her important, because no surviving text gives her a sufficiently demonic character.

For the sake of clarity it is best to consider first the character of the Fay Sebile in the surviving texts, and only then to examine her connection with the Cumean Sibyl. On both points the direct evidence is parlously scant, but it is certainly more than that which supports the theory of Andrea's inventing the Sibyl of Norcia.

The Fay Sebile has little independence in the surviving Arthurian material, but her persistent appearances accord well with the

---

32) Paton, (*op. cit.*), p. 52, note 2; *cf.* also Löhmann, p. 231.
33) Pabst, p. 61ff.

supposition that a largely lost narrative tradition (perhaps involving a subterranean paradise) surrounded her. In the extant texts she is used principally to provide a rival for Morgan and a foil for her enmity. Lucy Paton describes Sebile as a "shadow" of Morgan; the latter, it will be recalled, is widely associated with fairy-mistress stories of category *B*. Generally Sebile herself acts the part of an aspirant, but always frustrated, fairy-mistress, though this is no more than typical of all the Fays. It is in the nature of the literary works themselves that no adverse judgment is passed against her in an overtly Christian moral spirit; nowhere is she declared to be, or unequivocally shown to be, demonic. But she appears in a consistently unflattering light — she is bitter and vengeful in disappointment, and quite malicious in her punishment of Morgan. In the *Chanson d'Esclarmonde*[34] and the story of Alisandre l'Orphelin[35] which is related in a number of sources, she does little more than swell the ranks of attendant Fays. In the prose *Lancelot* she undertakes, together with Morgan and the Reine de Sorestan, the abduction of the hero; each of them hopes to win him as her lover, but Lancelot, taken in an induced sleep to a castle, roughly refuses them all and, to their intense chagrin, eventually escapes their efforts to hold him prisoner.[36] Sebile appears more than once in the *Prophecies de Merlin:* in the episode concerning Berengier de Gomeret she plots to gain the hand of this very eligible knight, but is thwarted by identical schemes on the part of the other Fays. In this case her rage is vented on Morgan.[37] In a further episode plans are hatched to abduct for her pleasure the knight Lamorat de Galles, but the outcome is not described.[38] Such a creature, whom no mortal seems to desire, certainly provides a plausible ancestress for the demonic lady of the mountain-paradise. A writer inclined to describe her character in more Christian terms, and anxious to derive from it some didactic capital, might very readily see in her a she-devil.

Incontrovertible proof of the original identity of the Fay Sebile and the classical Sibyl is of course impossible to find, but considerable weight must be given to the lack of any other explanation of the former's existence; this argument seems to have inspired the confidence

---

34) *Cf.* Paton, p. 253f.
35) *Les prophecies de Merlin*, ed. L. A. Paton (New York, 1926), p. 415.
36) *The vulgate version of the Arthurian romances*, ed. H. O. Sommer, vol. V (Washington, 1911), p. 91ff.
37) *Prophecies*, (*op. cit.*), p. 388f.
38) *Ibid.*, p. 402.

of Lucy Paton. The name, both with a Latin *i* and a French *e*, is quite un-Arthurian.

The Sibylline oracle in fact became a common part of the Arthurian legend well before the appearance of those texts which mention Sebile: Geoffrey of Monmouth alludes in his *Historia* to a Sibylline prophesy that three Britons were in turn destined to occupy the imperial throne at Rome — the last of them is understood to be Arthur.[39] This prophesy became a regular part of the story of Arthur's assault on Rome.[40] The prophetic powers of the Sibyl also seem to have led to her frequent coupling with Merlin; as prophetess she appears in the *Prophecies de Merlin* with the name "la roine Sebille".[41]

The immense popularity of Vergil's work ensured the existence in the Middle Ages of a thriving tradition concerning the Cumean Sibyl. Ovid, who was scarcely less popular than Vergil, described her nature as prophetic but not yet divine, and, most significantly, as tangible but yet immortal.[42] One may reasonably speculate regarding the category of beings to which such a nature might be assigned in the Middle Ages, since the Olympian Gods and their order were discredited. Only the fairy order and the demonic order can be seriously considered, and these two are frequently inseparable. It must also be remembered that prophecy is a common enough activity of the fairies. Moreover, her prophetic powers apart, the Sibyl is most famed for her surveillance of the gate to the Netherworld and to the Elysian Fields, where she led Aeneas. This classical but legendary realm obviously enjoys so many of the attributes of fairyland that it could readily be ascribed such a nature in the popular imagination; heroes dwell there in happiness, song and dance; like the Arthurian host in the *Wartburgkrieg*, they take the same pleasure in chariots and arms as they knew during mortal life; some drink the waters of Lethe in preparation for a return to earth; here mortal men, especially favoured by the Gods, may be brought in the flesh.

Thus we arrive once more at the question of the mountain-paradise and its origins. Although the evidence is of course mostly

---

39) Geoffrey of Monmouth, *Historia Regum Britanniae*, ed. J. Hammer (Cambridge, Mass., 1951), p. 167.
40) Cf. Wace, *Roman de Brut*, ed. I. Arnold (Paris, 1940), p. 571, v. 10,927f.; *Didot Perceval*, ed. W. Roach (Philadelphia, 1941), p. 303.
41) *Prophecies*, p. 339.
42) *Metamorphoses*, ed. M. Haupt, (Berlin, 1885), Lib. XIV, v. 100ff.

circumstantial, the Sibylline grotto nevertheless offers what is surely the most plausible single ancestor of the fairy-mountain; moreover, if that is indeed its origin, it is clear that the original lady of the mountain was derived from the Sibyl. Some doubt must remain as to the stage in the development of the fairy-mistress story at which it became associated with a subterranean location; but its connections with the Sibyl/Fay Sebile and the Sibylline grotto strongly suggest that this is not a late feature of the legend. In fact, the hollow mountain of the Tannhäuser-legend and of the Norcian tradition is unique among the fairy-mistress stories found on the continent of Europe in the Middle Ages. British fairyland tales not uncommonly involve a subterranean location — generally a hollow hill — but the idea does not seem to have found wide acceptance on the European mainland. Subterranean situations are by and large foreign to the stylised landscape of Arthurian literature, in which the Fays usually inhabit enchanted castles; conformity in this respect seems to have been imposed on the Fay Sebile in many of the texts. Thus it is quite reasonable to seek a specific and a different sort of source for the legendary mountain-paradise.

The *Wartburgkrieg* also affords early and important evidence connecting the Arthurian mountain with the Sibylline grotto. The most satisfactory explanation for the enigmatic allusion to "Sybillen kint" in the German poem has referred it to the Fay Sebile, since the context is manifestly Arthurian.[43] But it is also significant that the manuscripts give the classical *y* and not the French *e* in their orthography of her name. Moreover Sibyl/Sebile is not the only Vergilian figure present in the mountain. The text states that Juno dwells there with Arthur, and it is she, as goddess, who is summoned to explain their manner of life. No satisfactory explanation has been advanced for her inclusion in the German text, but Vergil actually alludes to her at the crucial point in his epic where Aeneas is instructed by the Sibyl to obtain the Golden Bough which ensures his safe passage through the grotto and into Hades: "... ramus, Iunoni infernae dictus sacer".[44] This Vergilian passage, too, has perplexed scholars, for no mythological connection between the Queen of Olympus and the Underworld is known. However that is of no

---

43) *Cf.*, F. Neri, "Le tradizioni italiane della Sibilla", *Studi Medievali,* 4 (1912/13), p. 228; "Felicia", the Sibyl's child, remains enigmatic and is perhaps intended allegorically: but in the 14th century romance *Perceforest* Sebile, an "enchanteresse" variously known as "Sebile du Lac" and "Sebile du chastel Vermeil" weds Alexander the Great and bears him a son called "Remanant de Joie"; *cf.* J. Lods, *Le roman de Perceforest* (Geneva, 1951), p. 29.
44) *Aeneid*, VI, 137f.

consequence; it is sufficient that, on the basis of Vergil's words, a subsequent classical and medieval tradition evolved, in which Juno and Avernus were quite distinctly associated.[45]

It is admittedly hazardous to assert from such simple evidence that the Sibylline grotto underlies the mountain of the *Wartburgkrieg*, and hence, presumably, the *Venusberg* too. But it is a theory which grows stronger in the light of all the circumstantial evidence connecting Sibyl/Sebile with the mountain-paradise. It serves, moreover, to explain the continuing existence of the tradition of a Grail-mountain or *Venusberg* in the vicinity of Avernus, recorded by Dietrich von Nieheim and Johann Fischart.

There is in fact one other rather indirect piece of evidence connecting the mountain-paradise and the Sibylline Grotto; it is described here rather for the sake of completeness than because it is felt to be particularly compelling. One of the most popular 13th century French works belonging to the cycle of Charlemagne was the anonymous *Huon de Bordeaux*; at one point in this lengthy text the hero visits a castle, the residence of a hostile giant, where he finds the door guarded by two artificial men of steel, who continuously and mechanically swing metal flails in such a way that entry is impossible. Huon's arrival is observed by a maiden held captive in the castle, who arrests the machinery and admits him; her name is Sebile.[46] The similarity to Antoine's "portes de metal, qui batent sans cesser" is unmistakeable, and the maiden's name confirms the likelihood of some common source. But the same flailing automata, in this case using hammers, are found in the so-called *Visio Beati Pauli*: arriving in Rome, St. Paul is disappointed to discover that Vergil, the great poet who prophesied the coming of Christ, has recently died, just too soon to become himself a Christian and to find salvation. Paul descends into his grave, where his way is barred by the two flailing figures. He does not succeed in passing, but sees beyond them the shade of Vergil at work among a vast heap of books.[47]

Pabst, ascribing without justification a compositional originality to Antoine which the author himself disclaims, supposes him to have taken his metal doors from *Huon de Bordeaux*.[48] But in fact the earlier

---

45) *Cf.* E. Norden, *P. Vergilius Maro: Aeneis Buch VI* (Leipzig, 1926), p. 175.
46) *Huon de Bordeaux*, ed. P. Ruelle (Brussels, 1960), p. 230f., v. 4743ff.
47) *Cf.* D. Comparetti, *Virgilio nel medio evo* (Florence, 1946), vol. 2, p. 182.
48) Pabst, p. 55.

text would appear to be more derivative: whereas the "reine Sibylle" in the *Paradis* is readily explained by the Norcian Sibylline tradition, "Sebile" in *Huon* is a gratuitous name, for the maiden is neither Fay nor Seeress, but simply a wronged and otherwise unexceptional virgin. It seems likely she was borrowed from a source where the name had significance. Vergil's grave, where his shade is still so active, must surely be Hades, for a classical figure of such stature, this one in particular, could go nowhere else on death. Issuing from its entrance Paul encounters a gale of wind, corresponding presumably to that which proceeds from the Sibylline caves in the *Aeneid*; Guerino finds the same on entering the mountain, and Antoine's windy cleft may be a derivative of the idea. But admission to the Underworld is possible only with the aid of the Sibyl. Presumably these flailing automata traditionally guarded its entrance and were controlled by the Seeress herself. The author of *Huon*, who was demonstrably something of a plagiarist,[49] apparently drew on such a tradition, though rather for its colourful drama than for its intrinsic significance. Nearly two centuries elapsed before the same automata emerge, altered, as Antoine's beating doors; in fact they seem to have distributed their properties between the doors and the life-like dragons (Andrea's "demonio"). The metal doors may have been inspired by the metal gate of Hades in the *Aeneid*, while the automata were perhaps originally transposed from another mythical location.

There are thus fairly good grounds for supposing the original fairy of the mountain-paradise to be a derivative of the Cumean Sibyl. Medieval literature, the French literature in particular, contains a large number of other characters bearing the name Sibille or Sebile; mutual influence between these and the Arthurian and continuing classical traditions seems most probable. Presumably they too for the most part derive ultimately from the classical Sibyl. The prophetess was commonly taken to have been a Saracen queen,[50] so it is not surprising to find a "reine Sebile" as queen of the heathen Saxons in the *Chansons des Saisnes*, a work of the Charlemagne-cycle.[51] Her most outstanding attribute is an exceptionally violent sexual passion for Baudouin, who is one of Charlemagne's paladins engaged in a protracted war with her husband. She pursues the gratification of this passion with all

---

49) *Cf.* Ruelle's edition, (*op. cit.*), p. 68ff.
50) *Cf., e.g., Li Romans de Dolopathos*, ed. C. Brunet and A. de Montaiglon (Paris, 1856), v. 12511.
51) *Cf.* L. Gautier, *Les épopées françaises* (Paris, 1880), vol. 3, p. 650ff.

unscrupulousness, and the fact that her feelings are fully reciprocated does little to redeem her character, although it does permit her to enjoy the object of her lust on various occasions, despite the seemingly unpropitious circumstances. She, at least, provides a good example of the association of the name Sebile with a character depraved beyond all measure.

Quite the opposite is the character of "reine Sibille", spouse of Charlemagne, and chaste, but maligned, heroine of another romance of the period. The original version of this work, in which the queen bore this name, does not survive, for in France she subsequently became known as Blanchflor.[52] But the original name is not subject to doubt: a version of the story, which was outlined by Alberich des Trois-Fontaines, was translated and printed in Holland in the 16th century as the tale of the "Koningin Sibille".[53] The same name, much corrupted, even appears in a Scandinavian version.[54]

At least it is clear that one need not seek far to explain Antoine's title "reine" for the lady of the paradise. Not only the wives of the Saxon ruler and Charlemagne have regal status; the prophetess herself, according to her alleged Saracen origins, is a queen, and even the "Sebile l'enchanteresse" of the Arthurian works is occasionally styled "la reine". In a French text the title would be almost more conspicuous by its absence.

It seems very likely that, by the 15th century, the Fay Sebile was no longer a figure of general familiarity. Some awareness of her original identity with the classical Sibyl had perhaps never been lost. At all events Antoine de la Sale immediately assumes that his story concerns a Sibyl, despite her uncharacteristic role, which mystifies him. With a scientific deliberation that must arouse the sympathy of scholars, he endeavours to establish the falsehood of the story by methodically accounting for each of the ten recognised Sibyls, and showing that none of them had any association with the Norcian mountain. Concerning the Cumean Sibyl, he states as fact the belief that she is dead and entombed in Sicily, a tradition which was apparently so widespread that

---

52) *Ibid.*, p. 684ff.
53) Alberich, (*op. cit.*), p. 712.
54) *Cf.* A. H. Krappe, "Une version noroise de la reine Sibille", *Romania*, 56 (1930) 585-8.

Andrea Barberino felt compelled to deny it, in order to lend credibility to Guerino's adventure.

It is also worth noting that Andrea, although his Sibyl is expressly the one from Cumea, actually depicts his hero castigating her as "rinigata fada", a term which surely betrays her other, suppressed nature.[55]

In Germany alone, where the legend was to enjoy popular success, the different identity allotted to the demonic fairy-mistress seems to have entirely obscured Sibyl/Sebile, if indeed she was ever known there in this capacity.

---

55) *Cf. supra*, p.47.

V
THE DEMONIC FAIRY-MISTRESS

The most crucial single development denoting the emergence of the Tannhäuser-legend from the medieval fairy-mistress story is, of course, the demonisation of the fairy. The fairy of pagan folklore, originally a more or less amoral creature, suffered no more than a general deprecation at the hands of medieval Christianity as a whole. But in the legend that deprecation is put to a powerful figurative use: the fairy and her realm are made to represent the diabolical temptations of an evil world, and the story illustrates in appropriately universal and didactic terms the consequences of such sin for human life. In this respect the legend differs fundamentally from the courtly romances of about the year 1200. There the fairy, rather than demonised, has been humanised, and emerges as the courtly lady whom the knight serves. Accordingly, his love for her is first and foremost an instance of common human love, although it may of course have further figurative significance in a possible wider meaning of the individual work. Moreover, this human love is conceived in the terms peculiar to the chivalric age and characteristically viewed in a positive light. Far from being censured as sinful, the knight's love is a consequence of his noble nature, and its consummation is the reward of his chivalric worthiness. In the Yvain-romance those very vicissitudes of love which supply the typical fairy-mistress structure are the result of the hero's developing moral qualities and of his lady's initially wrong assessment of them. The moral ideal in such works has a primarily social and secular character, despite its deeply Christian foundation: the knight generally achieves progress by combatting the evils which oppress his fellow-men. In the legend the moral pre-occupation is doctrinally religious, and therefore more individual: the issue is the salvation from a world of sin of a single, though representative, human soul. The Tannhäuser of the ballads confronts no social moral problems, indeed he has no dealings with other men as fellow humans in the strictest sense. He encounters only an allegorical figure of temptation and a Pope in whom, for all the question of the pontiff's possible human guilt, the hero sees only the *vicarius Christi*.

However, pure fantasy increasingly occupied the imaginations of romancers in the 13th century, and this era saw a growing number of works in which fairies and fairy-mistresses appeared with their original fairy natures unchanged. Many of these texts, as well as many earlier medieval fairy-mistress stories, exhibit a clear critical tendency towards the fairy, even while they evince little overt inclination to pass Christian moral judgments. Such an attitude plainly underlies the more extreme development in the legend. It will be recalled for instance that the fairy herself is generally responsible for initiating her amorous relationship with a mortal; she it is who magically entices him, binds his love with the spell of her superlative beauty, and thereby naturally deprives him of some freedom. A romantic liaison with a fairy is not always seen as a desirable matter, indeed it is one which the greater heroes of Arthurian romance generally see fit to avoid where possible. Fairies are not entirely beneficent towards men, nor are they necessarily endowed with pleasant traits of personality. They prove jealous and vengeful when crossed, and their possessiveness can be particularly detrimental to the normal activities of a knight-errant, for they show a certain predilection for imprisoning the beloved in an enchanted castle or other fairyland location, where they hope to enjoy his company in seclusion. No doubt the Middle Ages saw reflected in this possessive jealousy some comment on the nature of love and of women; the point is not unrelated to the moral of the Tannhäuser-legend. It is no mean compliment to the virtue of the 13th century Arthurian knights that the Fays, despite their incessant scheming, remain for the most part mateless.

Examples from the Arthurian texts are numerous. Lucy Paton argues ingeniously that the enmity between Arthur and Morgan, which runs throughout the Arthurian matter, originated in his refusal of her love; the motif presumably came to be obscured before they were reputed siblings.[1] The fate of Merlin casts a similarly doubtful light on Niniane, his fairy-mistress: having gained the enchanter's love purely in order to learn his powerful arts, she employs them to seal him for ever in a magic prison.[2] In the tale of Alisandre l'Orphelin the hero is lured with the help of a drug to Morgan's castle, where she hopes to win his love. But he resents this capture, and with the help of one of Morgan's maidens he eventually hatches a successful plot to betray and destroy the castle, thus effecting his escape; Morgan is furious at her loss.[3] In *Claris et Laris*, the two heroes are led by an apparently innocent maiden

---

1) Paton, (*op. cit.*) p. 13f.
2) *The vulgate version* ... ed. H. O. Sommer, (*op. cit.*), vol. II, p. 209ff. and p. 451f.
3) *Prophecies*, (*op. cit.*), p. 413f. and 421.

to a fairyland valley from the Forest of Broceliande, and they find themselves confronted by twelve Fays, the senior of whom is Morgan.[4] She informs them that they may never leave the valley again, although every conceivable pleasure is available to them there. However, in exchange for a promise of love, the Fay Madoine later secretly shows them a path from the place. These tales tell of a situation similar to that met with in the German Tannhäuser-ballads, indeed a situation implicit in the rigorous prescriptions governing times of departure from the mountain-paradise: mortals are enticed to an enchanted place and there retained against their will. The escape effected with the aid of a subsidiary maiden in both *Claris* and the tale of Alisandre parallels closely Guerino's departure from the mountain-paradise: he is led to the door by one of the Sibyl's maids.

The prose *Lancelot* tells how the hero is lured to Morgan's castle by the pretence of an adventure which awaits him. Morgan holds him prisoner in hope of winning his love, but, such is his yearning for Guinevere, that he bursts the bars and escapes.[5] In the *Bataille Loquifer* the hero Renoart is abducted to Avalon while searching for his lost son. After a few days of happy mutual love with Morgan, he insists on proceeding with his quest, to the intense anger of the Fay. She contrives to wreck his boat, but he is rescued and then regrets the entire escapade as soon as he thinks of his wife.[6] Both these works include the theme of enticement and retention, and the mention of the hero's human love recalls incidentally stanza 6 of the High German ballad.[7] Renoart's short-lived reciprocation of Morgan's love aligns his story still more strictly with the legend.

Such parallels reveal something more of the extensive narrative tradition to which the legend broadly belongs. But the extreme degree of demonisation characterising the legend in particular is expressed principally through the two motifs which, significantly enough, actuate the turning-points of the story. These are the weekly transformation of the fairy and the knight's confession of his sinful love to a priest. Both motifs are to be found in earlier fairy-mistress stories, and their previous history rewards investigation.

---

4) *Claris et Laris*, ed. J. Alton (Tübingen, 1884), p. 97ff., v. 3571ff.
5) *Vulgate version ...*, vol. V, p. 215ff. and p. 221f.
6) *Cf.* Paton, (*op. cit.*), p. 49ff.
7) *Cf.* Appendix IV, Text *B*, stanza 6 (= Text *A*, stanza 5, Text *C*, stanza 7).

The first of them is comparatively well-documented, so that something quite specific may be said of its sources in the legend. A certain tendency of devils to manifest themselves in the form of serpents is of course a well-attested and very widespread literary phenomenon of immense antiquity, but the regular weekly occurrence of the metamorphosis in the mountain-paradise proves to be a more useful feature: it is the principal motif of the Melusine-story.[8]

The tale is first recorded in the 12th century by Walter Map, though the fairy's name, Melusine, does not appear at that date.[9] In a grove on the Norman coast a youth bearing the name Henno cùm Dentibus (on account of his large teeth) finds an exceptionally beautiful maiden claiming to be the shipwrecked and reluctant bride of the King of France. Henno marries her himself and she bears him children; but his mother is disconcerted to notice that her new daughter-in-law invariably shuns attendance at the consecration of the Host on Sundays and also assiduously avoids contact with Holy Water. She is secretly observed during mass on one such occasion and seen to withdraw to her bath, where both she and her maid are transformed into loathsome dragons. Their suspicious aroused, mother and son seize them and sprinkle them with Holy Water; unable to bear its virtue, the demons leap through the roof with a great cry and disappear.

Essentially this is a fairy-mistress story of category A, although it lacks a third stage and the discovery of the fairy's transformations serves the part of the customary disobedience to a tabu. Just as in the Tannhäuser-legend, the metamorphosis betrays the woman's character and leads to the separation, the turning-point of the story. Map leaves no doubt at all as to her demonic nature, but both the detail and the structure of the tale clearly show that she is simultaneously a fairy. Indeed a certain disparateness of character results from the combination: prior to her disgrace she bears Henno children whose beauty bespeaks their half-fairy nature, and she displays the benevolence characteristic of fairies in such happy circumstances, surpassing even Henno's mother in the diligent performance of works of charity. But the metamorphosis then betrays her true nature: fairy

---

8) *Cf.* in general L. Hoffrichter, *Die ältesten französischen Bearbeitungen der Melusinensage* (Halle, 1928); K. Heisig, "Über den Ursprung der Melusinensage", *Fabula*, 3 (1960) pp. 170 181.
9) *De Nugis Curialium* (*op. cit.*), Div. III, cap. ix, p. 175f.

and demon are shown to be one. The essentially Christian quality of the transformation described in this story, whatever its possible pagan origin in folklore or myth, is indicated by the weekly occurrence: God's weekly presence in the Host at mass compels the demonic being to reveal itself.[10]

From some form of this story the motif evidently passed into the Tannhäuser-legend, indeed there is much justification for regarding the first part of the legend as a variant of the Melusine-story: the two concur in form and substance (the fairy-mistress story), in theme (the mortal's disillusionment), and in motif (the transformation). It is also worth noting that in *Guerino*, too, the transformations are quite explicitly stated to coincide with the papal mass at Rome.[11] Unfortunately only few other versions of Map's tale survive from the Middle Ages, although it plainly enjoyed popularity. Gervase of Tilbury records a story that is in many essentials the same, and actually introduces the motif of a broken tabu. The fairy is still unnamed, but the mortal is now Raimundus, Lord of Russetum in the Province of Aix. The fairy forbids him to see her naked body. When, after years of happiness and prosperity, and following the birth of beautiful children, he one day beholds her naked in a bath, he sees her transformed into a serpent and watches her sink below the water, never to be seen by him again. In this version there is no clear suggestion that the transformations occur weekly.[12] Later in the same century Vincent of Beauvais summarises the tale, but supplies so little detail that his testimony is worthless, except as an indication of popularity. He too does not specify a weekly occurrence of the metamorphosis.[13]

The next surviving versions are found only at the end of the 14th century. The fairy is now named Melusigne, and the material has been much expanded to incorporate a 'history' relating the origins of the House of Lusignan. The fairy-wife seems introduced largely in order to enhance with supernatural origins the prestige of the family. Interestingly, the three earlier versions also adumbrate this aspect of the

---

10) *Cf.* Reinhard, (*op. cit.*), p. 137, who points to the earlier existence of the motif as a pagan *geis*.
11) *Guerino*, cap. 147.
12) *Otia Imperialium* (*op. cit.*), Dec. I, cap. 15, p. 896; Gervase's rubric for the chapter runs "De oculis apertis post peccatum".
13) Vincent of Beauvais, *Speculum naturale* (Douai, 1624; rprt. Graz, 1964), lib. II, cap. 127, col. 157.

THE TRAGEDY OF KNIGHTHOOD 79

story by their insistence that the demon-fairy's progeny still survive. Two versions of the longer 14th century story are extant, both of them in French; the first by Jean d'Arras (prose, 1387) and the second by Couldrette (verse, c. 1401).[14] In the sections treating the fairy-mistress they are very similar indeed, and evidently used a common source, although this is thought to date from only about 1375. They contain a number of details otherwise found exclusively in either Walter Map or Gervase of Tilbury, but not in both; it is thus reasonable to conclude that the material had a more complex earlier history than may be reconstructed simply from the surviving evidence.

The apposite parts of these two versions may be summarised as follows: — Presine (or Persine), the sister of Morgan, marries a mortal, imposing on him a tabu: he may not visit her during her lying-in. She bears him three beautiful daughters, of whom the eldest is Melusigne, before he eventually breaches the tabu. She then leaves him to dwell in Avalon with her young daughters. When the latter reach adulthood, they are told of their father's misconduct, which so incenses them that they magically imprison him forever inside a mountain. But Presine in fact still loves her husband and, learning of her daughters' action, angrily punishes their cruelty by pronouncing a curse on each of them: Melusigne is destined to be transformed into a serpent from the waist downwards every Saturday. If, however, she marries a mortal, she may live a normal life, provided her husband agrees to avoid seeing her on Saturdays and to reveal nothing of her transformed state; if he breaks this tabu, she must live in her serpentine form until the Day of Judgment. Eventually Melusigne does marry a mortal, Remondin, but every son she bears carries some ominous physical deformity. Despite his great love for her, Remondin is finally provoked to break the tabu by an allegation of her infidelity. At first, he simply observes her in the shape of a serpent, but later anger at the grave misconduct of his son, Gieffroy au Grant Dent, prompts him to denounce her publicly as a "faulse serpente". In obedience to the curse, Melusigne then leaves him forever.

This whole narrative might be described as a duplicated fairy-mistress story, although the first part, treating Presine, seems designed

---

14) Jean d'Arras, *Mélusine, Roman du XVIe siècle*, ed. L. Stouff. Publications de l'Université de Dijon, fasc. V, (Dijon, 1932); Couldrette, *Mellusine*, ed. F. Michel (Niort, 1854); cf. L. Stouff, *Essai sur Mélusine* (Paris, 1930), esp. p. 52ff; the German version (1456) of Thüring von Ringoltingen is based on that of Couldrette.

simply to explain the curse that falls on Melusigne and causes her own unusual conditions of marriage in the second part. It can be seen that the original logic of the weekly transformation has been obscured or suppressed. The half-mortal Melusigne is decidedly not portrayed as a demon, a nature which would ill accord with the authors' objective regarding the ancestry of the House of Lusignan; indeed Melusigne is renowned for her building of churches. Her metamorphosis, rather than devilish, is akin to the motif of the Loathly Lady: she is cursed and must endure a hideous transformation until the prescribed act of kindness by a mortal lifts the spell. While the motif of the Loathly Lady is perhaps not entirely unrelated in its origin to the demonic transformation, its significance is quite distinct.[15] Evidently something unquestionably sinister, expressed in the notion of the fairy's retributive curse, attaches to Melusigne's nature. Presine herself sees the half-fairy constitution of her daughter as blight from which, but for her youthful hardness towards her father, she might have escaped, to be virtually human. The deformities of her sons further betray something uncanny. But her metamorphosis provokes in Remondin a reaction which above all reveals how it is felt to be a demonic motif, however much the general contention of the work seeks specifically to show this as unjust for Melusigne. On first beholding her transformed, Remondin is full of remorse at the broken tabu and at his wrongful suspicion of her infidelity. Later, when Gieffroy has destroyed a monastery and killed his own brother, a different mood inspires in Remondin a very different chain of thought: "Par la foy que je doy a Dieu, je croy que ce ne soit que fantosme de ceste femme, ne ne croy pas que ja fruit qu'ell ait porté viengne a perfection de bien; elle n'a porté enfant que n'ait apporté quelque estrange signe sur terre ... Et ne vy je leur mere, le samedy ... en forme de serpente du nombril en aval? Si fiz, par Dieu. C'est aucune esperite ou c'est toute fantosme ou illusion qui m'a abusé".[16] He later regrets this view, which is of course altogether unjust. The reader's sympathy is intentionally won for Melusigne; she is a benevolent, but long-suffering and maligned half-fairy, in a tale which makes no real attempt to explain the status of such a creature in an otherwise essentially Christian universe.

---

15) E. Frank, *Der Schlangenkuss. Form und Geist*, 9 (Leipzig, 1928).
16) Jean d'Arras, (*op. cit.*), p. 253: "By the faith which I owe to God, I think this woman is only a fantasy, and I believe that no fruit she has borne may come to perfection; she has not brought a child into the world who does not bear some strange sign ... And did I not see their mother on Saturday ... in the form of a serpent from the navel downwards? I did, by God. It is some spirit, or it is all a fantasy or an illusion which has deceived me."

The appearance in this story (to which convention has given the title *Melusine*) of the fairy's injunction to secrecy regarding her true nature is another matter of some interest for the evident connection with the Tannhäuser-legend. It might be regarded as an inconsistency or a structural flaw in the work that, whereas Presine's curse apparently specifies the mere witnessing of the transformation to be a breach of tabu, it does not in fact prove effective as such; only Remondin's subsequent indiscretion causes their separation. In the legend, too, the knight's disclosure of her wicked nature in the confessional breaches the lady's ruling that he must sing her praises; here there is no attempt to prevent his witnessing her transformations, indeed it is essential to the story that he does so throughout his stay.

Melusine also introduces the theme of papal confession and forgiveness, though they are used in a manner different from the legend. Throughout the narrative, forgiveness plays a prominent role. The curse pronounced on the fairy results from her hard-heartedness towards her father, and its consequences are condign, if movingly tragic: she must endure perpetual separation from her own erring husband, even though she herself earnestly desires to forgive him. When she announces her final departure, Remondin entreats her pardon, but she replies simply that, while she pardons him from her heart, true forgiveness comes from God alone. As a result of these words, Remondin subsequently journeys to Rome in search of pardon, confesses to Pope Benedict "Qu'il s'estoit parjurez envers sa femme",[17] receives absolution, and ends life as a hermit.

In the presence of so many common motifs, a reasonably close genetic relationship between *Melusine* and the Tannhäuser-legend may hardly be doubted. But it is scarcely possible that this elaborate fairy-mistress story can itself have been the source of the legend, and have given to it the themes of forgiveness and papal confession, for the charge of diabolism against the fairy, which is so purposefully waived in Melusine is crucial to the legend. The persisting thematic residue of diabolism in the French text suggests rather that the unknown author of the 14th century work (describing the history of Lusignan, and used by both Jean d'Arras and Couldrette) had before him a version in which the fairy was still unquestionably a demon, in the manner of Map's tale and the later legend. The seemingly unsatisfactory integration of the

---

17) *Ibid.*, p. 270: "... that he had perjured himself towards his wife."

papal confession in *Melusine* further leads one to suppose that it had a more essential function in the source. This putative story must then have resembled in very many important aspects the one which underlies both Hemmerlin's account and, apparently, *Guerino il Meschino*: the mortal repented of his love, when the fairy's transformations revealed her true nature as a demon, and he journeyed to Rome to confess and seek absolution. The nameless 14th century writer adapted and rearranged these motifs for his own end: — the whitewashing of the fairy-mistress in the interests of a reputable and virtuous genealogy for the House of Lusignan.

The same original demonic fairy-mistress story was plainly also a literary ancestor of the Tannhäuser-legend. However it is clear from *Melusine* that this postulated source identified the lady as a fairy, and gave her neither the name nor the attributes of Venus. There is no positive evidence, furthermore, that a hollow mountain-paradise was involved, though the idea may quite possibly have been simply suppressed, due to a specific desire to locate the events at the traditional homes of the House of Lusignan. There is also no hint that the source described a third stage of the story, in which the mortal regained, or returned to, the demonic fairy; indeed the texts of *Melusine*, like Hemmerlin and *Guerino*, suggest that his quest for absolution met with success, which would virtually preclude a third stage.

Unfortunately our knowledge of this presumed source is much too indirect to permit any greater precision with regard to its contents. Neither *Melusine* nor the surviving versions of the Tannhäuser-legend are its immediate descendants, and the intervening unknowns reduce to mere speculation any endeavour to establish their relationship more accurately.

The papal confession in *Melusine* is more or less extraneous to the fairy-mistress structure. It is not directly connected with a turning-point of the story, for Remondin seeks forgiveness only after he has offended his fairy-wife and breached the tabu, and he does not win her back as a result of his pardon. Above all the confession does not serve as a demonisation-motif, for he feels guilt precisely at having wrongfully accused her of diabolism, not because she is in truth a devil. However another text of the Middle Ages includes the motif of confession, and employs it more or less as a demonisation-motif in the manner found in the legend. This testimony strongly supports the contention that the motif initially entered the fairy-mistress story as a confession of sinful love for a demon. The text involved is the French *Lai de Désiré*, which dates probably from the 13th century and closely follows the other fairy-mistress *lais* (particularly *Lanval* and *Graelent*) in its form.[18] The hero, Désiré, who excels in the chivalric arts, encounters his fairy in the forest, and successfully sues for her love. The instructions which she gives for the continuation of their liaison depart a little from the usual pattern: she insists that his sustained activity as a knight is vital to their mutual happiness, and that it must above all be encouraged and promoted by his love for her; on no account should his knighthood be compromised by their relationship: "ne vos chargiez por moi de rien" she instructs him:

>Ainz que vos eussiez m'amor,
>Fustes vos de molt grant valor;
>N'est mie droiz a chevalier
>Que por amor doie empirier.[19]

She gives him a ring, with the warning that its loss involves the irrevocable termination of their liaison. A period of both happy love (with the birth of two children) and successful military activity for the knight ensues, but eventually Désiré confesses himself to a hermit, giving an account of his fairy-mistress. The poem reveals nothing at all of the thoughts that prompted this action. He receives absolution and departs, only to notice immediately the absence of the ring from his finger. Full of foreboding, he hastens to the rendezvous, but finds it deserted, and his cries and pleas bring no response. Near to despair, but realising clearly what he has done, he calls out "Li hermite me confessa/Onques de vos n'i mesparla".[20] Then, just like Tannhäuser in the Low German ballads, he roundly curses his confessor. For a full year he sees no more of the fairy, and his health so declines that his life is feared for; finally his mistress comes to him, full of both compassion and reproach:

>Tu te feis de moi confes,
>Sin me recovreras ja mes.
>Estoies tu de moi chargiez?
>Ce ne fu pas si granz pechiez;

---

18) *Désiré*, ed. Grimes (*op. cit.*).
19) *Ibid.*, v. 251: "Do not encumber yourself on my account."; "Before you had my love you were of the greatest valour; it is not proper that a knight should worsen because of love."
20) *Ibid.*, v. 355f.: "The hermit heard my confession, he never spoke ill of you."

> Je ne fui onques espousée
> Ne fianciée, ne jurée,
> Ne fame espousée n'en as.
> Je croi tu t'en repentiras.
> Quant tu confession queroies,
> Bien sai que de moi partiroies.
> Que vaut li pechiez a gehir,
> Qui ne se puet mie partir?
> Soventes foiz as tu douté
> Que je t'eüsse enfantosmé;
> N'aies tu ja de ce regart,
> Ne sui mie de male part.[21]

In order to prove her virtue and innocence she undertakes to appear beside him at mass and partake of the Host, as in fact subsequently occurs. Their love is then restored and later, after Désiré's son and daughter are introduced to the human world, and to knighthood and a human marriage respectively, the couple are themselves formally united (in an ecclesiastical ceremony) before departing to fairyland and perpetual happiness.

There can be no doubt that Désiré's confession is felt to be a demonisation-motif: the fairy herself infers as much from it, although the hero's thoughts remain unknown. But, at the same time, it is striking how the general tendency of this work, as of *Melusine*, is to deny the validity of the motif. In fact the proof of innocence employed by Désiré's fairy reverses exactly the original logic of the transformation-motif: she demonstrates that she may attend the consecration of the Host without suffering any hideous revelation of a wicked nature. Thus both works, *Melusine* and *Désiré*, use the demonisation-motifs in a more or less polemical way, introducing them only in order to discredit them: Jean d'Arras emphasises throughout his work the virtue of his patrons' fairy-ancestress, while the author of *Désiré* actually inverts one of the traditional motifs precisely in order to exonerate his harmless fairy.

---

21) *Ibid.*, v. 417ff.: "You made confession of me, and you will never recover me. Have you encumbered yourself on my account? This was not such a great sin; I was never married, nor affianced, nor am I subject to an oath; nor do you have a married wife. I think you will repent this. When you sought confession, I knew well that you would leave me. What use is it to confess a sin from which you cannot part? Many a time you have thought that I bewitched you; pay no heed to that   I am not of evil nature."

The matter of the tabu in *Désiré* is somewhat less simple. Clearly the hero's confession breaches the fairy's instructions and, by actuating the first turning-point of the story, assumes the role of the breach of secrecy found in many fairy-mistress stories of category *A*. But Désiré's immediate cry "Onques de vos n'i mesparla" betrays his own understanding that the confession arguably involves his lady's defamation. His reaction therefore corresponds better to Venus' words in the German ballad, "Mein lob das solt ir preysen",[22] than to the less precise instructions of his own fairy. Accordingly, it seems possible that the simple and customary requirement of secrecy in most of the fairy-mistress *lais (Lanval, Graelent, Pulzella Gaia)* underwent alteration in a diabolical version of the story: the demon-fairy, anxious perhaps to lure further souls to her snare, or perhaps from simple vanity, is concerned for her reputation in the world and demands that the knight speak no evil of her, or even that he sing her praises. This requirement is then implicitly breached in the confessional. Such a suggestion can at least explain Venus' odd demand in the ballads, to which, in the earliest surviving version, Tannhäuser warmly assents. In *Désiré*, where the attempt to prove the fairy's innocence dominates, the motif seems to have been imperfectly integrated with the main theme, which is a quite sophisticated one. The author displays an overriding concern with the rightful conduct and true proprieties of *amour courtois*, which he treats in a didactic manner. In the first passage quoted above, free and noble love is defended in the face of moral criticism; it is important not simply that the knight should continue to display his chivalric prowess while enjoying a lady's favours, but also that such noble and freely given love is actually essential to his success — parted from his beloved, Désiré rapidly becomes worthless as a knight. It appears, then, that in *Désiré* the components of a demonic fairy-mistress story were, as in *Melusine*, not required for their own sake. By clearing his fairy of the charge of diabolism, the author achieves a neat defence of courtly love.

One more medieval fairy-mistress story must be considered in some detail, on account of its affinity with the source-material of the legend: it is the Middle Scots romance *Tom the Rymer,* which Krappe believed to be a close relative of the Celtic source of the legend.[23]

---

22) Appendix IV, Text *B*, stanza 15.
23) *Op. cit.*; *cf.* also Löhmann, p. 239ff.

Tom the Rymer espies the Queen of Elfin-land by Huntley Banks, and hastens to meet her at Eldoune Tree.[24] Overwhelmed by her beauty, he at first takes her for the Blessed Virgin; but on her correcting this error he at once proceeds to request her amorous favours. She warns that this will cause instant loss of her beauty, but he persists, swearing her an oath of fidelity:

> Now, lufly ladye, rewe one mee
> And j will euer more with the duelle;
> Here my trouthe j will the plyghte,
> Whethir though will in heuen or helle.[25]

Finally she relents, although one manuscript shows him first obliged to promise secrecy — an undertaking soon broken it appears, for the first fifty lines of the work actually use the first person. Following the consummation of a passion that is evidently mutual, the Queen becomes instantly transformed into a hideous hag, and one manuscript depicts Tom reacting to this with the horrified belief that she is the devil incarnate.[26] On the one hand, this point plainly corresponds to his earlier and contrasting error as to her identity, for she once more promptly reassures him.[27] But it has also been suggested that the short passage showing Tom's reaction to her transformation is in fact a clumsy interpolation, a view which is well supported by the manuscript evidence.[28] Ugly as she now is, Tom is bound by his earlier oath and dutifully follows at her command. She leads him "jn at Eldone Hill",[29] where it is dark as midnight, and for three days he must wade through water to his knee; the lady of course rides her palfrey. Complaining of hunger, he is led to an orchard of fruit, but simultaneously warned that his soul will burn in hell-fire if he pluck any. Then, resting his head upon the fairy's knee, he is enabled to see the separate roads to Heaven, to Paradise, to Purgatory and to Hell, as well as the castle of the Elfin Queen herself. Before they enter it, Tom is instructed to remain quite silent, and then the Queen suddenly undergoes a reverse

---

24) *The romance and prophecies of Thomas of Erceldoune*, ed. J. A. H. Murray, Early English Text Society, O. S., no. 61 (London, 1875).
25) *Ibid.*, v. 105ff; the text quoted is that of the Thornton ms.
26) *Ibid.*, p. 9; (the Landsdowne ms.).
27) The earlier error is not without precedent in other texts, and can scarcely have been included simply to parallel the second one: Ogier, encountering Morgan for the first time, takes her for the Virgin; *cf.* also P. Sebillot, *Contes populaires de la Haute Bretagne* (Paris, 1880), vol. II, p. 31.
28) J. M. Burnham, "A study of Thomas of Erceldoune," *Publications of the Modern Language Association*, 23 (1908), p. 382.
29) *Romance*, v. 169.

transformation, so that she regains her former peerless splendour. Their reception at the castle is something of a stately affair: "Than ladyes come, bothe faire and gent/With curtassye to hir knelande".[30] Music and minstrels play, and the spoils of the chase are brought in, while knights play and dance. For three years Tom dwells with the Queen, though it seems to him no more than as many days. Finally she tells him that he must leave at once, for "To Morne of helle the foulle fende/Amang this folke will feche his fee";[31] the devil will assuredly choose Tom, who is large and handsome. The Queen leads him back to Eldoune Tree where, in parting, he requests a token of remembrance. She offers him the gift to "Harpe or carpe", but Tom declines the first: "Harpynge kepe j none;/ffor tonge is chefe of mynstralsye".[32] She then makes a further offer:

> If thou will spelle, or tales telle,
> Thomas thou sall neuer lesynge lye
> Where euer thou fare, by frythe or felle,
> I praye the, speke none euyll of me.[33]

He requests her to tell him some "ferly", whereupon she embarks upon a long 'prophetic' account of events from Scots border-history in the late 13th and 14th centuries, obviously written retrospectively.

The five manuscripts preserving the text are of considerably varying quality, but all belong to the 15th century. J. A. H. Murray, who edited the work, demonstrated that the complete version must date from the early years of the same century, but such dating is based solely on evidence contained in the prophecies. The romance itself could be earlier; Murray suggests that it could date from as early as 1333.[34] But this should be seen as a *terminus post quem*; there is certainly no evidence to place its composition in the 13th century, a supposition made purely in order to bring its date closer to that of the historical Tannhäuser.[35]

The belief that the work is composed of authentic and pure Celtic material, and that it arose in this form among Scottish Celts without alien admixture or alteration, was fundamental to Krappe's theory. But

---

30) *Ibid.*, v. 255f.
31) *Ibid.*, v. 289f.
32) *Ibid.*, v. 315f.
33) *Ibid.*, v. 317ff.
34) *Ibid.*, p. xxiiiff.
35) *Cf.* Löhmann, p. 240, note 55.

it is manifestly impossible to make such a claim confidently. The romance is a pastiche of elements, nearly all of which are recorded in some form on the continent of Europe at dates earlier than its composition.[36] Moreover, there is no trace at all of a previous Scots history for the material. While it is indubitably of a generally Celtic nature, the aristocratic social setting it displays indicates that it is at least well adulterated. It probably represents a *rifacimento* of narrative material derived from the continent at a time when contact between Scotland and Europe (France in particular) was strong. Such a view explains its similarities with the Tannhäuser-legend more readily than may Krappe's theory, which proves virtually untenable on close analysis.[37]

The similarities with the Tannhäuser-legend are undeniable. But they are either of a very general nature (the subterranean fairyland and the typical narrative structure of the fairy-mistress story), or a matter of incidental detail (such points are discussed below). The principal and definitive features of the legend — *i.e.* the fairy's demonic nature, the knight's disenchantment, and his voluntary departure from the mountain in order to procure absolution — are either altogether missing from the Scots text, or present only in rudimentary and inconsequential form. Tom's supposition that the lady is the devil certainly recalls the form of the demonisation-motif found in the ballads, but it is summarily brushed aside — "fende of hell am I none"[38] — and does not reappear, for it has no relevance to the story. The lady's transformation is quite undemonic in its aim: it is the motif of the Loathly Lady and serves simply to test Tom's honourable obedience to his oath.

Unlike the legend, Tom's story is not a psychological and theological one of sin, remorse and forgiveness; it recounts quite naively Tom's experience with his fairy-mistress. As the surviving manuscripts show, its purpose was connected with the prophecies which follow it. Tom the Rymer, whose real name was Thomas of Ercildoune, lived in the latter half of the 13th century and was probably a poet,

---

36) *Cf.* Burnham, (*op. cit.*), p. 386ff.
37) I referred the question to a Celticist, Professor B. K. Martin, who shared this opinion and expressed extreme doubts whether such a work could have played a seminal role in the development of the Tannhäuser-legend.
38) *Romance*, v. 150.

although none of his work actually survives. His reputation in the late Middle Ages rested entirely on the immense number of political prophecies which circulated under his name, and which related true or false events occurring after his lifetime. (Attempts to see in him a figure analogous to the historical Tannhäuser and inspiring the latter's role in the legend seem rather forced; while Tom's reputation as a political and prophetic poet explains his alleged encounter with a fairy-mistress, Tannhäuser was never known for such works.)[39] The real authors of these prophecies were of course keen to establish the veracity of their utterances, and to convince sceptics — it is noteworthy that Thomas, whose legend and prophecies are widely known today, still bears the sobriquet "True Thomas". The romance constitutes an attempt to demonstrate the reputability of Tom's prescience by indicating its source: it is plausibly revealed as the gift of a fairy, who was at one time his mistress. The fairy's particular gift of truth renders all his sayings quite unassailable. It is some indication of the quite subordinate role of the fairy-mistress story that it fills less than half of the surviving text.

However, the unknown author of the romance evidently used source material involving a subterranean fairy-mistress. Further parallels establish beyond all reasonable doubt that he in fact drew on the same narrative tradition as the Tannhäuser-legend. Apart from such obvious similarities as Tom's momentary belief that his lady is the devil, his obligation to her under an oath, and her request that he speak no evil of her, an odd correspondence to the Low German texts of the ballad (but not the High German) occurs at the point of Tom's entry into the hill, when the fairy bids him "Take thy leue of sone and Mone".[40] The degree to which these points correspond textually to the ballads suggests that the common source was very possibly an actual text. In as far as it retains the lady's fairy nature, the Scots text may be said to stand closer to this common original than the Tannhäuser-legend; from that point of view, but from virtually no other, Krappe's theory has a slight core of validity. Everywhere else, *Tom the Rymer* shows quite drastic alteration of the source: the transformation-motif is given a new, and quite undemonic purpose, though Tom's reaction to it still indicates the original function; the subterranean realm, now almost innocent, was a devilish place in the original, for the fiend still takes his toll of its inhabitants — this has become a mere device to operate the

---

39) *Cf.* Krappe, "Die Sage vom Tannhäuser" (*op. cit.*), p. 114; Burnham, p. 390f.
40) *Romance*, v. 157; *cf.* Appendix IV, Text C, stanza 24.

second turning-point, and is without moral consequence. Tom is not
held guilty for his sojourn, and the Elfin Queen emerges as no demon,
but a benevolent and loving fairy.

The subterranean location in *Tom the Rymer* indicates that the
hollow mountain was almost certainly associated with the demonic
fairy-mistress story at a stage when the lady's fairy nature was still quite
explicit, *i.e.* before she was replaced by the figurative character of
Venus, of whom there is no hint in the Scots work. This introduces a
further interesting aspect of the romance: the dual role of its heroine,
fairy-mistress and prophetess inhabiting a subterranean realm, brings
clearly to mind the shadowy figure of Sibyl/Fay Sebile. In fact, *Tom
the Rymer* contains some other points linking it firmly to the Norcian
grotto in such a way as to suggest that the Sibyl /Sebile of the Italian
mountain was indeed the original fairy of the story. The fee taken by
the devil from the realm of the Elfin Queen corresponds closely to a
part of the Norcian tradition recorded by Bercheur and later by
Leandro Alberti:[41] the devil exacts a yearly due of one soul from those
who visit the place. In his *L'Italia liberata* Trissino describes a journey
to the Norcian Sibyl, in the course of which the visitors, when they are
already underground, are obliged to wade for four hours through a
shallow lake.[42] As far as is known this motif is exclusive to the Italian
work and the Scots romance, and, in view of the general association of
the Tannhäuser-legend with Norcia, some joint source appears certain.
The Vergilian connection of the Norcian grotto permits one perhaps to
see in the shallow lake a derivative of the Marsh of Styx, traversed by
Aeneas and the Sibyl in Charon's flimsy corracle. One may even
conjecture on further Vergilian elements in *Tom the Rymer:* Tom's
vision of the roads to Heaven, Hell *etc.*, mysteriously granted by his
lady's lap, is found in no other text, but is distinctly reminiscent of the
manner in which the Sibyl, leading Aeneas to Elysium, indicates the
fork for the road to Tartarus.

Such evidence is slight indeed, but it adds what weight it has to the
supposition that Sibyl/Sebile was in fact the original demonic fairy-
mistress of the mountain-paradise.

---

41) *Cf.* Alberti, fol. 278v; Bercheur, (*op. cit.*) p. 611.
42) *Op. cit.*, lib. XXIV, fol. 108v.

THE TRAGEDY OF KNIGHTHOOD 91

These two chapters have demonstrated that the Tannhäuser-legend arose from a medieval fairy-mistress story which portrayed the fairy as a disguised demon, and showed the mortal consequently seeking absolution of the sin of loving her. In all, three distinct narratives have been discussed which show a similarity to the legend in sufficient points to justify speaking of closely related source material: *Guerino il Meschino*, the late 14th century versions of the *Melusine-story*, and *Tom the Rymer*. The degree of their correspondence with the legend varies, as do also the precise points of agreement, but the number of features which the legend shares with at least two of them is considerable: the demonic fairy in a subterranean realm who takes a mortal lover; her serpentine metamorphosis which warns of her true nature; the danger to the mortal of exceeding a certain term in the mountain; the need to absolve the sin; the papal confession; *etc*. What all these works most conspicuously lack, apart from a mention of the hero's final return to the mountain, is any suggestion at all of a figurative role for the fairy and her realm. Even in *Guerino*, the most pedagogically moral of the three, the Sibyl and her mountain represent for the hero no more than one specific test by temptation in the course of a long career. In the other two works, if only to a lesser extent in *Guerino*, the lady is still unmistakeably a fairy, as she therefore presumably was in the sources which they share with the legend. There is certainly no hint she was ever conceived as Venus, or as Fro Minne, allegorical figures representing carnality, worldliness, *etc*.

The dating of the three narratives is also a significant matter. Apart from some uncertainty surrounding the Scots romance, which allows the possibility that it appeared a little earlier, the evidence points to the latter part of the 14th century as the period when the source-material of the Tannhäuser-legend was influential elsewhere. Certainly there is no evidence that the definitive motifs of the legend were employed together as early as the 13th century.

VI
THE GERMAN BALLADS

In two recent publications J. W. Thomas has advanced with great assurance the theory that the Tannhäuser-legend began life as a German ballad (he had in mind the High German ballad) in the late 13th century, soon after the death, or perhaps even still in the life-time, of the historical Tannhäuser.[1]

One or two considerations arising from the preceding chapters tell against this suggestion at once. Such a ballad would naturally have included not only the figure of Tannhäuser himself, but also that of Venus, the allegorical Fro Minne; but neither name appears in conjunction with a demonic story of the fairy-mistress type before the 15th century, when the legend's obvious popularity ill accords with a supposed previous existence lasting more than a century in total obscurity. The relatively late appearance of other texts which used the same sources as the legend is also unfavourable to the theory of its early origin.

Thomas' conviction in dating the ballad so early is founded almost entirely on one point: the appearance of the name Urban IV in the final lines of the High German text.[2] He points out that Tannhäuser and Pope Urban IV were indeed contemporaries, and he concludes from their joint appearance in the ballad that a genuine incident concerning them underlies the legend, or that it at least reflects some historical relationship between them.[3] This question is best considered more fully later, but it should be stated at once that none of the early texts — the Essen ballad, the *Paradis*, and Hemmerlin's narrative — mentions Urban IV at all. However, from the same coincidence of these two

---

1) J. W. Thomas, *Tannhäuser: poet and legend* ... (*op. cit.*); "Walther von der Vogelweide and the Tannhäuser ballad," *Neuphilologische Mitteilungen*, 74 (1973) 340-7.
2) Essentially his view revives an argument of earlier scholars, *e.g.* Schmidt, (*op. cit.*) p. 27; R.M. Meyer, "Tannhäuser und die Tannhäusersage", *Zeitschrift des Vereins für Volkskunde*, NS 21 (1911), p. 14; and H. Schneider, "Ursprung und Alter der deutschen Volksballade", *Vom Werden des deutschen Geistes: Festgabe G. Ehrismann* (Berlin, 1925), p. 122; Siebert (*op. cit.*), p. 239.
3) Urban IV was Pope from 1261 to 1264; Tannhäuser died after 1265.

historical contemporaries, Thomas proceeds to contend that the High German ballad must be the oldest and most original version; a certain circular quality in this argument cannot be altogether denied.

He further suggests that the unknown author of the ballad was extensively influenced by a work of the renowned German poet of the late 12th and early 13th centuries, Walther von der Vogelweide: "Fro Welt, ir sult dem wirte sagen".[4] But the similarities in the two works are insufficient to support the claim convincingly. Like the early part of the ballad, Walther's work involves a dispute between the poet and an allegorical figure of temptation, Fro Welt. However this is by no means a rare theme in medieval literature, and the arguments used in works of the type are too commonplace, even too standardised, to permit readily such claims of close dependence. In this case there is no compelling textual evidence for the ballad's derivative status, although comparison of the two works is certainly interesting.

Thomas is not the only scholar to give preference to the High German text of the ballad. There has indeed been a general tendency to see this version, which was printed with great frequency in the 16th century, as both the definitive and the most authentic one.[5] But it is an assumption with no real justification, and it has contrived to maintain itself largely by causing neglect of the other versions. Principally by reason of the familiarity of its language, the High German text is the best known today, but its numerical predominance among the surviving early prints is certainly no indication of its superiority in any sense; the factors governing incidence of survival obviously have no necessary connection with a text's authenticity, and the situation in this case may be readily explained by the comparative total outputs of Southern and Northern presses, relative popularity, *etc.* It seems, moreover, that the printers operated by simply pirating existing broadsheets, *i.e.* without recourse to variant sources, for textual variation among the High German prints is, with the exception of a few insubstantial points, merely a matter of printer's errors.[6] The existence in the 15th century of

---

4) *Die Gedichte Walthers von der Vogelweide*, ed. H. Kuhn (Berlin, 1963), p. 138 (100, 26ff.).
5) *Cf. e.g.* Pfaff, (*op. cit.*) p. 104, and Amman, (*op. cit.*) p. 13, who terms it the *Vulgatfassung*.
6) An exception is the text of the *Ambraser Liederbuch* (1582) and the *Frankfurter Liederbüchlein* (Barto, Appendix, text XVI); though in High German, it closely resembles the Low German prints as to its content.

differing versions, now lost, need scarcely be doubted: not only the Low German versions, but also those collected from oral tradition in more recent times, show how very amenable the text was to variation. Although the dissemination and textual variation of the ballad was presumably at first to a large extent oral, the loss of all but one manuscript version of the 15th century should probably be blamed on the subsequent cheapness and ease of production of the broadsheets, for these would render an earlier manuscript of little value. The extant High German version is therefore simply the one which first happened to be printed in South Germany; it is not recorded before 1515, and has no particular title to authenticity. Nevertheless, the 16th century printers in the South adhered to it with such fidelity that it is unnecessary to reproduce more than one text of it in Appendix IV (*i.e.* text *B*).[7]

Printers in North Germany apparently adopted the same procedure as those of the South, using a different though quite closely related text (*C*): all three surviving Low German impressions give essentially the same version, of which a faithful translation was printed, at least twice, in Denmark.[8]

In the Appendix two further texts are given which, although also closely related to the prints, are nevertheless quite distinct. One of them is the Low German version of twenty-three stanzas found in the Essen manuscript (*A*); plainly more doubt attaches to its date of origin than is the case with many of the prints, but there has been unanimity in ascribing it roughly to the middle of the 15th century; that is to say, it is conceivably as early as the *Paradis*.[9] However, although it is certainly the earliest, it is also seemingly the most corrupt version textually, containing blatant errors of order, omissions, and repetitions — though

---

7) The most comprehensive list of texts is still that of Barto, (*op. cit.*) Appendix, 1. 149ff., who reproduces a wide selection including no fewer than ten of the High German version (texts VIII-XV, XVII and XVIII); he omits none of the early texts except the vital Essen manuscript. The one printed here in Appendix IV is from the earliest dated broadsheet, 1515. *Cf.* also the selection reproduced in *Deutsche Volks lieder mit ihren Melodien: Balladen*, ed. J. Meier, vol. 1, pt. 1 (Berlin, 1935), p. 145.
8) Barto, III V, *cf.* also the version of the *Ambraser Liederbuch* (Barto, XVI); the Danish texts: Barto VI and VII.
9) *Cf.* K. Ribbeck, *Danuser: eine alte niederdeutsche Fassung des Tannhäuserliedes. Erster Druck des Essener Bibliophilen Abends* (Essen, 1926); R. Jahn, "Die ältesten Sprach- und Literaturdenkmäler aus Werden und Essen," *Beiträge zur Geschichte von Stadt und Stift Essen*, 60 (1940), p. 98f.

in fact no surviving text of the ballad is altogether without some obvious corruption. The fourth text is a Dutch version of twenty-one stanzas, preserved in the so-called Antwerp Song-book (*D*).[10] Barto, who was unaware of the existence of the Essen manuscript, argued that this last text corresponds closest of all to the original legend;[11] but his premises have been largely proven incorrect, or are at least very doubtful, and subsequent textual analysis has shown quite definitely that this version is derived from the prints, with the small addition at its end of some unauthentic material.[12] Another Dutch text of eight stanzas, to which is appended a description in prose of the story's conclusion, was also published by Barto; it, too, is evidently derived from the other versions and can contribute no independent evidence.[13]

Obviously the derivative nature of text *D* greatly limits its usefulness, whereas the contents of *A* have a particular value on account of its patently greater antiquity; but, these points apart, there is no immediate reason for preferring any one text at the cost of the others. Generally speaking, the balladic material is best considered at first as a single body of evidence. The close similarity of all the texts points unmistakeably to their common ancestry.

An interesting attempt has been made to reconstruct, from a working text of twenty-seven stanzas, an original or "archetypal" version of the ballad.[14] Twelve "original" stanzas were identified, which relate the story in full; the remaining fifteen were held to be later additions, since they were apparently superfluous. But for this endeavour no use was made of evidence external to the ballad itself; the criteria applied were either textual, or drawn from a general theory of the development of folksong. The fundamental assumption was that the original version told only the physical, and not the psychical, events and developments of the story. Most of what was judged superfluous in

---

10) Barto, I.
11) *Ibid.*, p. 72ff.
12) *Cf.* S. Hirsch, *Studien zum Antwerpener Liederbuch vom Jahre 1544* (diss. Tübingen, 1922), p. 166ff.; H. Grüner Nielsen, *Danske Viser*, vol. 4 (Copenhagen, 1919), p. 190.
13) Barto, II.
14) S. Hirsch, "Die älteste Gestalt der Ballade vom Tannhäuser", *Jahrbuch des Vereins für niederdeutsche Sprachforschung*, 56 7 (1930 31) 194 204; significantly the text chosen was that of the High German prints, necessarily supplemented by one stanza (3) from the Low German prints: Hirsch gives no justification for this choice of text.

fact comprised dialogue, no fewer than twelve of the fifteen "inessential" stanzas belonging to Tannhäuser's initial dispute with Venus. However, this dialogue is used throughout the ballad for revealing the hero's state of mind, and thus for describing the psychological changes that carry much of the moral meaning. There is no ground at all for postulating the existence of an original ballad which related only the superficial events, for the very figures involved — Venus, the repentant knight, and the Pope — are largely intrinsic to its deeper significance.

At the same time, the ballads patently tell a simpler tale than that of the *Paradis*; indeed, the immense amount of sophisticated symmetry, protracted description, and closely analysed psychology in the latter could scarcely find room in a ballad, even were it all readily compatible with the balladic style, which characteristically prefers dialogue and abrupt action. It was suggested earlier that the story related in the *Paradis* had an ultimate source of some sophistication, presumably existing in literary form. But this cannot have been any of the surviving versions of the ballad, indeed it is most unlikely to have been anything so simple as a ballad at all. Thomas, in defence of his thesis of the legend's balladic origins, draws a parallel with other German narratives relating the fictitious adventures of historical poets;[15] but the only instance recorded as early as the 13th century uses the rhyming couplets characteristic of chivalric literature at that time.[16] The nature and content of German folk-ballads in the 13th century is an altogether speculative matter, for which the evidence concerns less courtly than heroic and other tales.[17] There is no positive evidence for the existence of ballads relating such moral stories as that of Tannhäuser in the 13th century.

In fact some authentic fairy-mistress elements have obviously been lost in the ballads. One example is the weekly transformation, whose original place in the legend is confirmed not only by its appearance in *Guerino* and the *Paradis*, but also by its inclusion in some of the ballads collected from Alpine regions in the last century: a St. Gallen version speaks of Frau Vrene and her ladies, and tells how "am Suntig sind

---

15) *Tannhäuser*: ... (*op. cit.*), p. 61.
16) *I.e. Der Welt Lohn* of Konrad von Würzburg: *Kleinere Dichtungen Konrads von Würzburg*, ed. E. Schröder (Berlin, 1968).
17) *Cf.* Schneider, *op. cit.*

s'Otre und Schlange";[18] a text from the Aargau runs "Sie ist ob em Gürtel Milch und Bluet/Und drunter wie schlangen und chrotte", recalling more precisely the appearance of the 14th century Melusigne.[19] Another omission of unassailable authenticity is the fairyland element of time-distortion, attested by both Antoine and Hemmerlin. Yet another, of less certainty, is the fairy ring, which only Antoine mentions, but which has a respectable history in fairy-mistress stories. These points alone are sufficient to disprove the claim of R. M. Meyer, an advocate of the German origins of the legend, that Antoine's deviations from the ballad all constitute later additions to the story.[20] Both the ballads and the *Paradis* are ultimately descended from a common ancestor which Antoine, to the extent that his version is more complete, reflects more exactly. Since no surviving version follows the original with demonstrable fidelity, its exact form and contents cannot be known. However the general characteristics of Antoine's story point decisively away from a balladic source.

The essentials of the moral and psychological tale told in the *Paradis* are nevertheless adequately conveyed in the German ballads. It is important to bear in mind the extent to which they are implicit in the story and its characters. The figurative significance of a knight's entry into the *Venusberg* must be seen in this light. By the 15th century the literary figure of a knight presents a somewhat stylised aspect: noble, proud, and devoted to the equally noble but worldly love-service of his lady, he occupies himself with strange and often unreal adventures whose essentially moral nature is usually evident enough. Tannhäuser's positive qualities as a knight are not to be doubted — "Danhueser was eyn Rydder gudt/he wolde wunder schouwen" — but like Antoine's knight, whose identical quest for "les merveilles de ce monde" led him into the devilish mountain, he comes directly "Tho Venus yn den berch,/tho andern schoenen Frouwen".[21] The devilish nature of Venus and her mountain are clear enough from what follows, but the lady is of course simultaneously *Fro Minne*, the allegorical embodiment of that love to which every knight naturally aspires. In this respect the early text *A* is especially interesting for its reading in the first stanza: "myt syner hoeffscher mynnen". All the later versions eschew the word

---

18) Barto, XXI, stanza 3.
19) Barto, XX, stanza 4.
20) *Cf.* Meyer, (*op. cit.*) p. 11.
21) Text *C*, stanza 2.

"höfisch"; indeed this line seems generally more subject to variation than any other in the first part of the ballad. It appears possible that the 16th century urban audience was less interested in any narrowly chivalric and courtly significance in the situation, although two versions have changed the line only to "Mit Venus der Edlen Minne".[22] Venus embodies here simply carnal pleasure and lust; no specific allusion to any non-sexual pleasure appears in the ballads. Moreover, the manner of the knight's sexual gratification contrasts with that in the *Paradis* where, with the utmost decorum and courtly discretion, he selects an unattached lady to be his lasting *compagnon*; the Venus of the ballads, like the Sibyl in *Guerino*, offers her own body to regain the disenchanted knight. Nevertheless, though the expression "hoeffsch" is in process of elimination, evidence enough remains of the original's courtliness: Venus invites Tannhäuser to her chamber to "spilen der edlen minnen" (*B*, 11,4; = "hoveschen mynnen" in *A*, 8,4), and Tannhäuser refers to her as "vrolyn saert" (*A*, 11,3), "Fraw Venus edle frawe zart" (*B*, 12,3) and "eddele frouwe tzart" (*C*, 9,3).

The knight's disillusionment with the *Venusberg*, which is handled in the *Paradis* with such skill and elaboration as to timing, causation, *etc.*, is treated in the ballads summarily and almost entirely in retrospect. Text *C* includes the line "syne suende beguenden 'em tho leyden", in a stanza which seems so crucial that it is possibly simply lost from the other texts. Otherwise, all versions proceed immediately to depict Tannhäuser already in dispute with Venus, at a point when his disillusionment is complete and he seeks to escape her clutches. For twelve stanzas (more than half the text in *A*, and nearly half in the prints) the situation remains physically static, while thoughts and reactions are expressed and exchanged: the pleasures of the mountain are made apparent, Tannhäuser's reasons for repudiating them become clear, and the force of his will to depart is evidenced. In this way the essential facts concerning his disenchantment are revealed. Venus alleges that he swore her an oath, recalling the promise given by Tom the Rymer to his Elfin Queen as well as the conditions of life inside Antoine's mountain which his knight had been obliged to accept. Three times Tannhäuser is tempted with sexual rewards, but his fear of hellfire prompts abhorrence of such offers, and he feels his life degraded by his presence in the mountain. At first he endeavours, as does Antoine's knight, to treat Venus with some semblance of courtly

---

22) Barto, VIII and XII.

respect and propriety, but finally only a frank vilification — "Ir seyt ein Teuefellinne", — denying her every honour, enables him to break away. This direct charge is all that remains in the ballad of the transformation-motif.

The theme of repentance, which occupies the second part of Antoine's story, appears quite naturally as early as the third stanza of the ballad. It is implied throughout the dispute, and is reinforced with constant appeals to Christ or the Blessed Virgin, as well as with the direct statement that Tannhäuser left the mountain in "iamer vnd in rewen" (B, 16,2). In the printed versions his confident expectancy of enjoying God's grace and a papal absolution is expressed in direct speech (B, 16,3 - 17,4; C, 18). There is also some hint that his plight is figurative, representing the generally human predicament of sinfulness, for Tannhäuser, just like the knight in the Paradis, confesses to the Pope the accumulated sins of his entire life.

The Pope's response introduces the motif of the dry staff, and marks the point at which the ballads and the Paradis diverge, rendering further comparison difficult. A. Remy, writing in 1913, pointed out that the Pope's words differ significantly in the High and in the Low German texts: in the former the pontiff roundly declares the impossibility of absolution, and employs the apparently dead staff as a figurative measure of that impossibility: "Als wenig es begrünen mag/Kumpst du zu gottes hulde". In the Low German, the greening of the staff is simply a measure of the time necessary for forgiveness; the Pope does not deny (or indeed express any opinion of) the likelihood of the forgiveness: "So de staff nu groenen wer/schoelen dyne ssuende vorgeuen werden". Without pursuing the matter further, Remy asks whether perhaps the Low German represents the original, which did not know the "figure of the cruel unforgiving Pope".[23] This important question, on which hinges the true reason for the knight's return to the mountain, has been entirely ignored, largely on account of the prejudicial preference shown to the High German text. The evidence is insufficient to answer the question with any certainty, but it certainly merits full examination, if only in order to demonstrate the weakness of the general assumption that a grossly culpable and subsequently

---

23) A. Remy, "The origin of the Tannhäuser-legend," *Journal of English and Germanic philology*, 12 (1913), p. 73; cf. also the work of Moser, (*op. cit.*) p. 12ff., who also asserts the Pope's blamelessness in an original version, but considers only the text of the High German prints.

damned Pope was always responsible for Tannhäuser's tragic fate. There is in fact a very good case indeed for the prior existence of a story in which the confessor acted with every propriety.

It should first be noted that the knight's final return to the mountain is not related in any other story concerning the demonic mountain-paradise, although it certainly corresponds to a normal part of the fairy-mistress narrative structure; neither *Tom the Rymer* nor *Guerino il Meschino* includes a second entry of the visitor, and in the latter, as well as in Hemmerlin's account of Simplicianus, he actually receives absolution. Nor indeed does any version of the Melusine-story show the mortal and the fairy finally reunited. Thus there is no other text to which one may turn for an explanation of the knight's last action. Moreover, it appears that the final stage of the story was a highly unstable element, for no two texts of the legend agree as to precisely what occurred. In the early text of the ballad, *A*, the Pope's words correspond to those in the Low German print: "Wen hye rode rosen drecht,/so synt dy din sunde vergeven", and very similar wording is used in the derivatory text *D*.[24] But from this point all the versions diverge. The *Paradis*, though it depicts the Pope summarily dismissing the knight "comme homme perdu", is certainly not truly anti-papal in intent, as was seen earlier, for the Holy Father expressly intends to grant absolution finally, and withholds it only temporarily, and for the most honourable reasons. Thus the High German text, whose existence, it should be recalled, can be confirmed only after 1515, is not merely the sole text to name Urban IV, but also the only one to portray a Pope manifestly guilty of wilfully damning a sinner's soul.[25] Felix Faber's description of the ballad, which includes the words "denegata fuit sibi absolutio", seems to suggest a similar understanding of the story, although his cursory account leaves a margin for uncertainty; but even the acceptance of such testimony brings the version of the High German ballad back with certainty only to 1483.

The staff-motif itself has a long history, and various late instances of it have been adduced in explanation of the legend.[26] However, in

---

24) *Cf.* also the text of the *Ambraser Liederbuch* (Barto XVI): Wen der stecken bletter tregt/so sein dir dein sunden verziegen: "When the staff bears leaves your sins will be forgiven."
25) *Cf.* Meyer, (*op. cit.*) p. 11.
26) *e.g.* F. Pfaff, "Das Stabwunder," *Quellwasser für das deutsche Haus*, 5 (1880/81), p. 552; Löhmann, (*op. cit.*) p. 248; U. Junk, *Tannhäuser in Sage und Dichtung*

order to throw light on its original form in the story, the argument should scrupulously confine itself to instances only up to the 15th century.[27] It is in point of fact not found in a form resembling that of any of the ballads until approximately the date of the German text *A*. Its appearance is also quite unsignalled in earlier sources depicting the demonic fairy-mistress of the mountain-paradise; there is no hint that it was known to Hemmerlin or to Andrea Barberino. The miraculous sign given by the burgeoning staff has been traced back to the biblical incident of Aaron's Rod,[28] while early medieval attestations of the motif seem to connect it invariably with Saints, hermits, and Holy Men. Gregory of Tours (6th century) tells the story of a recluse, St. Friardus, who "planted" a staff made from a windfallen branch.[29] Within two or three years it had become a fruitful tree, and the resulting fame of his hermitage attracted admiring crowds. God therefore struck down the tree as a warning against vainglory. But the hermit, "moved by compassion", prayed that the fruit it had borne might not perish and thrust the broken trunk into the ground, having first trimmed the roots and sharpened the point with his axe. Although rootless, it was soon restored to its original state, and the dried flower blossomed forth again. Gregory's own exegetic comment runs: "Credo ego de misericordia Dei, quod miraculum praesens exegit loqui, quia obtinere potuit hic oratione sua vitam mortuis a Domino impertiri, qui obtinuit arbores aridas in rediviva viriditate frondescere".[30] The theme of God's compassion is already conspicuously present; in fact the story appears to reflect something of the metaphor of the Rod of Jesse (*Isaiah* 10 and 11), when the Lord in his wrath cuts down the branches of the sinful, but the branch which grows from the Root of Jesse is the House of David, from which is born Christ, the incarnation of God's compassion

---

(Munich, 1911), p. 17f.; Thomas, *Tannhäuser* ... (*op. cit.*), p. 64f.; Schmidt, (*op. cit.*), p. 33; *cf.* the immense list of later folk tales incorporating some form of the motif in L. Mackensen, *Handwörterbuch des deutschen Märchens*, vol. 2 (Berlin, 1940), p. 550; and J. Bolte and G. Polivka, *Anmerkungen zu den Kinder und Hausmärchen der Brüder Grimm*, vol. 3 (Hildesheim, 1963), p. 463ff.

27) At the same time, the attempt of J. Haupt, "Die Sage vom Venusberg und dem Tannhäuser," *Berichte und Mitteilungen des Altertum Vereins in Wien*, 10 (1896) 315 22, to derive it from Germanic heroic legend, has no foundation, and the suggestion of Thomas, *Tannhäuser* ... (*op. cit.*), p. 65 that it is taken from the *Leich* of Walther von der Vogelweide has just as little evidence to support it.
28) Numbers, xvii; *cf.* Schmidt, p. 33; Thomas, *Tannhäuser* ..., p. 64f.
29) *Vitae Patrum, Patrologiae Cursus* ... (*op. cit.*), vol. 71, col. 1057f., cap. 10.
30) *Ibid.*: "I believe that, in interpretation, this miracle concerns God's mercy, for he who caused the dry trees to burgeon with renewed verdure could bring it about by his prayers that God bestowed life on the dead."

for man. It is He who accordingly overcomes the mortality that is the consequence of sin.

Elsewhere Gregory tells of a man who makes a stool, utilizing the wood of a tree sown by a Holy man, and, having used it for two years, is filled with remorse: "Vae mihi quia peccavi".[31] Cutting the legs from the stool he buries it, and finds in the following spring a blossoming tree, replacing the one he first destroyed. Remorse thus wipes out all trace of his sin.

In the hagiographical tradition the motif may signify nothing more than the divine presence, or the power of God. St. Christopher is directed by the Christchild, whom he has borne over the river, to set his staff in the ground, and the following day it bears flowers, leaves and fruit in testimony of his visitor's identity.[32] Later the Saint successfully repeats the miracle and effects a mass-conversion by thus demonstrating God's omnipotence. The second incident is also told of St. Savien.[33] Gervase of Tilbury gives the story of a novice, commanded to water a dry staff until it becomes alive. In due course it does so, "quasi testimonium virtutis divinae".[34]

Two German manuscripts, both of which are only roughly dateable to the mid-15th century, relate a tale in which the motif appears in much the form found in the Tannhäuser-legend. It tells of a son striving to procure the absolution of his repentant mother's sins. He journeys to Rome in search of papal assistance; "sanctus Silvester tollens ramum aridum dedit ei dicens: Hunc ramum portes in monte Celion, et cum habuerit fructus et poma, matri tue poteris suffragari".[35] He obeys, and after three years spent as a hermit, he finds the branch has become a tall tree bearing eight apples. Three of these he brings to the Pope, who

---

31) *Liber de Gloria Confessorum*, cap. 23, *ibid.*, col. 847f.: "Woe is me, for I have sinned".
32) Jacobus a Voragine, *Legenda Aurea* ... ed. T. Graesse (Leipzig, 1850), p. 432f.
33) *Ibid.*, p. 576.
34) *Otia Imperialium* (*op. cit.*), Dec. III, cap. 35, p. 972: "... as a witness of God's power."
35) J. Klapper, *Erzählungen des Mittelalters*, Wort und Brauch, no. 12 (Breslau, 1914), no. 194, p. 397: "... St. Sylvester gave to him a dry branch he was carrying, saying: 'Take this branch to Mount Celion, and when it bears fruit you will have succoured your mother' "; *cf. ibid.* p. 9, for dating.

then declares: "... hoc iudicium dei misericordie est".[36] According to one of the manuscripts it is the Pope himself who plants the staff, just as in the Low German ballads.[37] In this story the purpose of the motif is evident: forgiveness is granted only after a suitable penance, by which the necessary atonement is performed. The penance is a hermit's life of self-abnegation, whose duration must remain unknown until God, using the traditional sign of the fruitful staff, declares himself satisfied. The motif may fairly be viewed as an extension of the metaphorical Stem of Jesse: the fruit or flower of the Stem is Christ, through whose ultimate incarnation man is finally redeemed from sin.

The simultaneous appearances in this story of the staff-motif, of the journey to Rome, and of the Pope's central role, justify the assumption that it either shared some source with the legend or was, in some form, itself the legend's source. Strikingly, it employs the motif in the manner of the Low German ballads, not the High German text — the staff is simply a measure of the time which must pass before absolution is granted. Yet in the light of the earlier evidence this is surely the more original form of the motif: it arises naturally from the stories of Gregory's sinner and Gervase' novice, with the Pope assuming the role of the abbot in the latter, and the tale of a Pope who virtually defies the staff to flourish with respect to a particular sinner, certainly seems to presuppose one in which he intended only an appropriate delay in order to allow atonement. The manuscripts containing the tale of the atoning son are simply collections of material intended for sermons, and the story is therefore presumably older; however, it need not be very much older, and there is no positive reason for dating it before the first half of the 15th century. Thus, it is once more striking how the thematic material of the legend first appears, in a form which developmentally would precede the legend, only shortly before the latter's emergence in the mid-15th century.

In every version of the legend, the actual consequence of the Pope's response is to delay a forgiveness which is eventually nevertheless

---

36) *Ibid.*; "... this is the verdict of God's compassion"; both the use of the staff-motif and the lack of any rejection of the sinner by the Pope position this story much closer to the presumed original of the Tannhäuser-legend than is the *Waldbüßer-Episode* which Moser (*op. cit.*, p. 83ff.) sees as the source for the legend's ending.
37) Klapper, p. 397, *cf. A*, stanza 17; *C*, stanza 21; *D*, stanza 12; this action seems incongruous, if the Pope's intention is simply to express through the utter lifelessness of the staff the hopeless plight of Tannhäuser's soul.

forthcoming. The delay intended to effect atonement, which is found in the tale of the atoning son, is also implied in most versions of the legend. In the *Paradis* the knight's resolute repentance and his trust in God's mercy are tested by the wait, and the words "eust il assez souffert" are actually employed. In the Low German ballads the same implication is to be found, though, due to the cursory style of the ballad, it is spelt out less clearly: Tannhäuser's premature return to the mountain within three days indicates a tragic unwillingness to persist with the period of penance, whose obligatoriness is implied by the staff-motif. Certainly the Pope's words suggest that the staff's blossoming is, as in the tale of the atoning son, no more than a matter of time. In *Guerino il Meschino*, too, the three days which the hero must spend petitioning for a papal audience appear to have provided, in the source, a test of his persistence in repentance: redundant as the point is in Andrea's narrative, he nevertheless emphasises Guerino's perseverance during this period.

Only in the High German ballad is the position different. Here Tannhäuser returns to the *Venusberg* because he is led by the Pope to believe it is God's will for him: "Ich wil zu Venus meiner frawen zart/Wo mich got wil hin sende", (23, 3-4). But in this the Pope commits a heinous theological error, for God is willing to forgive the gravest sin, if the sinner is repentant and his atonement adequate. Indeed this odious action of the Pope assumes such importance that it is awarded a climactic position in the last lines of the text: "Des must der vierte Babst Vrban/Auch ewigklich sein verloren" (26, 3-4).

Most of all, the general character of the legend indicates that this is not the original version. The first part of the story, as it appears in the *Paradis*, unmistakeably endows the knight with a universal figurative value, so that the sinfulness and remorse of all mankind are adumbrated in his experiences. The legend proceeds from *his* sin, advances through *his* realisation of guilt, to show *his* repentance and *his* search for forgiveness. He is the unquestionable centre of the story. It is surely appropriate, then, that his final tragedy should also result from his own nature, from a weakness that is also universally human. The abrupt change towards the end of the legend, which inculpates the Pope and deprives the knight of that control over his moral destiny which is the very point of the tale hitherto, is less than convincing; it is apparently the alteration of the 15th century, an age of increasingly fervent anti-papal sentiment.

Needless to say, a detailed and reliable reconstruction of the original ending is not possible. The staff-motif appears only in the ballads, and may possibly have been introduced only at that stage of the legend's history. On the other hand, the previous transmission of Antoine's story certainly admits the possibility that its conclusion was corrupted, even if the complete loss of this particular motif may not be readily accounted for at once; the remarkable pragmatism of the Pope's grounds for withholding absolution strikes a disharmonious note in a story otherwise so symbolic in character, and it may very well constitute an alteration. The object of the staff-motif is plainly to place the final responsibility of pronouncing absolution with God Himself. Theologically this is no more than proper, for God is the only true source of forgiveness; and it is perhaps all the more appropriate, if the knight's predicament is to be seen as instancing all human sinfulness. Thus the Pope's response, whether or not it involved the miraculous and symbolic staff, presumably conveyed the meaning that he himself, being nothing more than God's vicar, was not in the last resort empowered to absolve human sin, so that man must turn to God for ultimate pardon. One is reminded, and surely most pertinently so, of the last words of Melusigne, when she admonished her husband to seek forgiveness only from God Himself.[38] But in the legend God delays, imposing a period of atonement, or at least testing the strength of the sinner's repentance. If such was indeed the original story, Antoine has clearly lost the intention of the Pope's words, even if he has retained their vital result: the delay. The ballads, too, give an impression that Tannhäuser's return to the mountain is occasioned by the delay; he is portrayed leaving Rome still hoping and praying earnestly for forgiveness: "Nu helpet, Maria, reyne maget,/an u steyt all myn trowen" (*A*, 18, 3f.). Nevertheless, within three days he has drifted back into the sinful mountain, his persistence unequal to the wait, and there he must remain for ever: "Wrau Venus, edele vrowe myn,/ick moet hyr by u blyven" (*A*, 20, 1f.). Text *C* shows the knight confidently praying to Christ as he leaves Rome; here his confidence endures even inside the *Venusberg* again — this is a unique feature, and must be mentioned again later. Text *B*, in which the knight's despair should surely directly follow the pope's unambiguous repudiation of him, includes another unique stanza in which Tannhäuser apparently expresses the belief that, if he could but live for a further year, he would have atoned for his guilt and might find forgiveness (stanza 21). Thus

---

38) *Cf. supra*, p. 81.

even in this version he seems at first to hold out some hope of finding grace. The specified period of one year is especially interesting in that it reflects the same preoccupation with numerical and temporal symmetry which characterised the *Paradis*: the presumed period of atonement corresponds exactly to that spent inside the mountain in a state of sin.

This leads to another intriguing point: the latter part of the legend as given by the ballads (with the staff-motif in the form of the Low German texts), corresponds better to the first part of the *Paradis* than does the ending of the French text itself. Once again, it appears that Antoine's immediate sources had corrupted the tale at this point. In the *Paradis* the preoccupation with the number three (and its arithmetical derivatives) makes no further appearance after the knight's audience with the Pope. But in the ballad it reappears in the number of days which elapse before the miracle of the staff's burgeoning; the authenticity of this period of time is strongly supported by the early evidence of *Guerino il Meschino*. It may be recalled, moreover, that Antoine's knight confesses himself to a papal confessor, prior to gaining access to the Pope himself. The incident has no obvious consequence, apart from that of directing the sinner onwards to the higher authority of the Pope himself. But it would seem likely that the event had some meaning in the original story; its authenticity is further supported perhaps by the pattern of events in Hemmerlin's account, where Simplicianus obtains absolution only after first approaching Hemmerlin himself.[39] If the Pope, as second confessor, also declined absolution, in his turn directing the knight to a still higher source of forgiveness, it can be seen that Tannhäuser's confessors were actually three in number. Three times, in the *Paradis*, the knight is permitted to leave the mountain, but he avails himself only of the third; three times in the reconstructed original he seeks absolution, and only at the third is he successful — but then it is too late. With three confessors, it is reasonable to suppose there were three confessions, and it seems possible that the two-line prayer, offered as the knight leaves Rome (*A*, 18,3f.; *B*, 22,3f.; *C*, 22,3f.) is the remnant of a confession made to God himself; significantly, the knight entering the Sibylline paradise is requested three times to declare his identity and purpose, and on the last occasion his reply is addressed to the queen herself. But what is perhaps the most interesting point of all concerns the three days required for atonement. For three hundred days Antoine's knight

---

39) *Cf.* also the 19th century St. Gallen ballad (Barto, XXI), stanzas 5 and 6.

dwells in pleasure in the evil mountain, unmindful of God and his duty to his own soul, before he turns back to his Creator in remorse. So great is God's benevolence, that the period of atonement is reduced to only one hundredth of that spent in sin. However even this drastically foreshortened term proves too much for the moral weakness of man, for he has already relapsed into temptation and sin.

Much of the evidence, then, seems to suggest that an original version of the legend held no real criticism of the Pope, and that his declining to grant absolution was both a deferential admission of his own limited powers in such matters, and a referral of the sinner to the true fount of forgiveness.

But it is nevertheless true that no surviving version of the legend is altogether free from criticism of the Pope's action. The story which has been tentatively reconstructed here may have served as a source for *Guerino il Meschino* and Hemmerlin's brief narrative. But plainly it could all too readily be interpreted (or distorted) to become the basis of an attack on the Papacy: "I cannot absolve you" is easily understood as either "I will not absolve you", or simply "Your sins are unpardonable". The anti-Roman reformatory spirit which swept Europe, and Germany in particular, in the 15th century naturally seized upon this aspect of the legend.[40] Anti-papal sentiment had already invaded the story by the mid-15th century when it first emerges in Germany; indeed it may have done so even before the tale was associated with Tannhäuser, since his name first appears only with these versions. Certainly this sentiment played a major part in the legend's popularity in Germany. In the *Paradis* the Pope's conscience is afflicted by the consequence of his words, and there is no doubt that he is not held altogether blameless for what occurred. Antoine's source apparently reflected something of the hardness later found in the High German ballad, since the Pope "comme homme perdu, le chassa de sa presence".[41] The explanation that this was simply pragmatic dissemblance appears to have been a device, aimed at combining a wrongful or misleading papal utterance with the original pattern of events, where absolution is simply delayed in order that the sinner persevere, and thus atone.

---

40) *Cf.* Dübi, (*op. cit.*) p. 257.
41) *Paradis*, p. 35: "... drove him, as a man lost, from his presence."

In text *A* of the ballad, which is perhaps more or less contemporary with the *Paradis*, there is no indication whatsoever of anti-papal feeling until the two final stanzas. The first lines of stanza 22, which are essentially the same as in the final stanza of *B*, simply relate the story's conclusion as it appears in the *Paradis*. The ensuing lines: "des mote dye pawes vervloget syn/al yn der hellen grunde" are ambiguous in meaning, since the precise force of "vervloget" is not clear; most literally they suggest that the Pope was subsequently cursed by Tannhäuser from the depths of Hell, but they may also be understood as a statement that the Pope suffered in Hell as a consequence of his action.[42] Tannhäuser's maledictions, corresponding to those of *C*, stanza 23, may very well be quite authentic, for even in *Désiré* the unhappy knight cursed his innocent confessor when the consequences of his confession were apparent. *A* concludes with the stanza:

> Darumb ensal gheen pawes watdoen
> hye ensulle sick wal bedencken
> als eyn sunder rowen heyfft
> des ensal men nummer krencken.

This sentiment is remarkably similar to that which might be inferred from the *Paradis*: the Pope acted thoughtlessly and improperly in not encouraging the sinner to persevere in hope. This is mild criticism, if the action is nevertheless considered worthy of eternal damnation. It seems possible that this stanza, and perhaps also the preceding two lines were simply appended to the story in order to make appropriate moral comment; it is noticeably the only point in this text at which the balladist offers a personal opinion of the events he describes.[43]

---

42) Neither the Middle High German dictionaries nor the Middle Low German dictionaries cite an instance of this verb meaning "to condemn to"; the dative *e* of "grunde" (*cf.* stanzas 5 and 6) would favour the first interpretation, although it is only slender evidence in a text so generally corrupt; the rhyme is impure to the point of non-existence.

43) The rather late text of the *Ambraser Liederbuch* (Barto, XVI), gives a remarkably similar ending: stanza 24 corresponds closely to *A*, 21, but the two ensuing stanzas run:

> Da was er wider in den berg
> darin sol er nun bleiben
> So lang bis an den jüngsten tag
> wo jhn Gott wil hin weisen (*cf. B*, 24,4)

> Das sol nimmer kein priester thun,
> dem menschen misstrost geben,
> Wil er buss und rew empfahn,
> sein sünden sind jm vergeben.

"He was back in the mountain, where he will now remain until the Last Day, whither God will send him. No priest should ever do that: discourage a man. If he seeks confession and a penance, his sins are forgiven him."

Text *C*, of indeterminably later date, includes a whole stanza after Tannhäuser's departure from Rome in which he roundly curses the Pope, accusing him of seeking to deprive God of a soul. The sentiments echo those of the letter left by Antoine's knight before his final disappearance: "... celuy a qui le Pappe ne voulut pardonner ...".[44] In this text of the ballad, too, criticism of the Pope is related to Tannhäuser's case alone, and its injustice is made amply clear by the last stanza:

> De Pawes bedroeuede sich gantz s'er
> he hefft geb'eden alle stunde

These lines are missing in the other versions and are probably unauthentic. However, text *C* displays a tendentiousness all its own: the tragedy of Tannhäuser's loss is underplayed, in order to emphasise the bounteousness of God's mercy in forgiving him. In a manner quite inconsistent with his returning there at all, Tannhäuser is still hopeful of absolution when back inside the *Venusberg*: "Noch bydd ick Christum van Hemmelrick/he leth my nicht bliuen voenralr" — these lines are unique and must also be considered of doubtful origin. The stanza depicting the staff's greening and the despatch of messengers to seek out the knight, which is found in all other versions, is here divided. The miracle of the staff is highlighted by further expansion — "Eer dat tho Vesper qwam/de staff droech loff vnd blomen" — while the despatch of the messengers is complemented with an emphatic statement of Tannhäuser's redemption : "He ys geloeset vth suenden bandt/doerch Christum vnsen Heren". There is no mention of the fact that he is now irretrievably inside the mountain, and therefore lost. His repentance, here persistent to the end, finds its reward, a magnificent testimony of God's benevolence. This change not only produces the gross inconsistency of Tannhäuser's return to the place of sin, but the papal criticism of stanza 23 also strikes a discordant note. In fact the final stanza is very possible intended to exculpate the Pope from such charges, and may have been inspired by an awareness that the story was commonly construed in such a way. Text *D* has adopted stanza 23 from *C*, but extended it to a statement of the deleterious effect of papal actions on the souls of men in general (stanza 13). A strongly protestant spirit underlies these lines. Tannhäuser's return to the mountain is an act of despair prompted by the Pope's rebuff — "die paus hefft mi sulken troost ghegheven/ewelick van god te sijn ghescheiden" (17, 3f.)

---

44) *Paradis*, p. 38: "... he whom the Pope would not forgive ..."

— however the conclusion seems to be a fanciful addition, not without facetiousness.

In text *B*, this same protestantism has produced the very well-known version, in which the Pope is truly, and apparently quite maliciously, culpable. Assuming more or less the role of Luther's papal anti-Christ, he actually deprives God of Tannhäuser's soul, seducing it away from salvation by means of ignorance. The textual changes required to accomplish this alteration were in fact few. The Pope's words have been modified (significantly but only slightly), and the final stanza has been adjusted, in order to place the Pope's damnation in a climactic position. It is indeed possible to see the final lines of *B* — "Des must der vierte Babst Vrban/auch ewigklich sein verloren" — as a modification of *A*, 22, 3f.

Such comparisons at least show quite clearly that the conclusion of the story, particularly the extent of the criticism levelled at the Pope, is not a fixed component. The earlier versions are decidedly less vehement in their criticism of the papal action. It is perhaps not unreasonable to see in this variability the surviving evidence of a process by which a fine moral story of the Middle Ages became travestied to supply anti-Roman propaganda for the presses of Southern Germany in the 16th century.

THE TRAGEDY OF KNIGHTHOOD   111

VII
TANNHÄUSER AND VENUS

The German versions of the legend — not only the ballads but also the other sources which are discussed in this chapter — identify its three principal characters as Tannhäuser, Venus, and Pope Urban IV; no source from outside Germany mentions any of these names.

The textual evidence favouring the authenticity of the last of them is very slight; there is altogether little evidence regarding a precise identity for the Pope. Apart from the High German ballad only one source mentions Urban IV specifically: a poem of three strophes (*cf. infra*) composed as late as 1549, at a time when the High German prints were already circulating in very large numbers. The High German ballad is not only one of the last versions of the legend to appear but, as was shown earlier, it is also perhaps one of the most altered versions; furthermore, the Pope is identified only at its conclusion, where the alteration seems greatest. Text *C* gives simply the name "Vrban"; the early text *A* gives him no name at all; and Antoine actually proposes two quite different Urbans (one of them confusedly) from the 14th century. Certainly the contemporaneity of Urban IV and the historical Tannhäuser is striking, but is it not sufficient justification for attributing the legend to the 13th century, as J. W. Thomas does, particularly in view of the poor textual evidence in favour of Urban IV and the total lack of any other evidence for the legend's existence at so early a date.

It is quite possible, for instance, that the name "Urban" was originally that of either Urban V (1362-1370), whom Antoine correctly identifies and suggests, or Urban VI (1378-1389), whose name Antoine seems to have transferred to the person of Gregory XI;[1] the first of these two was a popular Pope of a mild but ineffectual disposition and the second, though more belligerent, largely retained the allegiance of Germany in the Schism. At that stage the story presumably contained little or no anti-papal sentiment. The vehemently anti-papal author of *B* possibly had a source giving only the name "Urban", like *C*, so that he

---

1) *Cf. supra*, p. 31; also K. Nyrop, *Tannhäuser i Venusbjaerget*, Fortids sagn og sange, vol. 6 (Copenhagen, 1909), p. 77.

was free to specify Urban IV, who was not only a suitable object of hatred in Germany, due to his antagonism to the Hohenstaufen family,[2] but was also the only Pope of that name to have reigned within a century of Tannhäuser's lifetime. All this is no more than speculation, of course, but it serves to underline the weakness of the case for the authenticity of Urban IV.

No fully satisfactory explanation has been advanced for the identification of the 13th century *Minnesänger* with the hero of the legend. The miniature in the famous Manesse manuscript, a major source for Tannhäuser's own works, depicts him clad in the robes of the Order of Teutonic Knights, a religious touch which has been tentatively and far from convincingly connected with his legendary role.[3] There need be no doubt however that the poet, and no other Tannhäuser, was held to be the legend's hero.[4] Yet the literary works for which Tannhäuser's authorship is generally accepted give no adequate reason for this. Tannhäuser emerges from his own poetry as a worldly, self-indulgent figure, even a wanton libertine, such as might well be portrayed entering the *Venusberg*.[5] But, although he shows some slight interest in religious matters, he displays no trace of remorse or repentance for his sins.[6] When he laments, it is for the passing of more pleasurable times, not for the jeopardy of his soul. It is true, of course, that such a character affords ideal material for a medieval moralist, who is free to supply the subsequent repentance from his own pious imagination.[7]

But further evidence, linking the poet and the legend, has been found in other German works containing allusions of varying detail and explicitness to Tannhäuser's sojourn in the *Venusberg*. Unfortunately none of these texts can be reliably dated before the middle of the 15th

---

2) Thomas (*Tannhäuser* ... p. 62) overlooks this point when he describes the Pope as "obscure"; Urban initiated negotiation with Charles of Anjou over the seizure of the Kingdom of Sicily, a measure which was rapidly to destroy all German imperial power in Italy.
3) E. Jammers, *Das königliche Liederbuch des deutschen Minnesangs* (Heidelberg, 1965), p. 74; *cf.* also the reproduction and commentary in *Minnesänger: achtzehn farbige Wiedergaben* ... Einleitung von K. Martin (Baden Baden, 1953).
4) *Cf.* M. Lang and H. Naumann, "Zu Tannhäusers Balladengestalt," *Jahrbuch für Volksliedforschung* 5 (1936) 123-130; Meyer, *(op. cit.)* p. 13f.
5) The standard edition is that of J. Siebert, *Der Dichter Tannhäuser (op. cit.)*, which also includes some of the unauthentic works.
6) *Cf. e.g.* the poem Siebert XVI:
7) *Cf.* Siebert, p. 238.

century, *i.e.*, before the time which saw the appearance of the *Paradis* and text *A* of the ballad. Some of them may indeed be of earlier date, but they are for the most part poems of only moderate length, affording little or no internal evidence of their date of composition.[8] They may have been influenced by texts of the ballad; in many cases this would seem quite likely. Only one of them tells a substantial part of the legend in any completion: this is the work which names Urban IV, and was composed as late as 1549. The remainder are, for the most part, not primarily narrative in character, and contain nothing more than imprecise allusions to situations or events in the legend.

It is incorrect to see the historical Tannhäuser as a quite obscure figure, and to reason that a legend which concerns him must therefore go back to his time.[9] Manuscripts from the centuries following his lifetime contain many works which are either falsely ascribed to him, or are assigned melodies which he allegedly composed; his reputation lived on in this fashion, as did the reputations of some other German poets of his time.[10] Very many of these works have no connection whatsoever with the legend and show that his fame did not rest simply on a story connected with his name. There is therefore no need to date his association with the legend as early as the 13th century; it may quite reasonably be seen as the consequence of his reputation as a poet in the 14th and 15th centuries. Prominent among the unauthentic works appearing under his name is the type of the *Bußlied* (Song of Atonement, or, more descriptively, Song of Repentance), a *genre* in which the poet vents his extreme contrition at past sins, and prays to heaven for pardon. The surviving number of these is sufficient to justify the claim that the name of Tannhäuser was generally associated with such works, to the point at which he was widely envisaged as a conscience-stricken and prayerful figure, persistently laying bare his soul in verse. A number of *Bußlieder* survive which, though connected with the name Tannhäuser, contain no explicit allusion to the legend at all; it is particularly noteworthy that the only *Bußlied* which can with some confidence be dated reasonably closely to the poet's lifetime is of this type. Conversely, the *Bußlieder* which refer unequivocally to the legend are, without exception, found only in manuscripts of the late 15th century or afterwards, *i.e.* from the period of the ballad. It is

---

8) The manuscripts are mainly of the late 15th century.
9) *Cf.* Thomas, *Tannhäuser* ... p. 62.
10) *Cf.* Siebert, p. 194 249, esp. p. 247ff.

therefore not at all improbable that the figure of the contrite Tannhäuser, rather than deriving from the legend, actually preceded it and caused his name to be introduced into it. The point does not admit of final proof of course, but closer examination of some of the texts supports it, and it certainly provides a plausible transitional stage in the otherwise remarkable change from the character of unashamed sensuality in the authentic works to the remorse of the legendary knight who journeyed to Rome.

A Jena manuscript of the mid-14th century contains a *Bußlied*, ascribed in a modest rubric to the poet himself; his authorship of it is most doubtful, but it has been assigned, very tenuously and on linguistic evidence alone, to the 13th century.[11] However the work contains nothing whatsoever to suggest that its author had any knowledge of the legend; indeed there is nothing in the text to connect it specifically with Tannhäuser. It is in four strophes, and contains conventional expressions of guilt, sorrow, and apprehension at the grave consequences of the poet's undisclosed sins, prayers for aid, and declarations of trust in the redemptive power of Christ's Passion. Even the words "ich habe gesvndet myne tage/vnd ist myr noch vil selten e beruwen",[12] loosely reminiscent as they are of the knight's predicament in the legend, are nothing more than the customary plaint of a penitent. It appears most improbable that such a work can have been written with the legend in mind, particularly when it is put beside other *Bußlieder* with their quite explicit allusions. Of course, it is also possible that it had no original connection with Tannhäuser, for the ascription may be no older than the manuscript. But even that would indicate that the figure of the remorseful Tannhäuser was known to the scribe in the mid-14th century, before there is any evidence at all of the legend. The miniaturist of the Manesse manuscript (early 14th century) may perhaps have conceived the poet as a penitential figure, but he too gives no hint of the legend.

Examination of some of the other *Bußlieder* reveals that the allusions they make to the legend are late insertions into the text. The

---

11) *Ibid.*, p. 207ff. and p. 237; a facsimile of the ms. page, showing the rubric, is found in *Tannhäuser — die lyrischen Gedichte der Hss. C und J: Abbildungen ...* ed. H. Lomnitzer and U. Müller (Göppingen, 1973), p. 29   to judge from appearance, the inconspicuous words "der tanuser" may well have been added as an afterthought.
12) Siebert, p. 208, v. 27f. : "... I have spent my days in sin and never repented hitherto."

Kolmarer Liederhandschrift contains a group of three multi-strophic poems, all in the same metrical form, with the following rubrics respectively: "In tanhusers heupt ton oder gulden tone", "Ein anders, von vnser frauwen", and "Ein anders vnd ist tanhusers endliet".[13] One connection of these works with Tannhäuser is thus their use of a melody attributed to him. The first of the three must be discussed later. The second is a quite unexceptional *Bußlied* addressed to the Virgin, and contains no allusion to the legend. However the same poem also appears in the Wilten manuscript with the superscription "Tanhauser III lied" (referring to the number of strophes). Here the lines:

> Ich was betrogen hart,
> gemacht zu ainem toren.
> Venus die schon hat mich ser verraten,[14]

are substituted in the middle of the last strophe. But this personal utterance intrudes grossly into a description of the Crucifixion, which, by contrast, is evenly and logically maintained in the Kolmar text. The latter surely preserves the more original text, for there is nothing else in the poem to support the intrusive statement in the Wilten manuscript. The third Kolmar text contains in strophe 2 the lines "ach daz fraw venus ie gesprach/'du edler tanhusere' ", and, in strophe 3, "verwappent in den tot hat mich eins priesters hant".[15] But these verses also bear no true relationship to the remainder of the poem, a *Bußlied* conceived in very general and conventional terms. Once again the same work is preserved in another source, a Nürnberg manuscript, from which the quoted lines are absent, so that a more even, and presumably a more original, text results.[16] In the Nürnberg manuscript the rubric runs: "Ins don heusers haubt don 3 lieder".

Both these works appear to have originally had no overt textual connection with Tannhäuser; the emendations linking them with the legend were made simply to support the supposed authorship of the knight of the legend. But since both of them also have a primary link with Tannhäuser in their metrical form and accompanying melody, one is not obliged to account for the emendations simply by their character

---

13) *Ibid.*, p. 210ff.; these texts are also reproduced in M. Lang, *Tannhäuser*, Von deutscher Poeterey, no. 17, (Leipzig, 1936), p. 171ff.
14) *Ibid.*, p. 218: "I was greatly deluded and made a fool. The lovely Venus has betrayed me".
15) *Ibid.*, p. 219, v. 36f.: "Alas that Lady Venus ever spoke: 'Thou noble Tannhäuser' "; p. 220, v. 63f.: "A priest's hand has consigned me to death."
16) *Ibid.*, p. 220, text 4b.

as *Bußlieder*. A further hypothesis may be advanced, though it remains a tentative one. It seems possible that a strophic form or melody (or melodies), either invented by Tannhäuser himself or later ascribed to him, was particularly suited to *Bußlieder*; as the poems subsequently became loosely attributed to him, the poet acquired a consequent image of resipiscence. This then led to his assuming the role of the penitent hero of the legend, and the *Bußlieder* underwent consequent alteration, so as to include scraps of his new biography. Some of the weaknesses of such a theory are all too obvious in the tenuous arguments by which it was reached. But the musical link with the poet is a particularly weak point. The manuscripts ascribing the *ton* to Tannhäuser are all relatively late, and the melody (given in the Kolmar manuscript and in other sources) is thought to be a product of the 14th or 15th centuries;[17] thus the question remains as to why it was ascribed to Tannhäuser at all, though false attributions of this sort are common enough. It is nevertheless possible that *Bußlieder*, using some melody and form ascribed to the poet, were being written in the period prior to the appearance of the Manesse and Jena manuscripts. (The melody and form of the Jena *Bußlied* are quite dissimilar to the *Hauptton* of the Kolmar manuscript). It seems unlikely that further progress can be made in this matter without new evidence.

Attempts to derive from the *Bußlieder* further information concerning the legend's contents, particularly regarding its original conclusion, bring little success; both the late date of the manuscripts and the fleeting quality of their allusions to the legend greatly weaken their testimony. The lines quoted previously from the Wilten manuscript indicate no more than that Tannhäuser was duped by Venus. But the statement "verwappent in den tot/hat mich eins priesters hant", from the last of the Kolmar poems certainly suggests that the 'priest' has denied absolution. However the Kolmar manuscript was written only a few years before the first appearance of the High German ballad, at a time when the anti-papal aspects of the legend were presumably already being lent emphasis. There is noticeably no mention of the staff, and it is far from clear just what the knight was told by the priest. Moreover, it is consonant with the nature of a *Bußlied* that the knight does not yet despair but still looks to heaven for pardon, so that one may only guess at the reasons for a despair which must come later.

---

17) *Cf.* R. J. Taylor, *The art of the Minnesinger* ..., vol. II (Cardiff, 1968), p. 232; the melody is reproduced *ibid.* vol. I, p. 150.

The first of the Kolmar *Bußlieder* is decidedly the richest in allusions to the legend, but it is at the same time the most confused, corrupt and enigmatic of the texts.[18] It seems certain that neither the Kolmar manuscript nor the Wilten manuscript, which preserves three strophes of the same work, gives the original text with much fidelity. Strophes 2 and 3 contain only one line suggestive of the legend, and otherwise make a reasonable, though uncertain, impression of belonging to a conventional *Bußlied* with no particular relevance to Tannhäuser. They are absent from the Wilten version (which gives only strophes 1, 4, and 5), and may represent a different work. The remainder (there are seven strophes in all) apparently describes a marvellous journey through diabolical realms of temptation, in which most of the names are fantastical, and where the text is often distorted beyond all coherence. There seems little prospect of deriving dependable information from such a work. Venus is not mentioned, but there is ample sentiment of an anti-ecclesiastical type. However this criticism is oddly generalised, for the poet does not fulminate against the Pope or any individual priest, but rather at a plurality of clerics. In the first strophe he declares at once, "mit bicht macht mich mang priester mat",[19] calling to mind not a single papal rebuff, but rather the series of confessions made in ever higher places, a series which may be said to conclude with the confession made to God Himself, in this poem. Later, in strophe 3, he declares "zwar trost ist mir von pfaffen gar vnkunde", and again subsequently "wie gern ich gotte wonet by!/die pfaffen mir daz wenden".[20] The latter unambiguously indicates a plurality of priests, and the former probably does the same. But once again there is no clear statement of what the priests said to the knight, and it appears likely that the *delay* and the continuing penance in fact provoke his exasperated remarks, rather than a categorical refusal and denial of hope. The couplet "clein wart mir busz gegeben da ze rome,/des bin ich in den sunden gar vertome" does nothing to adversely affect that probability.[21] Certainly Tannhäuser has not yet been driven to despair, but still trusts in God's mercy. Just as in the third of the Kolmar poems, a persistent stress is laid on the knight's confidence in God, and in His boundless grace; indeed, beside that

---

18) Siebert, p. 210ff.
19) *Ibid.*, v. 6: "Many a priest exhausts me with confession."
20) *Ibid.*, v. 62: "The comforting of priest(s) is quite unknown to me"; v. 75f.: "How I yearn to dwell with God   the priests prevent me."
21) *Ibid.*, v. 84f.: "Scant was the penance I received at Rome, so that I am quite lost (?) in sin".

emphasis, the cavilling and inexplicit remarks at the cost of the priesthood are trivial. Once the priests have declared their inability to absolve him, Tannhäuser apparently turns to the only remaining and (theologically speaking) the only true source of forgiveness, and he gives no hint that his trust is anything but unshakeable.[22] In the first strophe he even expresses succinctly the vital theological doctrine at the core of the legend:

> ez wart kein missetat
> so grosz, gedenck ich mir,
> enpfehlt der sunder ruw,
> annemlich ist er dir.[23]

The *Bußlied* is static, corresponding to a point in the action of the legend at which the role of the priests and the Pope is already discharged. Since the knight is nevertheless still confident of pardon, the subsequent tragedy can only be caused by a spontaneous change within him: it must be his own moral strength which fails. To this extent, at least, the *Bußlied* presupposes a version in which the Pope was not the principal guilty party.

The poem from the collection of Wolf Bauttner is more informative concerning the details of the legend than are the *Bußlieder*.[24] By 1549 the High German ballad was decidedly the best known version in southern Germany, so that its influence on this work is indubitable. Here the Pope acts much as in the ballad, telling the knight "gottes gnad sei dir versagt merk eben".[25] But in general the work has more in common with the Meistersang-quality of the *Bußlieder*, sharing their use of the first person, their long strophe and their concentration on the hero's feelings of guilt and repentance. The knight remains confident of forgiveness, and defiant of the Pope's judgment — "got keinem sünder nie verseit"[26] — and the tragic conclusion is not described. The absence of the staff-motif has given rise to the suggestion that the text is "altertümlich", but it seems unlikely that, by 1549, the poet can have

---

22) It is conceivable that the verse "gib sture, reyne maget von jessya" (v. 81 = "Give succour, pure maid of Jesse") is a veiled allusion to the image of the staff, but appeals to the Virgin are stock components of *Bußlieder*, and this is one of her many standard metaphors.
23) *Ibid.*, v. 17ff: "No sin was ever so great, I believe, that the sinner is not acceptable to you, if he repents."
24) Barto, XXIV; *cf.* Siebert, p. 224.
25) Siebert, p. 233: "God's grace is denied you, mark well."
26) *Ibid.*: "God never refused a sinner."

been unaware of it.[27] The motif is simply redundant in a version which does not portray the tragedy at the conclusion of the legend; the author's preoccupation is with repentance and trust in God. Nevertheless the first half of his poem contains some details which no other German source knows, but which are corroborated by Antoine's *Paradis*. The moral significance of the *Venusberg*, for example, is made more explicit by the knight's statement that he was driven there by the hot blood and the adventurousness of youth. His splendid reception inside the mountain, and the marvellous nourishment available there are also mentioned briefly. Most interesting of all is the short description of Tannhäuser's disillusionment:

> Ich Danheuser sprich offenbar
> ein halbes jar bin ich gewest dar innen
> und etlich tag red ich für war
> ich dacht an mich und tet mich wol besinnen
> wie es mir würd ergan am jüngsten tag.[28]

This inexact period of time approaches at least closer to Antoine's precise three hundred days than does any other extant version; however, as in the ballads, Tannhäuser is obliged to remain the full fairytale term of one year, before he may depart. The High German ballad, the *Bußlieder*, and some further knowledge of the legend all seem to have combined in this version to give a text which is interesting, but of little scientific value.

The *Bußlieder* properly belong to the latter part of the legend, their theme being Tannhäuser's quest for absolution. But the theme of the early part, Tannhäuser's disillusionment with the temptations of Venus, also inspired a small group of further literary texts. These take the form of disputations between the knight and the lady and are fewer in number than the *Bußlieder*. They adopt the didactic stance of most medieval literature in this form: the time for Tannhäuser's self-indulgence is past, and he betrays with his words the falsehood and sinfulness of what Venus offers. She in turn displays an unmistakeably insidious character.

Traces of the disputation have found their way into various works: the poem of 1549, for instance, commences with a reproachful address

---

27) *Cf.* K. Goedeke, *Germania*, 28 (1883), p. 44; Schmidt, (*op. cit.*) p. 48.
28) Barto, XXIV, p. 232: "I, Tannhäuser, openly avow that I was there for half a year and several days, in truth. I thought of myself, and considered well what would befall me on the Last Day."

to Venus (Tannhäuser speaks throughout in the first person), but it is soon forgotten, and by the middle of the first strophe she is already relegated to the third person. The best of the disputations is a poem of nine strophes recorded in a Karlsruhe manuscript in the year 1453; whether its date of composition was in fact much earlier cannot of course be ascertained.[29] The rubric is simply "tanhusser", and the knight's sentiments at times approach those of the *Bußlieder* in his appeals to heaven. Strophe 4 in particular reechoes elements from the ballad, and the lines:

> der junckfrew wil ich lobes jehen,
> die hat vil menig sel erlost,
> bij der so wil ich ewig sin,
> bij irem lieben kinde zart,[30]

give some grounds for supposing that stanza 6 of the ballad (text *B*) is also intended to refer to the Virgin. Conspicuous among the temptations offered by Venus is that of the dwarfs who will serve the knight, and who seem designed to appeal to his love of courtly pursuits:

> ich han so vil der edlen zwerg,
> helt die muessen dienen dir
> mit stechen, singen, seitenspil ...[31]

Another disputation, probably of later date, is included by Keller in his collection of *Fastnachtspiele*; it seeks to emphasise the metaphorical nature of the temptress, by substituting Lady World (Fro Welt) for Venus.[32] There is of course ample precedent for such an allegorical portrayal of the World as a figure of temptation; apart from the well-known poem of Walther von der Vogelweide, the theme forms the basis of Konrad von Würzburg's *Der Welt Lohn*.[33] The ready affinity of such a figure with the lady of the mountain is quite evident from Antoine's

---

29) Barto, XXII; *cf.* Siebert, p. 224f.; the same ms. contains a further *Bußlied* "Tanhusers tagwise" (Barto, XXIII; Siebert, p. 222) containing no allusion to the legend.
30) Barto, p. 225: "I will praise the Virgin who has saved many a soul; I wish to remain with her and her dear Son for ever."
31) *Ibid.*, p. 224: "I have so many noble dwarfs who will serve you, hero, with jousting, singing and stringed music"; the dwarfs are presumably a folkloristic intrusion in the mountain paradise, *cf.* Remy, (*op. cit.*) p. 49f.
32) *Fastnachtspiele aus dem fünfzehnten Jahrhundert, Nachlese*, Bibliothek des literarischen Vereins in Stuttgart, no. 46 (Stuttgart, 1858; rprt. Darmstadt, 1966), no. 124.
33) *Cf.* supra p. 96; also der Guotaere, I, *Minnesinger: Deutsche Liederdichter* ... ed. F. von de Hagen (Leipzig, 1838), vol. 3, no. 13, p. 41f.

Paradis. In the *Fastnachtspiel* her part is in no way distinguishable from that of Venus in the legend, except perhaps when she includes the natural beauty of the world in her catalogue of temptations. At the conclusion of the work she actually refers to "Ffraw Venus" as a third person, speaking of the reception the knight would find from both her and her dwarfs, if he returned to the mountain. But he rejects the offer, echoing the ballad with the words "Ffraw Venus ist eyn teuffelinne".

Perhaps the most interesting aspect of these disputations is their obvious literary affinity with the first part of the ballad. Although textually quite distinct, the first fifteen stanzas of the ballad are of an identical type to the other two disputations described. Indeed the ballad might quite reasonably be described as a disputation which has been expanded to include a brief introduction and a summary of the story's conclusion. It is perhaps worth noting that the Karlsruhe text, the best of the dialogues, was recorded about the time of the Essen manuscript. Certainly, if the ballad was in fact composed on the basis of a preexisting tradition depicting Tannhäuser and Venus engaged in such disputes, the manner in which it oddly prefers static retrospection and indirect allusion for telling the intrinsically dramatic tale of the knight's sinfulness and disillusionment, is satisfactorily explained. This is not to suggest that the ballad itself was necessarily anything other than an originally integrated composition. But it further underlines the considerable distance between the German ballad and any full and authentic version of the legend; the German song appears to be based on a literary type which generally assumes prior knowledge of the entire story and disregards much of it, including the intense drama of the knight's undeceiving, to concentrate on one aspect only — his remorse.

Another important work of the same time as the Karlsruhe manuscript portrays Venus as a figure of dispute, though in a much more original, imaginative, and expansive fashion: this is the *Mörin* of Hermann von Sachsenheim, composed in 1453.[34] It employs a pseudo-autobiographical mode, but, with characteristic humour and self-irony, Hermann places himself more or less in the position of the disenchanted and struggling Tannhäuser. Yet the contest is given a legal form, which deprives Hermann of the freedom to escape enjoyed by the legendary

---

34) Hermann von Sachsenheim, *Die Mörin*, ed. H. D. Schlosser, Deutsche Klassiker des Mittelalters, N.F. Bd. 3 (Wiesbaden, 1974).

knight. He is captured by deceit, transported magically to the land of Venus (which is not a hollow mountain), and there made to face capital charges arising out of his past conduct. It is alleged that he was bound by oaths in his youth to serve Venus, but has since disregarded this obligation and practised treachery towards ladies. His successful defence is conducted rather by means of the niceties of legal procedure than by a proper refutation of the charges. Both the *Venusberg* and Tannhäuser are mentioned, and the latter is declared to be the spouse of Venus.[35] But no further specific reference is made to the legend, and Tannhäuser is later referred to simply as the "king". On the other hand, his character as monarch of this pagan realm (Venus is a Saracen queen, and particularly angered by Hermann's Christianity) is of some interest, for it accords well with that of the legendary knight who lacked the moral fortitude to atone fully for his sins. He is an outstandingly weak king, vacillating, irresolute, and henpecked by his wife; the text interestingly describes him as "wandelber" (unsteadfast).[36] There is no hint that his lasting presence here is the result of papal error or misconduct, indeed the work is entirely free of any anti-ecclesiastical sentiment.

During his involuntary stay in the realm of Venus, Hermann is befriended to his great advantage by the knight Eckhart, a figure who remains a consistent, though shadowy, feature of the subsequent German legend. He is later usually described holding a post at the entrance of the *Venusberg*, where he warns all seeking admission of the grave consequences they face.[37] In the *Mörin* he is depicted actually dwelling in the land of Venus, a Christian among pagans, where he loyally endeavours to assist his fellow-believer, Hermann. His role is wholly compatible with the later tradition: by his confidence and trust in God he fortifies Hermann's courage, and acts as his moral guardian when, desiring to witness a tournament, the latter risks the wiles of worldly temptation, and must be deterred. It is striking that neither Eckhart, nor any figure corresponding to him, is found in the non-German sources treating the mountain-paradise. On the other hand Hemmerlin's account of the Nórcian mountain includes the figure of the "senex" who, like Hermann's Eckhart, dwells inside the realm, and

---

35) *Ibid.*, v. 29; v. 156; v. 838.
36) *Ibid.*, v. 831.
37) *Cf.*, *e.g.*, J. Agricola, *Ander teyl gemayner deutscher sprüchwörter* (Nürnberg, 1529), fol. 137; Schmidt, *(op. cit.)* p. 29.

who warns visitors to depart in time.[38] He appears to be a metaphor for age and the passage of time, prompting in man the desire to care for his soul and to seek the absolution of his worldly sins. Such a character may have belonged to the legendary mountain-paradise at a very early stage of its development, and even be derived from the fairy beings who peopled it prior to its assuming a primarily moral character. In acquiring the German name Eckhart, the old man seems to have been identified with the guardian-figure of Germanic legend; this would account for his supposed position at the entrance of the mountain.

A figure of obviously much greater importance is that of Venus herself. While in the *Mörin* she is not actually identified with the devil, her hostility to Christianity nevertheless appears to motivate her more than anything else. She is depicted, just like the Sibyl, as a Saracen queen, while the moorish woman of the title is her helpmate and legal counsel whom, as the king (Tannhäuser) ironically remarks to his knights, she treats in the manner of a goddess.[39] In his plight, the wretched poet is urged to call on Mohammed for aid. But Venus also shows ambitions of worldly power — "Da tratt die küngin her gar kül/ als ob ald welt ir aigen wer"[40] — which seem to usurp the realm of religion: in their procession her followers parody the well-known crusading hymn — "In Fenus nammen faren wir".[41] The author evidently draws on the medieval tradition of anti-feminism in portraying her: she is vengeful, malicious and altogether unscrupulous in seeking to circumvent the proper course of the law for her own end: the destruction of Hermann.

Yet at the same time she remains essentially *Fro Minne*, the courtly personification of noble love, for it is purely in this capacity that she has arraigned Hermann. As the allegorical embodiment of love, Venus is a very common figure in the literature of late medieval Germany, wherever the values and character of Courtly Love and its proper conduct are discussed and upheld; numerous works survive in which Venus/Fro Minne serves as the advocate and arbitrator of noble and virtuous love, or forms with her retinue of subordinate allegorical ladies a court of appeal to which lovers turn for aid, advice and fair

---

38) *Cf.* Dübi, p. 252.
39) *Mörin*, v. 2588f.
40) *Ibid.*, v. 3406f.: "Then the queen coolly stepped forth as though all the world were her own."
41) *Ibid.*, v. 575: "In Venus' name we journey."

judgment.[42] A demonisation of this allegorical figure does not appear in texts before about the 15th century, indeed it may fairly be said to appear only with the emergence of the Tannhäuser-legend. Pabst suggested that the demonic Venus of the legend had her origin in the story of Venus' statue, which relates how a young man was unintentionally wed to Venus by thoughtlessly putting his ring on the finger of her statue.[43] But no real connection can be shown between this tale and the legend; it was apparently little known in Germany and, above all, it concerns only the classical goddess, not an allegorical figure. It is true that earlier poets, in deploring the cruel and disruptive power of love, figuratively depict Venus/Fro Minne as the butt of their attack. But such criticism is simply a rhetorical device employed to consider and debate the nature of love; Fro Minne is never declared to be diabolical, for the courtly poets of the High Middle Ages never conceive love as wholly bad from a moral point of view.[44] Only a later era of vernacular poetry, characterised by humanistic attitudes which depicted erotic love and morality unequivocally as polar opposites, could represent Venus in an entirely negative light. In the first years of the 15th century Heinrich Wittenwiler contrasts the counsels of Venus/Fro Minne with those of the Virgin: while the former urges his heroine to yield to erotic passion, the latter tells her to seek matrimony.[45] Yet even here Venus is less a devil than a wanton jade, whose base but inescapable promptings are best accommodated in the compromise which marriage affords. All in all, it seems most improbable that the utterly demonic Venus, who is so vital a part of the Tannhäuser-legend, existed in Germany prior to the late 14th century; she was perhaps known to Felix Hemmerlin at the time of his visit to Italy in the early years of the 15th century, but there is no earlier

---

42) *Cf.* in general O. Lauffer, *Frau Minne in Schrifttum und bildender Kunst des deutschen Mittelalters* (Hamburg, 1947).
43) Pabst, p. 116ff.
44) The instances cited by M. Lang, *Tannhäuser* (*op. cit.*), p. 160f., indicate only a particular awareness of the negative moral aspects of love; they never amount to a demonisation of Venus in the sense of the legend. The passage in Heinrich von Morungen, "Ich wene si ist ein Venus here" (*Minnesangs Frühling* 138, 33), expressly associated with the Tannhäuser-legend by both Carl von Kraus, *Heinrich von Morungen* (Bremen, 1924), p. 117 and H. Schneider, "Heinrich von Morungen, Venus und Helena," *Dichtung und Volkstum* 42 (1942), iv, 33, deserves especial comment. As indicated by Heinrich's own line "ja ist min geloube bose und ist wider got" (139, 11), the target of criticism is his own mind, which sees in love a God-like power appropriately expressed in the figure of Venus. While this certainly points towards the later demonisation of Venus, it still falls far short of it.
45) Heinrich Wittenwiler, *Der Ring*, ed. E. Wiessner (Darmstadt, 1964), v. 2295ff.

evidence for her whatsoever. It seems scarcely possible that she can have existed in a Tannhäuser-ballad from the late 13th century but left no trace of her character in German literature for more than a century.

But on the other hand one may not simply assert than an "author" of the legend removed Sibyl/Sebile from her place as lady of the mountain in the demonic fairy-mistress story, and substituted Venus /Fro Minne, whose allegorical nature supplied a broader metaphorical value. There is clear evidence that a perfectly innocent, allegorical Venus was associated with the legendary mountain-paradise quite independently of the legend; this development certainly pre-dates the first mention of the demonic *Venusberg*, and appears to precede any idea of a demonic Venus. Two German literary works of an allegorical type depict the court of Venus in association with a hollow mountain. One of them, bearing the title *Das Minneturnier*, is undated but belongs probably to the late 14th or early 15th centuries. The poet dreams of a visit to Frow Myn, whose court, like the land of Venus in the *Mörin*, consists of a group of tents in a paradise-like setting. But there is also a hollow mountain:

> eyn gebierg, sam wers gemeld,
> dar in der wunder seld
> meng faltig was behußt,
> vil stett und schloß verklußt
> fur alls benotten vest.[46]

The poet at first believes himself deceived by magic, and requests an explanation from an old man (Eckhart?), who advises him to consult the dwarf living in the mountain. He is eventually received as Venus' "hoffgesind", and is treated by her to a discourse on the nature of love. The other work, which was possibly the source for the mountain in *Das Minneturnier*, is Meister Altswert's *Der Tugenden Schatz* (c. 1380).[47] Here Venus and her court actually dwell in a hollow mountain, richly encrusted with jewels and guarded by a dwarf; it is not named, but specified to be that of Venus: "Dirre berg was fro Venus allein ..."[48]

---

46) *Mittelhochdeutsche Minnereden*, ed. K. Matthaei (Dublin/Zürich, 1967), p. 96ff., v. 87ff.: "A mountain, as if in a picture, wherein were housed the manifold joys of wonders; many a town and castle enclosed, secure from all attack."
47) *Meister Altswert*, ed. W. Holland and A. Keller, Bibliothek des literarischen Vereins in Stuttgart, no. 21 (Stuttgart, 1850), p. 70ff.
48) *Ibid.*, p. 83: "This mountain belonged to Lady Venus alone ..."

It can scarcely be doubted that these two works are connected with the legend of the mountain-paradise. The tournament referred to in the title of *Minneturnier* bears a marked resemblance to the chivalric game known as "Gral", which is described in some Low German sources of the period;[49] another work of the same time and type actually designates Venus' court of tents in its idyllic location ("als wer es das irdisch paradiß") as the "gral".[50] The existence of some link with the paradise-like Grail-mountain attested near Pozzuoli in 1410 seems undeniable.[51] Yet these allegorical mountains show virtually none of the fairyland features that underlie the character of the *Venusberg* in the Tannhäuser-legend. Apart from the old man and the dwarf, both of whom have only obscure connections with the legend, one detail alone seems to correspond in any way to the other accounts: the visitor to the mountain in *Der Tugenden Schatz* is required to accept new clothing prior to entry, just like the nameless knight in the *Paradis*. Some emphasis is placed throughout the work on the symbolic colours worn by the inhabitants of the place, and the poet's reclothing is apparently designed to conform with the prevailing symbolism. The point thus has more meaning here than in the French text, and this, rather than the *Paradis* may be the origin of the feature.

But in these two German works the entire mountain is given over to allegorical meaning in every other respect as well. In *Der Tugenden Schatz* the dwarf, who acts as guide to the poet, speaks of a large "Hofgesinde", but the inhabitants, apart from a host of nameless knights and ladies all suitably paired off in testimony of Venus' power, are exclusively allegorical in both name and function. The pleasure that is universally enjoyed there emerges as a figurative expression of the happiness bestowed by proper love, and the poet's visit is a purely educational experience, not a sensual one.

It is perhaps just possible that this allegorical mountain housing Venus' court was actually inspired by the Tannhäuser-legend. But it appears most improbable in view of the absence of any hint, even in the form of a refutation, of its diabolical nature. Surely the innocent, allegorical *Venusberg* precedes the demonic one, which acknowledges

---

49) *Cf.* Barto, p. 9ff.
50) *Mittelhochdeutsche Minnereden* (*op. cit.*), p. 1ff: *Der Minne Gericht*, v. 652: "... as if it were the Earthly Paradise"; *cf.* also v. 738 and v. 790.
51) *Cf.* supra, p. 6ff.

something of the character of its predecessor, but condemns it. The allegorical *Venusberg* does, on the other hand, seem to be another expression of the same simple idea which, in the form of a popular belief, was so severely criticised by churchmen like Dietrich von Nieheim and Johannes Nider: the notion of an other-worldly mountain-realm with paradisical attributes. Whereas the ecclesiasts condemned an ingenuous belief in its reality, the idea is used here for a literary object appropriate to its dream-land nature: the allegorical inhabitants, corresponding to the traditional perfections of the place, express in their rarified manner an ideal of secular morality and life.

Certainly *Der Tugenden Schatz* is the first dated surviving work to describe a *Venusberg*, in the sense of a mountain housing Venus/Fro Minne and her attendant ladies; Altswert himself may not have originated the idea, but it is reasonable to assume that an allegory of such a type first brought Venus into the hollow mountain. Scholars have been misled on this point by a traditional association of the classical goddess with mountain-tops. Claudian (*fl.* 400) situates her dwelling on a mountain in his *De Nuptiis Honorii et Mariae*, and this work was doubtless the source for the well-known allegorical passage in *Architrenius*, frequently mentioned in this context.[52] *Architrenius* may very well have had some influence on German texts describing the allegorical court of Venus, and even on its association with the mountain-paradise, but he does not himself describe a hollow *Venusberg*. Aphrodite's first home on the island of Cythera, confused with Mount Cithaeron in the Oedipus-legend, satisfactorily accounts for the much quoted lines from Gotfrid's *Tristan*.[53]

Is it possible, on the other hand, that the subterranean realm was introduced into the demonic fairy-mistress story only with the figure of Venus, *i.e.*, from the allegorical *Venusberg*? In the face of a lamentable paucity of evidence, this possibility cannot be entirely discounted, for all the surviving texts depicting a fairy-mistress in a hollow mountain may be of later date than the work of Meister Altswert. But it does seem

---

52) *Cf.* Claudii Claudiani, *Opera*, ed. P. Burmann (London, 1821), vol. I, p. 312, v. 49ff; Johannis de Altavilla, "Architrenius" in T. Wright, *The Anglo-Latin satirical poets* (London, 1872), vol. I, p. 240ff.

53) No particular mythological connection of Venus and Cithaeron is known, and Gotfrid's lines do not necessarily suggest he had a mountain in mind; "Zytherone,/ da diu gotinne Minne/gebiutet uf und inne" (v. 4808ff.) is surely the island and town of Cythera where Venus first rose from the sea, *cf.* Löhmann, p. 246.

highly improbable. Examination of *Tom the Rymer* showed that its source apparently involved a fairy, not an allegorical Venus, in a hollow mountain. Though it is perhaps a little more readily conceivable, it seems likewise improbable that Andrea's source for *Guerino* can have shown the lady of the mountain as Venus. In general, such a theory disregards the subterranean connections of Sibyl/Fay Sebile and her evident association with the earlier history of the material.

Moreover, the great majority of German works describing the allegorical court of Venus do not situate it inside a mountain. Thus, in combining the figure of Venus/Fro Minne with a fairy-mistress story which lacked the subterranean location, there would be no particular cause to introduce the hollow mountain at all — a group of fine tents (from the allegorical works) or a vague fairyland locality (from the fairy-mistress story) would seem more obvious choices for the lady's realm. It is noticeable that Herman von Sachsenheim, who knows of the *Venusberg*, nevertheless disregards it in favour of the court of tents. On the other hand it was shown earlier that the mountain-paradise, even in the 13th century, enjoyed a certain Arthurian fairyland quality which was eminently suited to a fairy-mistress story, but was largely lost in the allegorical *Venusberg* of the 14th century German works.

It is most probable, then, that the demonic fairy-mistress story and the figure of Venus/Fro Minne were each independently associated with a subterranean location prior to their combination in the Tannhäuser-legend. In very different literary ways, both were apparently connected with the same legend of a mountain-paradise, accessible to favoured men. Presumably it was this common feature which, when the idea of the allegorical *Venusberg* found sufficient acceptance, actually inspired the transfer of Venus into the fairy-mistress story: the two ladies of the mountain, each from her own narrative and moral sphere, were joined in one diabolical figure who, since Fro Venus was familiar enough, could take her name with no need to claim a fairy nature. This identification of the wicked fairy-mistress with the allegorical representation of worldly love profoundly enriched the demonic fairy-mistress story with metaphor.

CONCLUSION

The assurance and simplicity with which earlier authorities spoke of a single national origin of the legend were plainly unwarranted. The theory of its German origins is virtually inseparable from that of its genesis in the 13th century, for both are based almost entirely on its inclusion of the names of Tannhäuser and Pope Urban IV. If it could be shown that their introduction into the story occurred only in the 14th or 15th centuries, not only the presumed 13th century beginnings, but also the contention of its German origins in the narrow and exclusive sense widely visualised would lose all real foundation. The evidence does not permit this to be done quite unequivocally; it remains still possible that some incident or policy with which Urban IV and Tannhäuser were concerned underlies the legend, and that a tale representing its original form became attached to the poet soon afterwards, to be first recorded in written form much more than a century later. However, since the weaknesses of such a supposition — principally the totally inscrutable and unexplained veil of silence that shrouds the legend until the 15th century, and the apparent later date of its closest sources, in as far as these may be determined from related texts — can be supported by plausible suggestions as to why the named poet and the particular Pope were introduced at a later date, the scales of probability must be said to weigh heavily against the exclusively German origin and in favour of a later time.

The evidence affords little enough information for any absolute chronology:— The years about the middle of the 15th century saw a sudden flowering of interest in the legend, indeed very much of the crucial evidence concerning it dates from that time. The composition of the *Paradis* and of Hemmerlin's *Dialogus*, the testimony of Aeneas Piccolomini and Johannes Nider regarding the *Venusberg*, and the texts of the Karlsruhe disputation, Hermann's *Moerin*, and of the first version of the ballad all belong to this period. It seems reasonable to look for some positive event preceding and causing this burst of popularity: perhaps it was the composition and dissemination of the ballad, which was to prove so successful subsequently. At all events the retrospective evidence given in the *Paradis* and in Hemmerlin's account indicates that the legend had already existed for at least a few decades previously.

Descriptively, one might speak of the legend as a demonic fairy-mistress story in which Venus/Fro Minne, a figurative being of exclusive and quite specific moral significance, has been substituted for the fairy, a creature of simple fictional narrative, who is only loosely felt to be evil. If a definition based on that description and incorporating the appropriate fairy-mistress motifs is applied to the problem, a date in the later 14th or even the early 15th century is indicated. Only in the late 14th century is Venus first depicted inside a hollow mountain, indeed at that time she may still be so depicted without any hint of her demonic nature; and only after that time is she ever conceived or portrayed as diabolical in other texts. Similarly, even if the testimony is perhaps less unambiguous, other fairy-mistress narratives displaying collectively the motifs proper to the legend appear only from the 14th century, although the individual motifs are for the most part older.

It may be argued that a definition of the legend must also include the staff-motif, although the point at which it entered the tale in relation to other developments is obscure. It is not to be found elsewhere used in a manner analogous to the legend before the 15th century.

A full definition may not of course omit the name of Tannhäuser. But here the evidence fails completely: like the staff-motif, Tannhäuser has no discernible connection with the story before the mid-15th century, though he then seems quite well-established as its hero. If indeed legendary material already surrounded his name in the 13th century, it seems unlikely to have included many of the prominent features of the later legend, and it left no clear trace at all in any contemporary record. On the other hand, it is quite feasible that Tannhäuser's enduring reputation in the realm of poetry and song, perhaps in particular his association with *Bußlieder*, led to his identification with the knight of the legend in the late 14th or early 15th centuries.

The case for Urban IV is most slender; conversely, an origin in the late 14th century significantly corresponds to the dates of Urban V and Urban VI, two of the three Popes mentioned by Antoine de la Sale.

All in all, the argument for an early date of origin is a very weak one.

The question of national provenance involves two distinct matters, which were not always satisfactorily separated in past scholarship: firstly, the national or ethnic origins of elements more or less important to the legend; secondly, the language and homeland of the versions through which the material passed to become the final (exclusively German) legend of the knight Tannhäuser. Consideration of the latter point is hampered most of all by the paucity of evidence. From the inferential arguments permissible, it is not possible to distinguish the successive versions in the legend's evolution with anything approaching certainty; although the *Paradis* affords an indirect glimpse of a version which probably had a neatly rounded literary character, the general picture is of a story which, over a fairly short period of time, changes drastically with regard to at least three of its most important points:— the identity of the temptress; whether the knight returned to the mountain; and the extent of the Pope's implication. Not until the prints of the 16th century does the story overtly achieve stability of content, and at this point it may already be described as degenerate in many respects.

Any attempt to paint an overall picture of the legend's genesis calls for the extensive assistance of conjecture, so that the consideration of detail is a largely futile occupation. A very general summary is attempted here for the sake of completion, since nothing more precise seems possible; there is no question of blindness, wilful or otherwise, to its limited scientific dependability. But it may at least serve as a helpful basis for further critical examination of the question; the conjectures it calls for are substantially a matter of assessing probabilities, and such judgments are personal — others, with different knowledge and experience of the period, will hold different and perhaps more accurate opinions.

The fairy-mistress story whose structure underlies the legend initially spread into medieval Europe mainly in the form of Breton-French tales. But the development of this Celtic material into the Christian story of a man's wicked union with a demon seems to have occurred largely in France; or, at least, the principal motifs concerned are at first either geographically associated with France, or appear in French texts (*Melusine* and *Désiré*). By the 14th century they had spread to Italy, Germany, Britain, and doubtless elsewhere in Europe.

The hollow mountain with which the story was associated has less clear origins. No doubt widespread mythological ideas and tales of malicious and demonic beings inhabiting the interior of mountains both contributed to, and nourished, the concept. But it appears to have had a more specific source in the legend of a mountain-paradise offering perfect and abundant pleasures, to which men have conditional access. Whether this legend was always more popular in Germany than elsewhere cannot be determined from the evidence, but it does find its way into German literature as early as the 13th century, and in the 15th century, when the Tannhäuser-legend was becoming popular, it is the subject of ecclesiastical condemnation in Germany. Most of the evidence connects its physical existence with Italy, and there seems to be a good case for associating its beginnings with the Sibylline grotto and the Elysian Fields of Vergilian tradition. In this point, those who saw the legend's origins in Italy were perhaps correct. In Germany the mountain is early portrayed as the fairyland realm to which the immortal Arthur withdrew. But it is unreasonable to conclude from the lack of evidence that this conception was unknown in Italy. The 13th century German sources also depict it as the home of the Grail; later it is simply known as "Grail", and the name appears to have persisted in the 15th and 16th centuries alongside "Venusberg".

It seems most likely that the demonic fairy-mistress story was already connected with the hollow mountain before the substitution of Venus. The fairy was perhaps initially identified with the Fay Sebile, a descendent of the Sibyl, for both her capacity as seeress, and other Sibylline attributes, are in evidence at times. It is thus reasonable to postulate an anterior version (not necessarily in literary form) involving a demonic fairy-mistress in a mountain, together with the motifs of transformation and confession; it very possibly lacked the two interdependent elements of refused absolution and return to the mountain. There are no grounds whatsoever for connecting such a story with Germany in particular, indeed none of the relevant texts comes from Germany.

The only central elements of the Legend that are indisputably German are the names of Tannhäuser and Venus. The former is obviously of considerable interest, but of little necessary consequence for the legend itself, having been supplied most probably from a simple wish to lend a suitable identity to the penitent knight. Venus is plainly a more important figure. In the latter part of the 14th century some German literary works of allegorical type used the idea of the mountain-paradise as a new fictional home for the court of Venus and her ladies; the traditional perfections of the place were equated with the ideals of love and courtly conduct embodied in these allegorical personages. Previous traditions associating the Goddess with mountains no doubt aided this development, but the hollow mountain housing Venus' court is strictly a new phenomenon in the 14th century, and is not yet found outside Germany. It subsequently inspired in the mind of some literary German moralist her identification with the demonic fairy of the hollow-mountain.

It is certainly true that, since Venus is a purely German contribution to the legend, any increase in metaphorical content which she brought to it is likewise a German development. As her domain, the mountain-paradise acquires a metaphorical dimension it previously lacked. Essentially, Tannhäuser in entering the demonic mountain-paradise of the legend, and the poet in entering the allegorical *Venusberg* in *Der Tugenden Schatz*, perform the same act and encounter the same phenomenon: each seeks in the perfections of the place for the ideal object of his worldly aspirations. Only in the moral evaluation of that object do the two diverge. While the latter text affirms the ideal, portraying it as the highest values of secular virtue in allegorical abstraction, the former exposes it as a slough of mundane sensuality. When the legendary *Venusberg* is revealed as a sinful trap for the souls of adventurous men, the entire range of worldly values implied by the allegorical *Venusberg*, and by the allegorical Fro Minne, lie revealed as a devilish fraud — the evil inherent in love, courtly splendours and riches, sophisticated pleasures and pursuits, lies uncloaked.

This version, which may reasonably be called the original version of the Tannhäuser-legend, is broadly identifiable with the sophisticated text which was postulated as an indirect source of the *Paradis*, and it surely had literary form. It is reasonable to assume that it named Tannhäuser (though there is no actual evidence either for or against the assumption) and that it depicted his return to the mountain, since this involves the same thematic pre-occupation with *delay* as characterised the earlier parts of the story. Indeed, the staff-motif is so appropriate to that theme, that it too may very well have appeared in this version. On the other hand this original probably did not involve any criticism of the Pope, which would have been inimical to the universal moral spirit of the tale. It can scarcely have been a ballad, indeed its regrettable loss may perhaps be attributed to usurpation by a popular balladic text in the 15th century.

Superficially this outline is at variance with the evidence of the *Paradis*, where the legend's figurative nature is now in fact to be best seen, but where neither the name of Venus nor the staff-motif appears. But despite its informativeness, the status of Antoine's text as an authentic version of the legend must be called into question, on account of its previous transmission; although his own fidelity is not doubted, that of the loosely termed "gens du païs" who informed him must be. The undeniable subtleties of his story are scarcely of their invention and may therefore be generally presumed authentic. But other details of the anterior literary version may very well have been lost; the suggestion is all the more plausible since varying versions of the rapidly changing story must have become confused in the local tradition as they reached Norcia.

There can be no doubt that Antoine's "Reine Sibylle" is in character much more an allegorical Venus than either a fairy or a Sibyl. Moreover, the story he heard at Norcia was evidently a largely German one, brought no doubt by such travellers from the North as are attested for earlier years by Hemmerlin and later by others. Antoine's immediate informants are aware of the peculiarly German obsession with visiting the mountain's interior: not only the story's hero, but also the two men led in by the lunatic priest are said to be German. It is particularly hard to see why the knight should be inconsequentially known to the local inhabitants as a German if the story were a purely native one. But, coming from Germany, the story has imposed itself on a domestic tradition of the prophetic Sibyl, if not also on an indigenous fairy-mistress story of the Fay Sebile. It is therefore less than surprising to find that the "gens du païs" did not relinquish their own popular Sibyl in favour of the alien Venus, whose presence and name would have been quite unaccountable in terms of the necromantic connections of the place; after all, it was presumably these connections which first brought the legendary mountain-paradise of the Sibyl to Norcia at some time in the 14th century. One telling result of this confusion of names is presumably Antoine's own rather learned puzzlement at finding a Sibyl who plays such an uncharacteristic role. Hemmerlin, though he writes of it only later, makes it seem likely that the Norcian mountain was already known to some (presumably German-speakers like himself) as *Mons Veneris* at the time of Antoine's visit.

The same sort of confusion in the local tradition may account for other points in Antoine's narrative. It is quite understandable that his informants could not recall the actual name of the knight, despite all his efforts to discover it; to them it must have been both strangely foreign and unimportant. A similar explanation, if a less simple and certain one, may be advanced for Antoine's omission of the staff-motif, though it should also be borne in mind that this may possibly not have been a part of the German legend which had reached Norcia by 1420. An indigenous fairy-mistress tradition may not have involved the hero's return to the mountain at all, but showed him rather as the recipient of absolution, like Guerino and Simplicianus. The invading German version, though substantially that of the sophisticated literary original, was brought by simple travellers on whose lips it was tainted with criticism of the Pope. The resulting version, taken by Antoine from the local inhabitants, seems to be a compromise, reached with the help of reconstruction: a pragmatic motive, quite out of keeping with earlier parts, is ascribed to the Pope, in order to delay absolution and effect the hero's return to the mountain while at the same time questioning the responsibility of the Pope's part in the affair.

Anti-papal feeling was to determine increasingly the content of subsequent versions and effectively to obscure the original. The earliest ballad of Tannhäuser may have been free of such sentiment, but no such text survives and later variants intensify this aspect to the point at which, in Southern Germany, the story was virtually petrified in a piece of blatant anti-papal propaganda. Only in the remoter Alpine areas does it seem to have experienced further evolution, although no record of these changes survives before the 18th century.

The idea of the mountain-paradise, known generally as the *Venusberg* after the 15th century, continued to enjoy some independent popularity; in the intellectual climate of 16th century Germany it grew more like the Italian mountain of a century earlier, a haunt of necromancers and of the devils they conjure. It became a school where travelling scholars may acquire the black arts, as well as satisfy their baser appetites.

Not until the romantic 19th century was the simple medieval splendour of the legend once more recognised, its force only partly obscured by the shortcomings of the ballads. The finest result of this revival in interest is surely the work of Richard Wagner who, in his own way, restored to it some of the tragic power which must have characterised the original.

APPENDIX

I

Letter of Aeneas Silvius Piccolomini, written 15th January 1444 from St. Veit, Austria, to his brother in Siena. From: *Der Briefwechsel des Eneas Silvius Piccolomini*, Abt. I, Bd. I, *Privatbriefe*, ed. R. Wolkan (Vienna, 1909), p. 283ff. *Fontes Rerum Austriacarum, Diplomataria et Acta*, Vol. 61:—

Eneas Silvius, poeta imperialisque secretarius, salutem plurimam dicit Gregorio jurisconsulto, fratri suo.

Venit ad me hac hora lator presentium, ex me quesitum, an Veneris montem apud Italiam scirem, nam ibi magicam artem tradi dicebat, cujus avidus est herus suus, qui Saxo est, summus astronomus. dixi me scire portum Veneris, qui est prope Lunam inter Ligusticos montes, quo in loco tres noctes egi, dum Basileam peterem. inveni etiam apud Siculos montem fore qui Herix appellatur, Veneri sacer, sed in his locis nichil accepi magicum tradi. inter conferendum autem venit in mentem locum esse in Umbria, que provincia ducatus dicitur, non longe ab urbe Nursia, ubi preruptus mons ingentem speluncam facit, per quam aque fluunt. illic memini audisse me striges esse et demones ac nocturnas umbras, ubi, qui audaces animo sunt, spiritus vident alloquunturque et artes ediscunt magicas. hec non vidi nec vidisse curavi, nam quod peccato discitur, melius est ignorasse. sed Savinus, juris civilis peritus, qui apud Camilliam inter publica diversoria domum habuit, hec mihi vera esse asseveravit, locum nominavit et locum descripsit. sed ista ex memoria fugerunt, que labilior est anguillis. ideo te rogo, si Savinus vivit, hunc virum ut ad se ducas sibique eum commendes. nam et ipse mihi et tu in hoc rem gratissimam facietis. is enim, qui nuntium hunc mittit, medicus est ducis Saxonie, homo tum dives, tum potens.

Aeneas Silvius, poet and imperial secretary, sends to the lawyer Gregory, his brother, fullest greetings.

There has just come to me a bearer of presents, asking me whether I know a mountain of Venus in Italy, for he says the art of magic is taught there, which greatly interests his master, a Saxon and a supreme astronomer. I said that I know of Porto Venere, which is near Luna among the Ligurian mountains, where I spent three nights while I was travelling to Basle. I have also found a mountain in Sicily known as Eryx, sacred to Venus, but I have heard nothing of the teaching of magic in these places. However while we were talking, it came into my mind that there is a place in Umbria, the province known as the Duchy, not far from the town of Norcia where a rugged mountain has formed a huge cave through which waters flow. I remember having heard that there are witches there, and demons and nocturnal shades, where those who are of bold disposition may see and speak with the spirits and learn the magic arts. I have neither seen these things, nor desired to see them, for it is better to remain ignorant of what is taught by sin. But Savinus, a man most learned in civil law, who has a house in Camillia among the public lodging-houses, assured me that these things were true and named and described the place. But these matters have escaped my memory, which is more slippery than eels. Therefore I am asking you, if Savinus should still be living, to take this man to him and commend him to him. For both you and he will do me a favour in this. For he who sends this messenger is the doctor of the Duke of Saxony, a man both rich and powerful.

II

Felicis Malleoli, vulgo Hemmerlein; Decretorum Doctoris Iureconsultissimi. De Nobilitate et Rusticitate Dialogus. Sacre Theologie: Iurium: Philosophorum et Poetarum Sententiis: Hystoriis et Facetiis Refertissimus. (Basel, 1497). Cap. 26, fol. 93v.f.

... ex his omnibus infertur proprie prout legitur in historiis Tuscanorum quod inter urbes Senarum et Parusienis, prout sepe vidi, concernitur montanium alpibus altissimis et vallibus proclivissimis complicatum. Et dicitur communiter mons Sibille coniunctus civitati Nursie et castello montifortin; et his diebus per hominum transgressus ad eorundem montium iuga generatur illico, prout infra similiter dicetur c. xxxii, grandinum ventorum et tempestatum insultus nimium vicinis locis importunus; et ultra ut propositum continuemus prout vidi patenter et audivi signanter expertos, quod in eisdem montibus sunt cavernarum et speluncarum; et usque ad interiora montium pertuse concavitates et transitus meabiles. Et intantum quod ille dicitur communiter mons veneris, ex eo quia prout fertur Venus uxor vulcani venereum officium non sine calore perpetuo ibidem conficiat; et hoc non aliter provenire perpendimus nisi quod in hoc loco pronunc incubi sint et succubi id est spiritus muliebris speciei pulchritudinem simulantes viros undecunque venerint largiter indagantes. Et tempore Johannis pape .xxiii cum sua curia Bononie degentis vidi hominem simplicianum de terra switensium pro penitentia illic provenientem qui firmiter quod in dictis montibus et apud succubas videlicet mulieres et famellas veneris per annum libidine saturatus permanserat confitebatur. Et protunc penitentia ductus et contritus absolutionis beneficium in ecclesia sancti Petronii per certum pape penitentiarium me disponente recepit gratissimum. Et ibidem inter alia retulit simplici sermonum prolatione requisitus quod postquam cum duobus sociis sibi coniunctis de Alamania cavernas montium intraverat, reperit

THE TRAGEDY OF KNIGHTHOOD 139

... from all these matters it may be appropriately mentioned that a range of mountains with very high peaks and most steep valleys is to be seen between the cities of Siena and Perugia, as is told in Tuscan stories and as I myself have' often witnessed. And the mountain commonly called the Mountain of the Sibyl adjoins the town of Norcia and Castello Montefortin; and even today, as is discussed likewise below in Chapter 32, an onslaught of hailstorms, winds and tempests, most harmful to the neighbourhood, is caused by men crossing to the ridge of those mountains. But to continue further with the matter, as I have seen myself and heard from the express eye-witness accounts of others, there are in these mountains caverns and caves, and hollows and paths leading into and penetrating the interior of the mountains. And this is commonly called the mountain of Venus, in as much as because they say that Venus, the wife of Vulcan, there performs her carnal rite, and not without everlasting heat. This, we consider, can have no other cause but that *incubi* and *succubi* are now in that place, that is, spirits assuming the beauty of the female form and freely searching out men from wherever they may come. And at the time when Pope John XXIII was staying with his court at Bologna I saw a man Simplicianus*, from the land of the Swiss, who came there on account of his repentance and who confessed with some insistence that he had lived for a year, sated with lust, in the said mountains with the *succubi*, that is, with the women and maidens of Venus. But now, contrite and led by penitence, he received, at my arrangement, the most gracious Sacrament of Absolution from a certain penitentiary of the Pope in the church of St. Petronius. And there, questioned with the simple prompting of words, he told among other things how, after he had entered the caves of the mountains in the company of two friends from Germany, he found a

---

*"Simplicianus" is attested as a personal name, but was evidently chosen to suggest the man's simplicity.

amenissimi serenissimique loci planiciem; ac si foret quadripartitus angularis ambitus alicuius ecclesie maximus duodecim ianuis tergotenus distinctis, ad quamlibet partem tribus pulchriter ornatus per quas ad temperiem duodecim mensium totius anni pro hominis libito continuus fuit liber meatus; et quod tempore martis montem intraverat cum sociis; aperuit hostium de mense septembris omni fertilitate referti, et fuit fructuosissime saturatus. Item quod mox post ingressum ad exquisitarum famellarum species sibi copiose continuus fuerat solatiosus accessus; et omnium solationum humani conditioni saltem iuvenili placitorum ibidem fuera[t] compar agressus; et summarie conclusit omnium ibidem fore voluptatum vite mundialis libidinose delicate florideque redolentis ornatus. Retulit insuper quod postquam cum sociis per priores meatus fuerat ingressus per quem senem fideliter prout apparuit ne ultra presentis anni cursum permaneret fuit avisatus, aliis perpetuo prepeditus sibi liber non pateret egressus; et iterum anno finito idem senex hos accolas admonuit, qui perterriti; et quod vix per mensem solatia tenuerint ipsis firmiter apparuit. Unde sociis suis per miras narrationum suasiones feminarum convictis ibidem permanentibus ipse solus evasit. Item quod in eadem loca multas diversarum terrarum et presertim de Anglia desperatas viderit personas perpetuo permansuras, et inter ceteros quemdam virum antiquum et suum filium non aliorum more gaudentes. Simplicianus autem predictus videlicet switensis gravissimum in hoc cognovit suum reatum, quia dolenter confitendo retulit quod introitus sui tempore una cum sociis divine gratie dei q[uoque?] misericordie renunciaverit; ac adiutorium beatissime virginis et omnium sanctorum abdicaverit; et hec levatis manibus promissione firmavit; et finaliter corde contritus in ecclesia predicta absolutionis gratiam obtinuit.

level place, most beautiful and serene, and as it were the enormous circuit of four walls and corners of some church, beautifully decorated with twelve doors separated all the way to the back, three in whichever way one looked, through which the way was always open, at one's pleasure, to the climates of the twelve months of the whole year; and that he had entered the mountain with his friends at the time of March; he opened the door of the month of September, full with every fertility, and was sated with its fruitfulness. Furthermore, soon after his entry he was freely allowed continual and satisfying access to the sight of delightful maidens; and he similarly had available there every satisfaction for the human state, or at least of the pleasures of youth; in short he concluded that there was in that place the supply of every pleasure of mundane life, redolent with blossoming charm and wantonness. He reported moreover that after he had entered through the first passages with his companions, he was warned by a seemingly trustworthy old man that he should not remain there beyond the span of the present year, or the way out would not be made open to him, but barred forever; and again at the end of the year the old man warned those living there, who were terrified; and that it seemed plain to them that the pleasures had scarcely endured a month. And his friends, won over by the wonderful temptations described to them by the women, remained there, while he alone escaped. He saw moreover in that place many people from diverse lands, especially from England, who had despaired and would remain there forever, and among them a certain old man and his son, not rejoicing in the way the others did. Simplicianus, that is the aforesaid Swiss, acknowledged his grave guilt in this matter, for, in an anguished confession, he said that at the time of his entry with his friends he had renounced the divine grace and mercy of God, and had repudiated the intercession of the Blessed Virgiñ and all the Saints; and these things he avowed with raised hands in an oath; and eventually, with a contrite heart, he obtained the grace of absolution in the said church.

III

Felix Faber, *Evagatorium in Terrae Sanctae, Arabiae et Egypti Peregrinationem*, ed. K. Hassler (Stuttgart, 1849). Bibliothek des literatischen Vereins in Stuttgart, 4., p. 221.

Et moderno tempore vulgus rudis delirat de quodam Tusciae monte, non longe a Roma, in quo dicunt dominam Venerem deliciis frui cum quibusdam viris et foeminis. Vnde de hoc carmen confictum habetur, quod manifeste a vulgo per Alemanniam canitur de quodam nobili Suevo, quem nominant Danhuser, de Danhusen villa prope Dünckelspüchel. Hunc fingunt ad tempus in monte cum Venere fuisse, et cum poenitentia ductus Papae fuisset confessus, denegata fuit sibi absolutio, et ita regressus in montem nusquam comparuit, et in deliciis vivit, ut dicunt, usque ad diem judicii. Ecce, quam facile homines in errores ducuntur credentes fictionibus! Nam Venerem mortuam et haud dubium damnatam, quae vivens numquam Europam vidit, credunt in Tusciae montibus degere. In tantum autem hac fama dementati sunt Alemanni, ut multi simplices ad hos famatos peregrinentur montes, et dum contingit aliquem mori, amici sui famant, eum raptum a Venere in montem; alii redeuntes dicunt se vidisse, quae a phantasticis auditu didicerunt.

And nowadays the ignorant people rant about a certain mountain of Tuscany, not far from Rome, in which they say the Lady Venus enjoys delights with certain men and women. And concerning this a song has been made, which is openly sung by the people throughout Germany, of a certain Swabian nobleman, whom they call Tannhäuser, after the village of Tannhusen near Dinkelsbühl. They say he had been until that time in the mountain with Venus and when, led by remorse, he confessed himself to the Pope, pardon was denied him, and so, having returned to the mountain he was nowhere to be found and lives in pleasures, so they say, until the Day of Judgment. Behold, how readily are men led into errors and to believe lies! For they believe that Venus, who is dead and without doubt damned, and who never saw Europe while she was alive, is living in the mountains of Tuscany. The Germans are so obsessed by this talk that many simple men journey to these famed mountains, and when it happens that someone dies, his friends put it about that he was carried off by Venus into the mountain; others who come back say they have seen things which they spread about, to be heard by dreamers.

IV
THE GERMAN BALLADS

Text *A*:

Text of the Essen manuscript (mid-15th century); *Stadtarchiv Essen, Rep. 100 Nr. 2593*; printed in K. Ribbeck, *Danuser: eine alte niederdeutsche Fassung des Tannhäuser-liedes. Erste Druck des Essener Bibliophilen Abends* (Essen, 1926); J. Meier, *Deutsche Volkslieder mit ihren Melodien: Balladen* (Berlin, 1935), vol. 1, pt. 1, p. 147f.:—

1 Over wyl yck heven aen
van Danuser tho syngen,
wat hye wunderss heyfft gedaen
myt syner hoeffscher mynnen.

2 Dannuser, gy syt my warden leyff,
daran so sulle gy dencken,
gy hebt my eynen eyt gedaen,
gy enwylt nycht van my wecken.

3 Dannuser, gy syt my warden leyff,
gy sult hyr ummer blyven;
ich geve u mynen spelgenoten
tot eynen echten wyve.

4 Wro Venus, dat ys nycht also,
dat wyl yck wedersprecken;
spreck dat oick eymant met,
god solt my helpen wrecken.

5 Neyme yck nu eyn ander wyff,
dan ick heb yn mynen synne,
so moest ick nu ind to allen tyden
in der hellen grunt versynken.

6 Du segest my vel van der hellen grunt;
heyffstu den wal bevonden?
gedenck an mynen roter munt
Dye lacht to allen stunden.

1. I shall begin again to sing of Tannhäuser and the wonders he did with his courtly love.

2. Tannhäuser, you have become dear to me, you should bear that in mind, you swore me an oath that you would not part from me.

3. Tannhäuser, you have become dear to me, you shall remain here for ever; I shall give you one of my companions to be your true wife.

4. Lady Venus, that is not so; I deny it — if anyone further says that, God should help me avenge it.

5. If I now took another wife than she I have in mind, I would have to sink now and for all time into the depth of Hell.

6. You tell me much of the depth of Hell; have you known it then? Think of my red mouth which laughs at all times.

7   Iuwe roter mund bedreget my,
    dat voel yck yn mynen synne,
    wou dat yck dat seggen dorst,
    gy syt eyn duvelynne.

8   Dannuser, wu redestu also?
    bustu nycht woel by synnen?
    laet uns yn eyn kamer gaen
    ind plegen der hoveschen mynnen.

9   Iuwer mynne ergeer yck nycht
    sye ys my unwerdich sere,
    gyff overloff, vrolyn gued,
    ind yck wyl wederkeren.

10 Dannuser, wyl gy oerloff haen?
    ick enwyl neyn orloeff geven.
    blyff [by] my, dat rade ick dy,
    ind spar dyn junghe leven!

11 Myn leven ys my worden suer
    alhyr op dusse erden;
    gyff my orloeff, vrolyn saert,
    ind ick wyl wederkeren

12 Vyltu ummer orloeff haen,
    nym orloeff van den grysen,
    ind waer gy yn den landen syt,
    unsen loeff den suldy prysen.

13 Vrow Venenus, dede yck nycht also,
    ick heb nycht dan gued an u gewanden;
    juwen loeff, den wyl ich ummer prysen
    nu ind tho allen stunden.

14 Dannuser genck uyt den berghe
    myt jamer ind myt rouwen
    tho rome al yn dye guden stad,
    off hye des pawes mochte schauwen.

15 Her pawes, vader myn,
    my rowet myn sunde sere
    ....
    ....

7. Your red mouth is a hindrance to me, I feel in my mind; if I dare say it: you are a she-devil.

8. Tannhäuser, why do you speak thus? Are you not in your senses? Let us go into a chamber and practise courtly love.

9. I do not desire your love, to me it is most unworthy; give me leave, good lady, and I shall go back (return?).

10. Tannhäuser, do you seek leave? I shall give you no leave. Remain with me, I advise you, and cherish your young life.

11. My life has grown bitter here on this earth; give me leave, tender lady, and I shall go back.

12. If you still seek leave, take leave from the old man (men?), and wherever you are in the lands you shall sing our praise.

13. Lady Venus, did I not so (?), I have found nothing but good in you; your praise I shall always laud, now and at all times.

14. Tannhäuser went out of the mountain with sorrow and repentance, to the good city of Rome, (to see) if he might see the Pope.

15. Lord Pope, my father, I sorely repent my sin ...

16 Yck heb gesundigen seven jar
    myt Venus, myner vrowen;
    ick wolde gerne boten entfaen,
    dat ick god mocht schauwen.

17 Dye pawes had dar eynen dariken stock
    den stack hye yn dye erden:
    wen hye rode rosen drecht,
    so synt dy dyn sunde vergeven.

18 Dannuser genck weder uyt der staet
    myt jamer ind myt rowen:
    Maria, Maria, reyne maget
    an u steyt all myn trowen!

19 Was wellickkoem, Dannuser leyff,
    my heyfft so sere verlangen,
    gy sult oick dye allerleyffste syn
    darto so wal entfangen!

20 Wrau Venus, edele vrowe myn,
    ick moet hyr by u blyven;
    merck, dat ich nu spelen sal
    myt juwen sarten lyve!

21 Do dat quam op ther derden dach,
    dye staff bestont tho gronen;
    men sante boden over boven
    off Dannuser wer komen.

22 Dannuser was weder yn den bergh
    hye enmocht nycht wederkomen;
    des mote dye pawes vervloget syn
    al yn der hellen grunde.

23 Darumb ensal gheen pawes watdoen
    hye ensulle syck wal bedencken:
    als eyn sunder rowen heyfft,
    des ensal men nummer krencken.

16. I have sinned for seven years with Venus, my lady; I wish to receive penance, that I may look on God.

17. The Pope had a dry staff which he thrust into the earth: "When it bears red roses your sins will be forgiven".

18. Tannhäuser left the city again, with sorrow and repentance: "Now help, Mary, pure maid, all my trust is in you".

19. You are welcome, Tannhäuser dear, I have so longed for you; you shall be the dearest of all, and also well-received.

20. Lady Venus, my noble lady, I must remain here with you; see, now I shall play with your tender body.

21. When it came to the third day the staff began to green; they sent messengers and messengers (to see) where Tannhäuser had gone.

22. Tannhäuser was back in the mountain, he could not return; for that the Pope was cursed in the depth of Hell.

23. Therefore no Pope should do a thing without considering well: when a sinner shows repentance, that should never be spurned.

Text *B*:

Broadsheet of 1515 in the Library of Erlangen University; printed as Barto IX; Meier, p. 145f.; *cf.* the facsimile in G. Könnecke, *Bilderatlas zur Geschichte der deutschen Nationallitteratur*, 2nd edit. (Marburg, 1912), p. 124.

Das lyedt von dem Danheuser

1 Nun wil ichs aber heben an
  Von dem Danheueser zu singen
  Vnd was er hat wunders gethan
  Mit seiner fraw Venussinnen

2 Danheueser was ein Ritter gut
  Wann er wolt wunder schawen
  Er wolt in fraw Venus berg
  Zu andern schoenen frawen

3 Herr Danheueser ir seyt mir lieb
  Daran solt ir mir gedencken
  Ir habt mir einen aydt geschworen
  Ir woelt von mir nit wencken

4 Fraw Venus das enhab ich nit
  Ich wil das wider sprechen
  Wann redt das yemant mer dan ir
  Got helff mirs an jm rechen

5 Herr Danheueser wie redt ir nun
  Ir solt bey mir beleyben
  Ich wil euch mein gespilen geben
  Zu einem stetten weybe

6 Vnd nem ich nun ein ander weyb
  Ich hab in meynem sinnen
  So muest ich in der helle glut
  Auch ewigklich verbrinnen

7 Ir sagt mir vil von der helle glut
  Vnd habt es nie entpfunden
  Gedenckt an meinen rotten mundt
  Der lachet zu allen stunden

The song of Tannhäuser

1. Now I will begin again to sing of Tannhäuser and the wonders he did with his lady Venus.

2. Tannhäuser was a good knight, for he wanted to see wonders; he wished to enter lady Venus' mountain and to (see) the other fine Ladies.

3. Sir Tannhäuser, you are dear to me — you should bear that in mind for my sake; you swore me an oath that you would not part from me.

4. Lady Venus, that I did not, I deny it; and if any other than you says that, may God help me avenge it on him.

5. Sir Tannhäuser, what are you now saying? You should stay with me; I shall give you my companion as a constant wife.

6. And if I now take another woman — (than her?) I have in mind — then I must burn for ever in hellfire.

7. You tell me much of hellfire, but you have never known it; think of my red mouth which laughs at all times.

8   Was hilffet mich ewer roter mundt
    Er ist mir gar vnmere
    Nun gebt mir vrlaub frewlein zart
    Durch aller frawen ere

9   Herr Danheueser woelt ir vrlaub han
    In wil euch keinen geben
    Nun beleybent edler Dannheueser
    Vnd fristet ewer leben

10 Mein leben das ist worden kranck
    Ich mag nit lenger bleyben
    Nun gebt mir vrlaub frewlein zart
    Von ewrem stoltzen leybe

11 Herr Danheueser nit redet also
    Ir thut euch nit·wol besinnen
    So geen wir in ein kemerlein
    Vnd spilen der edlen minnen

12 Gebrauch ich nun ein frembdes weyb
    Ich hab in meinem sinne
    Fraw Venus edle frawe zart
    Ir seyt ein Teueffellinne

13 Herr Dannheueser was redt ir nun
    Das ir mich guennet schelten
    Nun solt ir lenger hierinne sein
    Ir muestent sein dick entgelten

14 Fraw Venus vnd das wil ich nit
    Ich mag nit lenger bleyben
    Maria mutter reyne maydt
    Nun hilff mir von den weyben

15 Herr Danheueser ir solt vrlaub han
    Mein lob das solt ir preysen
    Wo ir do in dem landt vmbfart
    Nembt vrlaub von dem Greysen

16 Do schiedt er wider auss dem berg
    In iamer vnd in rewen
    Ich wil gen Rom wol in die stat
    Auff eines Babstes trawen

8. What does your red mouth avail me, I care not for it. Now give me leave my tender lady, for the honour of all ladies.

9. Sir Tannhäuser, if you seek leave I shall give you none; now remain, noble Tannhäuser, and keep your life.

10. My life is grown wretched, I cannot stay longer; now give me leave, my tender lady, from your proud person.

11. Sir Tannhäuser, do not speak so, you do not consider well; let us go into a chamber and play the game of noble love.

12. If I now have a strange woman — (other than her?) I have in mind — Lady Venus, noble tender lady, you are a she-devil.

13. Sir Tannhäuser, what are you now saying, that you begin to curse me? If you were to stay longer in here, you would much pay for it.

14. Lady Venus, that I will not, I cannot stay longer; Mary, mother, pure maid, now help me from these women.

15. Sir Tannhäuser, you shall have leave; you shall sing my praise wherever you go in the land — take leave of the old man!

16. Then he departed out of the mountain in sorrow and repentance — I will go to the city of Rome, trusting in a Pope.

17   Nun far ich froelich auff die ban
     Got muess sein ymmer walten
     Zu einem Babst der heyst Vrban
     Ob er mich moecht behalten

18   Ach Babst lieber herre mein
     Ich klag euch meine sunde
     Die ich mein tag begangen hab
     Als ich euchs wil verkuende

19   Ich bin gewesen auch ein jar
     Bey Venus einer frawen
     So woelt ich beycht vnd buss entpfahen
     Ob ich moecht got anschawen

20   Der Babst het ein steblein in der handt
     Das was sich also duerre
     Als wenig es begruenen mag
     Kumpst du zu gottes hulde

21   Nun solt ich leben nur ein jar
     Ein jar auff diser erden
     So woelt ich beycht und buss entpfahen
     Vnd gottes trost erwerben

22   Do zog er wider auss der stat
     In iamer vnd in leyden
     Maria mutter reyne maydt
     Muss ich nun von dir scheyden

23   Er zog do wider in den berg
     Vnd ewigklich on ende
     Ich wil zu Venus meiner frawen zart
     Wo mich got wil hin sende

24   Seyt got wilkumen Danheueser
     Ich hab ewer lang entporen
     Seyt wilkumen mein lieber herr
     Zu einem bulen ausserkoren

25   Das weret biss an den dritten tag
     Der stab hub an zu gruenen
     Der Babst schicket auss in alle landt
     Wo der Danheueser wer hin kumen

17. Now I go cheerfully on my way — may God ever govern it — to a Pope called Urban, to see if he can save me.

18. Ah my dear lord Pope, I lament to you my sins that I have committed in my life, as I shall tell you.

19. I have also spent a year with Venus, a lady; so I wish to receive confession and penance, to find if I may look on God.

20. The Pope had a little staff in his hand that was quite dry: as little as it may become green can you find God's favour.

21. Now were I to live only a year, one year on this earth, then might I receive confession and penance, and win the consolation of God.

22. Than he left the city again in sorrow and distress: Mary, mother, pure maid, I must part from you.

23. Then he went back into the mountain eternally without end; I will go to Venus my tender lady, whither God will send me.

24. You are welcome Tannhäuser, I have long missed you; you are welcome my dear Lord, most excellent lover.

25. It endured until the third day: the staff began to green. The Pope sent out in all lands (to see) where Tannhäuser had gone.

26 Do was er wider in den berg
    Vnd het sein lieb erkoren
    Des must der vierte Babst Vrban
    Auch ewigklich sein verloren

                Gedrueckt zu Nuernberg
                 durch Jobst Gutknecht
                      M.CCCCC.Xv.

26. But he was back in the mountain and had found his love. Therefore Pope Urban IV was also lost for ever.

Text *C*:

Undated broadsheet (*c.* 1530?) without printer's name or place; from Barto IV, *q.v.*:—

Vam Danhueszer

1   Aver wil ick h'euen an,
    vom eynem Danhueser syngen.
    Und wat he wunders hefft gedan,
    wit Venus der dueuelynnen.

2   Danhueser was eyn Rydder gudt,
    he wolde wunder schouwen
    he toch tho Venus yn den berch,
    tho andern schoenen Frouwen.

3   Do eyn yar all vmme quam,
    syne suende beguenden 'em tho leyden.
    Venus eddele Frouwe fyn,
    ick wyl wedder von yw scheyden.

4   Her Danhueser wy hebben yuw gantz leeff,
    dar an schoele gy gedencken.
    Gy hebben vns eynen Eedt geswarn,
    gy schoelen van vns nicht wenken.

5   Frouw Venus des hebb ick nicht gedan,
    ick wyl dat wedder spr'ecken.
    Vñ spr'eke dat yemant m'er wen gy,
    ick wold dat an 'em wr'ecken.

6   Herr Danhueser wo r'ede gy nu also,
    gy schoelē mit vns blyuen.
    Ick g'eue yuw myner sp'elnoten eyn,
    tho eynem steden Wyne.

7   Neme ick den eyn ander wyff,
    wen ich dr'ege yn mynem sinne,
    so moeste jo jn der helle grūt
    myne seele ewichlyken bernen.

Of Tannhäuser

1. I shall begin again to sing of Tannhäuser and the wonders he did with Venus the she-devil.

2. Tannhäuser was a good knight, he wished to see wonders; he went to Venus in the mountain, and to other fine ladies.

3. When a year came round he began to grieve for his sins; Venus, fine and noble lady, I wish to part from you again.

4. Sir Tannhäuser, we hold you dear, you should bear that in mind; you swore us an oath, you should not part from us.

5. Lady Venus, I did not do that — I deny it; and if any other but you says that, I shall avenge it on him.

6. Sir Tannhäuser, why do you now speak thus? You shall stay with us; I shall give you one of my companions as a constant wife (*reading* "Wyve").

7. If I take another wife than (her) I bear in my mind, then my soul would have to burn for ever in the depth of Hell.

8   Gy seggen v'ele van der helle grunt.
      gy hebben der nicht befunden.
      Gedencket an mynen roter mundt,
      dede lachet tho allen stunden.

9   Wat helpet my yuwe roter mund,
      de ys my gantz vnm'ere
      G'euet orloff eddele frouwe tzart,
      Doerch aller Junckfrouwen Eere.

10   Danhueser gy wylt orloff haen
      my wylt yuw nenen g'euen,
      blyuet hyr by vns eyn Rydder gudt,
      vnd frystet yuwe yunge l'euen.

11   Myn l'euendt ys geworden kranck,
      ick mach nicht lenger blyuen.
      Na bycht vnd ruwe steyt myn beger,
      vnd yn bote myn l'euent dryuen.

12   Danhueser wo rede gy also,
      synt gy ock klok van synnen.
      So ga wy yn eyn k'emerlyn,
      gy schoelen doch nicht van hynnen.

13   Gy seggen my v'el vam k'emerlyn,
      vth yuwē valschen sinne.
      Ick se yd an yuwen ogen wol.
      gy synt eyn Dueuelynne.

14   Danhueser wo r'ede gy nu also,
      wil gy yo mit vns schelden.
      Schold gi lenger hyr by vns syn,
      gy moesten des dicke entgelden.

15   Frouw Venus des syth van my berycht,
      ick wil nicht lenger blyuen.
      Help my Christe van Hemmelrick,
      van dyssen boesen Wyuen.

16   Danhueser gy wylt orloff haen
      n'emet orloff van den Grysen.
      Wor gy yn den Landen varen,
      vnse loff dat schole gy prysen.

8. You speak much of the depth of Hell, and you have never known it. Think of my red mouth which laughs at all times.

9. What does your red mouth help me, I care not for it; give leave, noble tender lady, for the honour of all maidens.

10. Tannhäuser, if you seek leave I shall give you none; remain here with us, good knight and keep your young life.

11. My life has grown wretched, I can stay no longer; my desire is for confession and repentance, and to spend my life in penance.

12. Tannhäuser, why do you speak thus, you who are clever of mind? Let us go into a little chamber, you shall not go from here.

13. You speak much of the little chamber from your false thoughts. I well see from your eyes that you are a she-devil.

14. Tannhäuser, why do you now speak thus, that you curse us so? If you stayed longer with us here, you would much pay for it.

15. Lady Venus, know this from me: I will stay no longer. Help me Christ in Heaven, from these evil women.

16. Tannhäuser, if you will have leave, take leave from the old men; wherever you go in the lands you shall laud our praise.

17 He scheyde wedder vth dem berge,
    mit leue vnd ock mit leyde.
    Help Christe van dē Hēmelrick,
    lath my nicht van dy scheyden.

18 Nu wyl ick hen tho Rome gaen
    God moete dysse reyse walden.
    Thom Geystliken vader Pawes Vrban,
    de myn ssele mach behalden.

19 Ach Pawest geystlike Vader myn,
    ick klage yw all myne suende,
    der ick myn dage hebbe v'el gedan,
    so ick yuw wil vorkuenden.

20 Ick byn gewest eyn heyl gantz yar,
    yn ssuenden mit Venus der Frouwen
    Dat bychte ick nu fyr apenbar,
    Went all ssuend my sser ruwen.

21 Der Pawest hadd eynen droegen staff,
    den stoette he an de 'erden.
    So de staff nu groenen wert,
    schoelen dyne ssuende vorgeuen werden.

22 Danhuesser scheyde sick vth der Stadt
    mit leyde vñ ock mit ruwe,
    O Jesu Christ van hēmelrick,
    help my nu doerch all dyne truwe.

23 Vorfloecket syn de leydygen papen,
    de my tho der helle schryuen,
    Se wỹllen Gade eyne ssele berouen,
    de wol moechte beholden blyuen.

24 Do heē qwam all vor den bech
    he sach sick wyde vmme.
    Godt ges'egen dy Suenne vnd Maen
    Darto myne leuen Fruende.

25 Danhueser gynck wedder yn den berch,
    he waert gar wol entfangen.
    Segget vns Danhueser eyn Ridder gudt,
    wo hefft ydt yw gegang.

17. He departed from the mountain with joy and with sorrow. Help Christ in Heaven, let me not part from you.

18. Now I will go to Rome — may God govern this journey — to the Holy Father, Pope Urban, who can save my soul.

19. Ah, Pope, my Holy Father, I lament to you all my sins, of which I have committed so many in my life, as I shall tell to you.

20. I have been for a whole year in sin with the Lady Venus. I openly confess that now, for I sorely repent all my sins.

21. The Pope had a dry staff which he thrust into the earth: When the staff becomes green your sins will be forgiven.

22. Tannhäuser left the city with sorrow and repentance: O Jesus Christ in Heaven, in your faithfulness, help me now.

23. Accursed be the wretched priests who consign me to Hell; they seek to deprive God of a soul which might well be saved.

24. When he came to the mountain he looked round far and wide: May God bless the sun and the moon and also my dear friends.

25. Tannhäuser went back into the mountain, and he was well received. Tell us Tannhäuser, you good knight, how it has fared with you.

26 Als ydt my gegangen hefft,
    dat hedd ick wol vorswaren.
    Noch bydd ick Christum van Hemmelrick,
    he leth my nicht bliuen voenralr.

27 Do ydt qwam an den druedden dag,
    de staff beguende tho groenen.
    Eer dat tho der Vesper qwam,
    de staff droech loff vnd blomen.

28 De Pawes sende Boden yn alle Landt,
    Danhueser scholde weder k'eren.
    He ys geloeset vth suenden bandt,
    doerch Christum vnsen Heren.

29 De Pawes bedroeuede sick gantz s'er
    he hefft geb'eden alle stunde,
    Godt wyl erfuellen Danhuesers beg'er
    vnd verg'euen 'em svne suende.

26. How it has fared with me I could well have forsworn. Still I beg Christ in Heaven that he does not let me remain lost (*reading* "voerlarn").

27. When it came to the third day the staff began to green: then before vespers came, the staff bore foliage and flowers.

28. The Pope sent messengers into every land, that Tannhäuser should return. He is redeemed from the bonds of sin by Christ our Lord.

29. The Pope was sorely grieved, he raised prayers at all times, that God would fulfill Tannhäuser's desire and forgive him his sins.

(Textual emendations from: J. G. T. Graesse, *Der Tannhäuser und der Ewige Jude* (Dresden, 1861), p. 45ff.)

Text *D*:

Jan Roulans, *Liedekens-Boeck*, Antwerp, 1544, fol. 88r-89r; Barto I; reproduced here from Hoffmann von Fallersleben, *Niederländische Volkslieder*, 2nd edit. (Hannover, 1856), p. 26ff.:—

Herr Daniel

1 Wildi horen een goet nieu liet?
   ende dat sal ic ons singhen,
   wat heer Danielken is gheschiet
   al met vrou Venus minne.

2 'Oorlof, sprac hi, vrouwe waert!
   ende ic wil van u scheiden,
   ic wil gaen trecken te Romen waert
   al om des paus gheleiden.'

3 'Heer Daniel, wilt ghi oorlof ontfaen,
   ic en wil u niet begheven:
   laet ons in die camer gaen
   die hoochste minne pleghen.

4 'Dat en doe ic niet, vrouwe fier!
   mi dunct in alle minen sinne,
   uw oghen bernen al waert een vier,
   mi dunct ghi sijt een duivelinne.'

5 'Heer Daniel, wat ist dat ghi secht?
   ghi en dort u niet vermeten,
   coomt ghi noch weder in den berch,
   dat woort en sal ic niet vergheten.'

6 'Trouwen neen ic, joncfrou stout!
   nu noch te ghenen stonden
   en peise ic om dinen roden mont,
   die en achte ic niet tot allen stonden.'

7 'Daniel wilt ghi oorlof ontfaen,
   neemt oorlof aen die grisen,
   werwaert dat ghi henen keert
   onsen lof sult ghi altijt prisen.'

Sir Daniel

1. Will you hear a good new song? Then I shall sing us one, of what befell Sir Daniel with Lady Venus, Love.

2. Give me leave, worthy lady, he said, and I shall leave you. I shall travel towards Rome, to seek guidance of the Pope.

3. Sir Daniel, if you seek leave I shall give you none; let us go into the chamber and practise noble love.

4. That I shall not do, proud lady; in my mind I think that your eyes burn like a fire: you are a she-devil, I think.

5. Sir Daniel, what is that you say? You should not dare to presume so much; if you come back to the mountain I shall not forget that word.

6. Indeed, not I, bold lady, not now or at any time; I do not consider your red mouth, I care not for it at anytime.

7. Daniel, if you seek leave, take leave from the old men; wherever you may go, you shall always laud our praise.

8.   Hi nam een staf al in sijn hant
     ende hi streec te Romen binnen:
     'nu biddic Maria, die moeder gods,
     dat ic den paus mach vinden.'

9   Doen he quam voor den paus ghegaen,
     voor onsen eertschen vader:
     'here, ic soude mi biechten gaern
     ende roepe op god ghenade.

10   Ic soude mi biechten seer bevreest
     met alle minen sinne,
     ic heb seven jaer in den berch gheweest
     met vrou Venus die duivelinne.'

11   'Hebdi seven jaer in den berch gheweest
     met vrou Venus die duivelinne,
     so sult ghi bernen ewelijc
     al in die helsche pine.'

12   Die paus nam enen droghen stoc
     ende stac hem in die aerde beneven:
     'Wanneer desen stoc rosen draecht,
     dan sijn uw sonden vergheven.'

13   Vermaledijt moeten die pausen sijn
     die ons ter hellen driven!
     si hebben gode so menighe siele ghenomen
     die wel behouden mochten bliven.

14   Hi tooch te Ronsen opt hoghe huis
     om drie sijnder suster kinder,
     die nam hi al metter hant
     ende leidese bi Venus sijnder vriendinne.

15   Al doen den derden dach omme quam,
     dien droghen stoc droech rosen;
     men sant bode ende wederbode
     om heer Daniel te soeken.

16   Doen he voor den berch quam,
     vrou Venus die quam hem teghen:
     'secht mi, secht mi, Daniel fijn!
     hoe is die reise gheleghen?'

8. He took a staff in his hand and he journeyed into the city of Rome: now I beg Mary, the mother of God, that I may find the Pope.

9. Then he came before the Pope, before our earthly father: Lord, I wish to confess and call on God for grace.

10. I wish to confess in great fear, with all my mind: I have spent seven years in the mountain with Lady Venus, the she-devil.

11. If you have spent seven years in the mountain with Lady Venus the she-devil, then you will burn for ever in the pain of Hell.

12. The Pope took a dry staff and thrust it into the earth beside him: when this staff bears roses your sins will be forgiven.

13. Accursed be the Popes who drive us to Hell! They have deprived God of so many a soul that well might have been saved.

14. He went to Ronse to the castle for three of his sister's children; he took them by the hand and led them to Venus his beloved.

15. When the third day came round the dry staff bore roses; they sent messenger after messenger to seek Sir Daniel.

16. When he came to the mountain, Venus came to meet him. Tell me, tell me, fine Daniel, how did your journey go?

17 'Hoe nu die reise is gheleghen,
daer toe is mi so leide:
die paus heeft mi sulken troost ghegheven,
ewelic van god te sijn ghescheiden.'

18 Si sette hem enen stoel,
daer in so ghinc hi sitten,
si haelden hem enen vergulden nap
ende wilde Danielken schinken.

19 Hi en wilde eten noch drinken.
si wilde enen raet visieren,
hoe si in die camer soude comen
met seven camenieren.

20 Mer doen si uter camer quam
al lachende ende al spelende,
al had si ewelic ghespeelt,
heer Daniel die hadde ghesweghen.

22 Mer die dit liedeken eerstwerf sanc,
sijn herte lach hem in dolen,
hi was liever in Venus bedwanc
dan in helsche scholen.

17. It saddens me so, how the journey went: the Pope has given me such comfort that I must be parted from God for ever.

18. She set him a chair and he went and sat down; she fetched him a golden cup, and wanted to give Daniel to drink.

19. He wanted neither to eat nor drink. She considered how she could come into the chamber with seven chambermaids.

20. But when she came out of the chamber, laughing and playing as if she had always played, Sir Daniel had remained silent.

21. But he who first sang this song, his heart was in pain; he was rather in Venus' power, than among the hosts of Hell.

BIBLIOGRAPHY

The following is not a complete listing of the numerous works consulted in the course of this study, for very many of them relate to the Tannhäuser-legend only in point of the argument used, and full bibliographical details are supplied in the appropriate footnotes. The aim here is rather a compact and useful inventory of those studies which treat the legend itself and the ballads through which it is known. A few very early works of this sort have also been excluded as being of no conceivable further scientific value.

Amersbach, Karl. "Zur Tannhäusersage". *Alemannia*, 23 (1895) 74-83.
Amman, Adolf N. *Tannhäuser im Venusberg*. Zürich, 1964.
Barto, Philip S. "Studies in the Tannhäuserlegend". *Journal of English and Germanic philology*, 9 (1910) 293-320.
Barto, Philip S. *Tannhäuser and the Mountain of Venus: a study in the legend of the Germanic paradise*. New York, 1916.
Barto, Philip S. "The German Venusberg". *Journal of English and Germanic philology*, 12 (1913) 295-303.
Bechstein, Ludwig. *Der Sagenschatz und die Sagenkreise des Thüringerlandes*. Hildburghausen, 1835, I, pp. 34-44.
Bernhardt, E. "Vom Tannhäuser und dem Sängerkrieg auf der Wartburg". *Jahrbuch der Akademie gemeinnütziger Wissenschaften zu Erfurt*, Neue Folge, 25 (1900) 89-112.
Böckel, Otto. *Handbuch des deutschen Volksliedes*. Marburg, 1908, pp. 51-57.
Böckel, Otto. "Zur Sage vom Venusberg". *Alemannia*, 13 (1885) 141-42.
Cassel, Paulus. *Aus Litteratur und Symbolik*, Leipzig, 1884, pp. 1-17.
Burckhard, Max E. *Das Lied vom Tannhäuser*. Leipzig, 1889.
Denk, Otto. "Der Minnesänger Tannhäuser und seine Heimat". *Das Bayerland*, 28 (1916-17) 225-28.
Desonay, Fernand. "Der italienische Ursprung der Tannhäuser-Sage". *Universitas*, 3 (1948) 149-61.
Dübi, Heinrich. "Drei spätmittelalterliche Legenden in ihrer Wanderung aus Italien durch die Schweiz nach Deutschland". *Zeitschrift des Vereins für Volkskunde*, 17 (1907) 42-65, 143-60, 249-64.
Dübi, Heinrich. "Frau Frene und der Tannhäuser". *Zeitschrift des Vereins für Volkskunde*, 17 (1907) 249-64.
Eis, Gerhard. "Die Sage vom Tannhäuser bei Rudolf Rebmann". *Studia Neophilologica*, 33 (1961) 159-62.
Eis, Gerhard. "Die Tannhäusersage bei Gaunern und Walen". *Archiv*, 191 (1955) 221-23.
Elster, Ernst. *Tannhäuser in Geschichte, Sage und Dichtung*. Bromberg, 1908. (*Veröffentlichungen der Abteilung für Literatur der deutschen Gesellschaft für Kunst und Wissenschaft zu Bromberg*, 3.)

Franckel, Adolf. *Der Tannhäuser.* Weimar, 1854.
Geiger, Emil. "Bericht über die Verhandlungen der germanistischen Section der 49. Versammlung deutscher Philologen und Schulmänner zu Basel". *Zeitschrift für deutsche Philologie,* 40 (1908) 93-107.
Golther, Wolfgang. "Geschichte der Tannhäusersage und Dichtung". *Bayreuther Taschenbuch,* 7 (1891) 8-29.
Golther, Wolfgang. "Tannhäuser in Sage und Dichtung des Mittelalters und der neuen Zeit". *Walhalla,* 3 (1907) 15-67.
Götze, Alfred. "Tannhäuser und Venusberg". *Neue Jahrbücher für das klassische Altertum, Geschichte und deutsche Literatur,* 53 (1924) 57-58.
Graf, Arturo. "Un monte di Pilato in Italia". *Miti, leggende e superstizioni del medio evo,* Turin, 1892-3, II, pp. 141-66.
Grässe, Johann G. *Der Tannhäuser und der ewige Jude.* Dresden, 1861.
Grässe, Johann G. *Die Sage vom Ritter Tannhäuser.* Dresden, 1846.
Güntert, Hermann. *Kalypso: bedeutungsgeschichtliche Untersuchungen auf dem Gebiet der indogermanischen Sprachen.* Halle, 1919, pp. 101-110.
Hamerling, Robert. "Über die deutsche Venus-Tannhäuser-Sage. Mit Beziehung auf die Dichtung 'Venus im Exil' ". *Westermanns Monatshefte,* 79 (1896) 53-62.
Haupt, Josef. "Die Sage vom Venusberg und dem Tannhäuser". *Berichte und Mitteilungen des Altertum-Vereins zu Wien,* 10 (1869) 315-23.
Heinrich, Gusztav. "Die Tannhäuser-Sage". *Ungarische Revue,* 6 (1886) 827-29.
Heinrich, Gusztav. *Tannhäuser.* Budapest, 1915.
Hirsch, Selma. "Die älteste Gestalt der Ballade vom Tannhäuser". *Jahrbuch des Vereins für niederdeutsche Sprachforschung,* 56-57 (1930-31) 194-204.
Hirsch, Selma. *Studien zum Antwerpener Liederbuch vom Jahre 1544.* Diss. Tübingen, 1923.
Hoecker, Georg, *Der Tannhäuser.* Wien, 1898.
Jahn, Robert, "Die ältesten Sprach- und Literaturdenkmäler aus Werden und Essen. VII: Das Essener Liederheft. b: Das Tannhäuserlied". *Beiträge zur Geschichte von Stadt und Stift Essen,* 60 (1940) 104-23.
John, Alois. "Tannhäuser im Fichtelgebirge". *Literarisches Jahrbuch: Central Organ für die wissenschaftlichen, literarischen und künstlerischen Interessen Nordwest-Böhmens und der deutschen Grenzlande,* 3 (1893) 70-73.
Junk, Victor. *Tannhäuser in Sage und Dichtung.* München, 1911.
Kluge, Friedrich. "Der Venusberg". *Bunte Blätter.* Freiburg, 1908, pp. 28-61.
Kornmann, Heinrich. *Mons Veneris: Fraw Veneris Berg.* Frankfurt, 1614.
Krappe, Alexander H. "Die Sage vom Tannhäuser". *Mitteilungen der schlesischen Gesellschaft für Volkskunde,* 36 (1937) 106-32.
Krappe, Alexander H. "La légende de Tannhäuser". *Mercure de France,* 284 (1936) 257-75.

Kretzenbacher, Leopold. "Der Tannhäuser in der Volksdichtung Österreichs". *Volkslied, Volkstanz, Volksmusik*, 48 (1967) 2-7.

Lang, Margarete. *Tannhäuser*, Leipzig, 1936. (*Von deutscher Poeterey*, 17).

Lang, Margarete und Hans Naumann. "Zu Tannhäusers Balladengestalt". *Jahrbuch für Volksliedforschung*, 5 (1936) 123-30.

Levissohn, Robert. "Eine obersteirische Fassung des Volksliedes vom Tannhäuser". *Zeitschrift für deutsches Altertum*, 35 (1891) 439-40.

Liebleitner, Karl. "Ein Tannhäuserlied". *Das deutsche Volkslied*, 22 (1920) 34-35.

Liebleitner, Karl. "Ein Tannhäuserlied aus Kärnten". *Reichspost*, 192 (14.7.1935) 15.

Löhmann, Otto. "Die Entstehung der Tannhäusersage". *Fabula*, 3 (1960) 224-53.

Loomis, Roger S. "Morgain la Fée in oral tradition". *Romania*, 80 (1959) 337-67.

Lucas, C. "Über den Krieg vom Wartburg". *Historische und literarische Abhandlungen der königlichen deutschen Gesellschaft zu Königsberg*, 1838, no. 4, pt. 2.

Meier, John. *Deutsche Volkslieder mit ihren Melodien*. Berlin, 1935, I, i, pp. 145-61.

Meyer, Richard M. *Deutsche Charaktere*. Berlin, 1897, pp. 60-68.

Meyer, Richard M. "Tannhäuser und die Tannhäusersage". *Zeitschrift des Vereins für Volkskunde*, NF 21 (1911) 1-31.

Moser, Dietz-Rüdiger. *Die Tannhäuser-Legende: eine Studie über Intentionalität und Rezeption katechetischer Volkserzählungen zum Buß-Sakrament*. Berlin, 1977. (*Fabula*: Supplement Serie: Reihe B, Untersuchungen: Bd. 4).

Nodnagel, A. "Die Tannhäusersage und ihre Bearbeitungen". *Archiv*, 6 (1849) 119-40.

Norer, Jakob. *Die Tannhäusersage und ihre poetische Gestaltung*. Hamburg, 1897.

Nyrop, Kristopher. *Tannhäuser i Venusbjaerget*. Copenhagen, 1909. (Fortids sagn og sange, 6).

Oehlke, Alfred. *Zu Tannhäusers Leben und Dichten*. Diss. Königsberg, 1890.

Pabst, Walter. *Venus und die mißverstandene Dido: literarische Ursprünge des Sibyllen- und des Venusberges*. Hamburg, 1955. (Hamburger Romanische Studien: Reihe A, 40).

Paris, Gaston. "La légende du Tannhäuser". *Légendes du moyen âge*, Paris, 1903, pp. 111-49.

Pfaff, Fridrich. "Die Tannhäusersage". *Zeitschrift für deutsche Philologie*, 40 (1908) 97-99.

Puls, Alfred. "Tannhäuserlied und Maria tzart". *Jahrbuch des Vereins für niederdeutsche Sprachforschung*, 16 (1890) 65-68.

Reischl, Friedrich. *Das Buch von der schönen Stadt Salzburg*. Wien, 1923, pp. 134-147.

THE TRAGEDY OF KNIGHTHOOD 175

Remy, Arthur F. "The origin of the Tannhäuserlegend". *Journal of English and Germanic Philology*, 12 (1913) 32-77.
Reumont, Alfredo di. *Saggi di storia e letteratura*. Firenze, 1880, pp. 389-394.
Reuschel, Karl. "Die Tannhäusersage". *Neue Jahrbücher für das klassische Altertum, Geschichte und deutsche Literatur*, 13 (1904) 653-67.
Ribbeck, Konrad. *Danuser: eine alte niederdeutsche Fassung des Tannhäuserliedes nach einer Handschrift des Essener Stadtarchivs*. Essen, 1926. (Erster Druck des Essener Bibliophilen-Abends.)
Rostock, F. *Mittelhochdeutsche Dichterheldensage*. Halle, 1925, pp. 12-15. (Hermaea, 15.)
Rudolf, Adalbert. "Tanhäuser". *Archiv*, 68 (1882) 43-52.
Schlossar, Anton. *Deutsche Volkslieder aus Steiermark*. Innsbruck, 1881, pp. 351-52.
Schmidt, Erich. "Tannhäuser in Sage und Dichtung". *Charakteristiken*, 2nd edit., Berlin, 1912, vol. 2, 23-52.
Schmidt, Leopold. "Zur österreichischen Form der Tannhäuser-Ballade". *Jahrbuch des österreichischen Volksliedwerkes*, 1 (1952) 9-18.
Schmitt, Franz. *Stoff- und Motivgeschichte der deutschen Literatur*. Berlin, 1959, pp. 173-74.
Schneider, Hermann. "Ursprung und Alter der deutschen Volksballade". *Vom Werden des deutschen Geistes: Festgabe G. Ehrismann*. Berlin, 1925, pp. 112-24.
Siebert, Johannes. *Der dichter Tannhäuser: Leben, Gedichte, Sage*. Halle, 1934.
Simpson, Claude M. "Wagner and the Tannhäuser tradition". *Publications of the Modern Language Association*, 63 (1948) 244-61.
Söderhjelm, Werner. "Antoine de la Sale et la légende de Tannhäuser". *Mémoires de la Société Néo-Philologique à Helsingfors*, 2 (1897) 101-67.
Söderhjelm, Werner. "Eine tschechische Version der Reise ins Sibyllenparadies". *Neuphilologische Mitteilungen*, 10 (1908) 72-88.
Thomas, John W. *Tannhäuser: poet and legend*. Chapel Hill, 1974. (*University of North Carolina studies in the Germanic languages and literatures*, 77.)
Thomas, John W. "Walther von der Vogelweide and the Tannhäuserballad". *Neuphilologische Mitteilungen*, 74 (1973) 340-47.
Uhland, Ludwig. *Schriften zur Geschichte der Dichtung und Sage*. Stuttgart, 1865-73; II, 219-50; IV, 259-86; VII, 598.
Weller, Karl. "Zur Lebensgeschichte des Tannhäusers". *Beiträge zur Geschichte, Literatur und Sprachkunde vornehmlich Württembergs: Festschrift Karl Bohnenberger*. Tübingen, 1938, pp. 154-63.
Wiora, Walter. "Alpenländische Liedweisen der Frühzeit und des Mittelalters im Lichte vergleichender Forschung". *Angebinde: Festschrift John Meier*. Lahr, 1949, pp. 169-98.
Wis, Marjatta. "Ursprünge der deutschen Tannhäuserlegende: zur Geschichte

mittelalterliche Pilgertraditionen, I". *Neuphilologische Mitteilungen*, 61 (1960) 8-58.

Zack, Viktor. "Tannhäuserlieder aus Steiermark". *Das deutsche Volkslied*, 32 (1930) 77-80.

Zander, F. *Die Tanhäuser-Sage und der Minnesinger Tanhäuser: Zur öffentlichen Prüfung der Schüler des König Friedrichs-Collegiums.* Königsberg, 1858.

Zingerle, Ignaz V. "Zur Tanhäuser-Literatur". *Germania*, 5 (1860) 361-65.

Zoder, Raimund. "Tannhäuserlied aus Niederösterreich". *Das deutsche Volkslied*, 32 (1930) 80.

Zohner, Alois. *Die Verbindung der Eckhart- und Tannhäuser-Sagen.* Diss. Wien, 1909.

INDEX

Abel, Caspar 15n
Aeneid 40, 46, 48, 68ff., 71, 90
Alberich de Trois Fontaines 13, 72
Alberti, Fra Leandro 6n, 90
Albrecht von Scharfenberg 11, 16
Alisandre l'Orphelin 67, 75
Ambraser Liederbuch 93n, 100n, 108n
Amersbach, K. 8n, 15n
Amman, A. 2n, 93n
Antwerp songbook 95
Architrenius 127
Arthur, King 9ff., 27, 62, 68ff., 75, 132

Barberino, Andrea da *see: Guerino il Meschino*
Barto, P.S. ix, 5n, 6, 8n, 15, 93n, 94n, 95, 97n, 98n, 106n, 118n, 119n, 120n
Bataille Loquifer 76
Bercheur, Pierre 4, 42, 90
Bran, Voyage of 57n, 62f., 65
Burnham, J.M. 86n, 88n

Caesarius of Heisterbach 12f.
Charlemagne 14, 71f.
Chrétien de Troyes 51, 58
Claris et Laris 75f.
Claudian 127

Debility of the Ultonian warriors 61
Der Guotaere 120n
Der Tugenden Schatz 2, 125f., 133
Désiré, Lai de 55, 61, 64, 83ff., 108, 131
Detto del Gatto Lupesco 13
Didot Perceval 68
Diefenbach L. 15, 17
Dietrich von Nieheim 6ff., 12, 17f., 20, 70, 127
Dübi, H. 5n, 21n, 36n, 107n, 123n

Eckart 122f., 125
Essen ms. 94f., 121, 144ff.
Etienne de Bourbon 13n
Etienne de Rouen 14

Faber, Felix 3, 5, 9, 12, 17, 19f., 100, 142f.
Fay Sebile 66ff., 123, 128, 132, 134
Fischart, Johann 8, 15, 70
Floriant et Florete 13, 62
Frankfurter Liederbüchlein 93n
Frederick Barbarossa 14
Frederick II 13f.
Fro Venus (Fro Minne) 20, 38, 47, 66, 82, 90, 91, 92f., 97f., 109ff., 119ff., 129, 132
Fro Welt 120

Geoffrey of Monmouth 68
Gervase of Tilbury 12, 57, 78, 102f.
Gottfrid von Straßburg 2, 127
Graelent, Lai de 61, 83, 85
Grail 6ff., 10, 15ff., 126, 132
Gregory XI, Pope 31, 111
Gregory of Tours 101ff.
Gregory the Great 52
Guerino il Meschino vii, 3ff., 9, 17, 22, 39ff., 56f., 64, 66, 71, 73, 76, 78, 82, 91, 96, 98, 100f., 104, 106f., 128, 133
Guingamor, Lai de 61

Hartland, E.S. 58n, 60n
Hartmann von Aue 54
Heinrich von Meißen (Frauenlob) 16
Heinrich von Morungen 124n
Hemmerlin, Felix 2, 4, 6, 17ff., 20, 37, 42ff., 48, 56ff., 82, 92, 97, 100f., 106f., 122f., 124, 129, 134, 138ff.
Herla, King 63n
Hermann von Sachsenheim 121 ff., 128, 129
Huon d'Auvergne 48f.
Huon de Bordeaux 70f.

Innocent VI, Pope 31

Jacobus a Voragine 102n
Jean d'Arras 79ff., 84

Jena ms. 114
Juno 69f.

Karlsruhe ms. 120f., 129
Klapper, J. 102n, 103n
Kluge, F. 5n, 21n, 36n, 37n
Kolmar ms. 115ff.
Konrad von Würzburg 96n, 120
Krappe, A.H. viii, 14n, 55, 72, 85, 87ff.

La chevalerie Ogier 62n
La faula 16
Lancelot 54, 67, 76
Lang, M. 112, 115, 124n
Lanval, Lai de 61, 83, 85
Loathly Lady 80, 88
Lohengrin 10ff.
Löhmann, O. 2n, 9n, 39n, 48n, 51n, 55n, 66n, 85n, 87n, 101n, 127
Loomis, R.S. 12n, 14n, 55n

Mackensen, L. 54n, 101n
Maelduin, Voyage of 57n
Manesse ms. 112, 114, 116
Meister Altswert *see: Der Tugenden Schatz*
Melusine 77 ff., 84f., 91, 97, 100, 103, 131
Meyer, R.M. 37, 92n, 97, 100n, 112
Minneturnier, Das 125
Morgan le Fay 11, 62f., 67, 75f., 86
Moser, D.-R. xi f., 20n, 48n, 99n, 103n

Nider, Johannes 2, 3, 5, 12, 17ff., 20, 127, 129
Niniane 75

Olger (Ogier) the Dane 14, 62ff., 65, 86n
Osella, G. 39n, 40n
Otto of Freising 13
Ovid 68

Pabst, W. ix, 6f., 9, 11, 39n, 40n, 47f., 66, 70, 124
Paradis de la Reine Sibylle vii, 17, 21ff., 39, 47f., 56ff., 64f., 70ff., 92, 94, 96ff., 104ff., 113, 119f., 126, 131, 133ff.

Paris, G. 21n, 54f.
Partonopeus 62
Patch, H.R. 50n, 56n
Paton, L.A. 60n, 66ff., 75, 76n
Pfaff, F. 5n, 93n, 101n
Piccolomini, Aeneas Silvius 1, 3, 4, 5, 129, 136f.
Prophecies de Merlin 67f.
Pulci, Luigi 3, 5
Pulzella Gaia 61, 85

Reinhard, J.R. 54n, 58n, 78n
Remy, A. 99, 120n
Roman de Brut 68
Roman de Perceforest 69n
Romans de Dolopathos 71n

St. Christopher 102
St. Patrick's Purgatory 41, 49ff., 56
St. Savien 102
Sale, Antoine de la *see: Paradis de la Reine Sibylle*
Schmidt, E. 8n, 36n, 101n, 119n, 122n
Schneider, H. 92n, 96n, 124n
Sibyl *(see also:* Fay Sebile) 1, 3ff., 7, 9ff., 21ff., 36, 39ff., 65ff., 90,
    132, 134
Siebert, J. 29n, 92n, 112n, 113n, 114n, 117n, 118n, 120n
Sigibert de Gembloux 13
Sigismund von Birken 5n
Söderhjelm, W. 12n, 17, 57n

Tannhäuser (the poet) 37, 92, 111ff., 129, 130
Theoderic the Ostrogoth 13f.
Thomas of Eccleston 13
Thomas, J.W. vii, 92f., 96, 101n, 111, 112n, 113n
Tom the Rymer (Thomas of Erceldoune) 55, 85ff., 98, 100, 128
Trissino, Giangiorgio 3, 90

Urban IV, Pope viii, 33, 37, 92, 100, 104, 111ff., 129, 130
Urban V, Pope 31, 111, 130
Urban VI, Pope 31, 111, 130

Venus *see:* Fro Venus

Venusberg 1ff., 39, 55ff., 68ff., 90, 97f., 104f., 109, 112, 119, 122, 125ff., 129ff.
Vincent of Beauvais 78
Visio Beati Pauli 70f.

Walther von der Vogelweide 93, 120
Wartburgkrieg 9ff., 14, 16ff., 68ff.
Wenzel, King 14
Wigalois 54
Wilten ms. 115ff.
Wis, M. 3n, 39n, 42
Wittenwiler, Heinrich 124
Wolfram von Eschenbach 15, 54

www.ingramcontent.com/pod-product-compliance
Lightning Source LLC
Chambersburg PA
CBHW021156160426
43194CB00007B/760